MAKING A DIFFERENCE COLLEGE GUIDE

SO-AVW-897

"A great guide for college-bound young activists."
Julia Butterfly Hill

"I highly recommend this guide for students who care about the Earth."
David Brower, Friends of the Earth

"We are very excited that there is a guide to college whose basis is service to others and community concerns. This Guide is particularly rewarding. With our emphasis on service to others we are proud to be included."
Swarthmore College

"Buy this book. It's the bible for students who seek higher education for higher purposes - one of the most practical and insightful college selection resources today."
Marcy Hamilton, College Counselor, CA

"Commitment to community and caring about both our human and physical environments should be critical components of a student's educational experience. We feel fortunate to be considered with other colleges that emphasize consciousness about and responsibility for the future"
R. Shaw Jr., Dean of Admissions, Yale U.

"Our nation is fortunate that so many of its youth seek to contribute to a more just and sustainable future. The institutions profiled within this book offer academic preparation that enables students to promote social justice and environmental protection. And the guide is not only idealistic, but also pragmatically career-oriented so that students can go on to make a difference in the context of a decent job."
Rick Clugston, Center for Respect of Life & Environment

"So many students are being directed into corporate and business life which is soulless and will not serve their future. This extremely important book, however, could help them assist in saving the Planet."
Dr. Helen Caldicott

"Harnesses the idealism of today's college bound youth, and points them to relevant, value-based education, often filled with service programs - whether in local communities or abroad, and then tops it off with practical yet meaningful career-oriented studies!"
Youth Service America

"Targets those students who are dissatisfied with the prospects of a traditional, passive, and one-dimensional approach to higher education. Interesting, informative and well-written, this book can make a difference for us all."
Journal of College Admission

"Profiles hidden gem colleges that most students should know about but rarely do. It is the college guide for idealistic students, and fills a tremendous need"

"I'm honored to have the chance to extol the virtues of this book. It's about time a college guide addressed the really important issues in education today. This Guide profiles a unique cross-spectrum of schools offering a rich, empowering and relevant education."

"An excellent resource. It can help students find institutions that will deepen both their understanding of human problem-solving and their social commitment to a better world, and help ensure that they make the most of their college education."

"Oil spills, the vanishing rain forests, and the starving children in Rwanda all made you want to throw out your homework and pitch in. But first you had to finish high school. Now it's time for college, and with this guide's help in finding socially aware colleges, you may actually get that chance to help save the world."

"Until I read this guide, I had no interest in going to college. Now I've picked out a school which I am actually eager to attend."

"As a parent, I am grateful for this book, and urge all concerned parents to buy a copy. This book changes lives. I bought five more copies for my son's classmates."

"Like no other resource on the market. The colleges in the guide include the schools of choice for most of the young people with whom I have worked and is particularly strong for students who seek to be involved in high quality community service, who are creative and/or who do not look forward to four years of listening to professors lecture. As a college counselor, *Making A Difference* is my best reference. I have directed over three-hundred young people to colleges in the Guide and have found the schools remarkably responsive to their students needs. When I send a student to one of these colleges, I know s/he will have a life-affecting and satisfying collegiate experience."

"This guide is very much in line with our mission of idealism. There is no better way to "be the change you wish to see in the world" than to be armed with a values-based education and to surround oneself at a college campus whose intellectual environment, curriculum, and programmatic activities cultivate that."

"This guide is very difficult to rave about in just a few words. It makes me want to go back to college!"

More Praise

"Until the emergence of *Making A Difference College Guide*, high school students who care about the world blindly faced a bewildering array of questionable college options, but not anymore. Even thumbing through this book, you'll wonder how any intelligent student, parent, or guidance counselor could do without it."

Green Teacher Magazine

"At it's best, a college education helps students acquire the knowledge, skills and dispositions to change the world, to make it a better place. The institutions profiled in this book are among the best at helping students make this kind of difference. *Making A Difference College Guide* is a valuable resource."

Vito Perrone, Former Director, Teacher Education Program, Harvard

"*Making A Difference College Guide* is distinctive in that its criteria focus on what should be the fundamental purpose of our campuses: launching students, with heart and mind, to enhance life for present and future generations. The Guide's value-centered approach to college selection fulfills a much needed demand."

Doug Orr, Former President, Warren Wilson College

"I use this terrific tome constantly in my work at the Positive Futures Network. I connect with teachers and students to deliver inspiring news, and work to support their active engagement in shaping alternatives to current social, economic, and environmental ills. Your guide is an incredible resource -- it helps me connect with campuses and programs that emphasize creating the better world we all desire. Thank you again for this guide and the good green energy you bring to the world."

Kim Corrigan, *YES! Magazine*

"In a moment of discouragement, your words about social activism in context of spirituality moved me greatly and re-charged my commitment."

Robert Elkins, VA

Recommended. In spirit the Guide resembles the *Whole Earth Catalog*."

American Library Association *Booklist*

"This guide allowed me to find a smaller, more alternative college with a friendly atmosphere, a family-like structure and wonderful professors who enjoy their occupation. Ms. Weinstein's book led me to the path of a higher education."

Amy Mermin, CA

"Three of our children have found wonderful colleges through this guide that we would have never known about otherwise. Our children are inspired, and as parents, we are most grateful."

Richard & Marie Mermin, CA

"Thanks for making this book available. It is exactly like the kind of information I've been killing myself trying to track down in the library."

Ed Lawson, VA

"How wonderful it is that nobody need wait a single
moment before starting to improve the world."
Anne Frank

"Anyone can be great, because anyone can serve."
Martin Luther King Jr.

"When I was young, I was quite idealistic. We had the freedom in those days to
be idealistic and not necessarily to have to produce immediate results.... But the
reality is, you don't have the time, the world doesn't have the time for the sort
of idealism my generation enjoyed. You have to be so much more practical than
we had to be at your age. You must look at your idealism and not compromise it.
And yet, you must also be wise enough and smart enough and patient enough to
know how to go by steps...."
Theresa Heinz Kerry, Campus Earth Summit remarks

"I'll interpret the rocks, learn the language of the flood, stream and
the avalanche. I'll acquaint myself with the glaciers and wild gardens,
and get as near the heart of the world as I can."
John Muir

"If we really want this millennium to be happier, more peaceful and harmonious
for humankind we will have to make the effort to make it so. This is in
our hands, but especially in the hands of the younger generation. Along with
education, which generally deals only with academic accomplishments, we need
to develop more altruism and a sense of caring and responsibility for others in
the minds of the younger generation studying in various educational institutions.
... It in fact consists of basic human qualities such as kindness, compassion,
sincerity and honesty. We need to address the issue of the gap between the rich
and the poor, both globally and nationally. For the sake of our future generations,
we need to take care of our earth and of our environment."
The 13th Dalai Lama's Millenium Address

"It's better to light a candle than to curse the darkness."
Eleanor Roosevelt

"Religions are too pious, corporations too plundering, government too subservient
to provide any adequate remedy. In this situation, the university has a
special role.... to reorient the human community toward a greater awareness
that the human exists with the single great community of the planet Earth."
Thomas Berry

"To be free is to be able to enjoy the fruits of life in
a just, caring, and compassionate community."
Abraham Heschel

TENTH ANNIVERSARY EDITION

MAKING A DIFFERENCE COLLEGES

DISTINCTIVE COLLEGES TO MAKE A BETTER WORLD

Next
Generation
Scholars

- 781 LINCOLN AVENUE -
SAN RAFAEL - CA - 94901

MIRIAM WEINSTEIN

SAGEWORKS PRESS
SAN ANSELMO, CALIFORNIA

Weinstein, Miriam (Miriam H.)
    Making a difference colleges : distinctive colleges
to make a better world / Miriam Weinstein. – 10th
anniversary ed.
    p. cm.
    Includes index.
    Rev. ed. of: Making a difference college & graduate
guide.
    ISBN-13: 978-0-9634618-9-6
    ISBN-10: 0-9634618-9-3

    1. Universities and colleges–United States–
Directories. 2. Universities and colleges–Social
aspects–United States–Directories. 3. Universities
and colleges–Moral and ethical aspects–United States–
Directories. 4. Environmental sciences–Study and
teaching (Higher)–United States–Directories.
5. Vocational guidance.   I. Weinstein, Miriam (Miriam
H.) Making a difference college & graduate guide.
II. Title.

L901.W45 2007   378.73
                  QBI06-600309

Thank you to the following for granting permission to use their work:
    College Report Card, How To Test Drive A College © Martin Nemko
    What is Education For? © 1994 by David Orr
    From Knowledge to Wisdom © 2000 Matthew Fox
    Rethinking the Mission of Education © 1997 Jeremy Rifkin
    College profiles are copyright by the individual colleges.

Cover design and book design by Miriam Weinstein

Published by   SageWorks Press
                 P.O. Box 441
                 Fairfax, CA 94978
                 1. 800. 218.4242
                 www.making-a-difference.com

Please contact SageWorks for bulk discount pricing for non-profits, youth, social change,
environmental, service and other similar organizations.

Also by Miriam Weinstein:
Making A Difference Graduate Guide - Spring 2007
Making A Difference Scholarships (out of print)

For my children,
and
to Native Peoples struggling to maintain
their cultures and their lands,
and you, the reader, the hope of the future.

Acknowledgments

I'd like to give my sincerest appreciation to my daughter, Radha Blackman, who gave me exceptional support in many ways for this tenth editon. To Marty Nemko, who was a gracious mentor in many arenas when I was first starting the guide. Thanks to my childhood neighborhood - The Amalgamated in the Bronx- a hotbed of social consciousness, and to my beloved friend, the late Joanne Lukomnik who dragged me to many picket lines and demonstrations. I am indebted to the gracious thinkers and organizations for contributing essays and, in particular, I am honored to have thoughts from Matthew Fox, Jeremy Rifkin and David Orr.

I am especially grateful for the enthusiastic reception, cooperation, and faith I've received from the colleges and programs profiled in the guide, and for the valuable education they render.

Thanks to you, the readers for your desire to make a better world, despite all the challenges you face.

Thanks to my children for being my inspiration, and importantly, heartfelt gratitude to Mother Earth who sustains us all.

CONTENTS

MAKING A DIFFERENCE COLLEGES

DISTINCTIVE COLLEGES TO MAKE A BETTER WORLD

Every man must decide whether he will walk in the light of creative altruism or the darkness of destructive selfishness. This is the judgement. Life's most persistent and urgent question is, what are you doing for others?

Martin Luther King Jr.

INTRODUCTION

Global warming, deforestation, war in the Middle East, loss of democracy at home, over-priced health care while the rich are getting richer, and everyone else is getting poorer. You know why you chose this college guide.

I didn't decide to write this book, this book picked me. It picked me because I was committed to healing the Earth and it's inhabitants. I was a mother of four, armed with an "empow-ering" education from one of the colleges in this guide, which cares deeply about social justice. While doing a college search with my eldest child, I scoured the college guides and the viewbooks and wondered if we were living on the same troubled planet! Surely there had to be colleges that offered an education both relevant, inspirational and practical. The good news I found out through extensive research, is that is the answer is yes, there are wonderful colleges committed to the environment, peace, social change and service. This book is filled with them. Some of the colleges in this guide that offer a relevant, values-based education are true hidden treasures, others are among the nation's most well known and prestigious.

This book is graced with essays by three seminal, inspirational thinkers: Matthew Fox (*From Knowledge to Wisdom,*) Jeremy Rifkin (*Rethinking the Mission of American Education,*) and David Orr (*What Is Education For?*) I urge you, particularly parents, to read their thought provoking words. There is much to chew on in each introductory essay.

And you, students, do you feel your life has a purpose, do you have a desire to make a difference? Maybe you want to become a lawyer working to prevent logging of ancient forests, or a policy maker deciding how to best protect the water supply and still meet the needs of farm-ers and wildlife. Maybe you'd like to to be a peacemaker, or help inner-city kids make it through college. Maybe you don't have a clue, you just know you want to make a difference. But you real-ize that the right college education is essential.

For you then, choosing a college involves very different questions than the standard "Will I get a big name education?" "How's the football?" "Will I get a high paying job?" etc. Your ques-tions are also: "Will this college help me discover my calling?" "Will this college provide me with the tools to make a better world?" and "Does this college support my values?" You can use *Making A Difference Colleges* to find a college where most or all of the students are actively involved in community service and working to make a better world. You'll discover that most colleges in this guide are committed to and actively engaged in helping solve our world's complex and pressing needs, both in and out of the classroom.

When considering a college, of course you'll look at academic caliber, location and majors. But you'll also learn in this Guide if it has an ethic of service, concerns for peace and social justice, an environmental focus, and how these concerns are brought into the classroom and the world. The colleges and programs profiled here can give you the skills, tools, self-trust, and con-nections you'll need. Pick out several that pique your interest. Then use Martin Nemko's *College Report Card* to evaluate their general fit, and use *How To Test Drive A College* to conduct an "arm-chair" tour.

The spectrum of colleges profiled in this guide is truly unique. There are colleges dedicated to peace and social justice, strongly environmental colleges, and a Buddhist inspired college. There are work colleges, international colleges and travel programs. You'll even find colleges on coastal islands at opposite ends of the country. At the more alternative colleges you can take courses taught by teams of teachers from different disciplines or design you own major incorporating your own interests in your own particular way. Many of the colleges are very outdoorsy, perfect for those of you who like to commune with nature. Happily, many colleges and universities today are also seriously "greening" their campus practices. eco-built dorms and organic gardens are flourishing. I'll happily admit, that in the last two years, colleges have even surpassed my hopes in many areas. The movement, in particular, to use local and organic foods in the dining halls - a step with so many positive benefits - caught me unaware.

What else is different? At most of these distinctive campuses you'll find opportunities to learn while doing service or working in the field. Imagine working in a health clinic in remote Nepal, teaching sustainable agriculture in Central America, or building water cisterns at a rural African school. You can monitor a local river for pollution, save a threatened species, design affordable housing, tutor inner city kids or learn sustainable forestry using draft horses.

This is the kind of education some of your parents might have only dreamed of. If, however, your parents are worried that this doesn't sound sufficiently academic, put their fears to rest. More and more educators consider experiential and service-learning the most effective kinds of learning, and these programs are blossoming nationwide.

While the potential for awakening students to the value of social change is substantial, in many colleges, service becomes a "feel good" experience. Good service-learning programs are an excellent tool for both moral development and awakening a social consciousness. This guide takes the next step: to evaluating an education for deep-rooted pervasive social change and environmental stewardship.

Many socially committed colleges are small, undergraduate-centered, and have approachable faculty who care more about teaching than research grants. They generally have smaller classes, more personal attention, and a stronger sense of community. Universities, on the other hand, offer a mind-boggling array of majors, greater opportunities to participate in advanced research, vast resources, and often a more diverse student body.

There's also something to be said for being an outstanding student at a less competitive institution, rather than an average or struggling student at a very competitive school. If you are already looking ahead to graduate school, that strategy may prove even more helpful, as graduate schools are more interested in the top student at a middling college, than in a low ranked student at a prestigious college.

While some schools in this guide are characterized as only moderately selective or even "non-selective" in their admissions process, be aware that 'selectivity' is a function of the number of applications received. It is not a direct reflection of a quality undergraduate education. The truth is, the most competitive universities are often be surprisingly disinterested in their undergraduates, and some recent studies indicate that attending a top college doesn't provide greater "success" in life. In the end, it doesn't matter how prestigious or selective a college is, what matters is if it's the right college for you, and gives you what you seek.

As you read this guide, you'll notice its emphasis on meaningful career-oriented studies. The more specialized your area of study, the easier it is to find work initially. But experts are quick to note that liberal arts students often find greater flexibility in career opportunities over the years. And although studies such as social work, peace, urban planning, and natural resources are the ones listed here, students who major in traditional liberal arts such as literature gain critical thinking skills beneficial in many careers, and often specialize further in graduate school. Of course, if you'd like to design your own major —say — Watershed Management and Sustainable Forestry, or Women's International Health - you'll find plenty of opportunities for that too!

Interdisciplinary studies - such as women's, peace and environmental studies were often considered inferior step-children at many colleges and universities. As the complexity of environmental and social problems become more evident, this prejudice is giving way, and interdisciplinary studies are becoming as common. Personally, I think they are the answer. The world is complex and interrelated, and studies should be as well.

Many parents fear that making a difference means a life of poverty, but these fears are unfounded. The *Making A Difference Careers* section lists hundreds of career pathways corresponding to the myriad studies noted in this guide. This is a practical career-oriented college guide. A college degree doesn't always guarantee a secure, interesting, or high paying job, but if you're looking to make a better world, there is meaningful work waiting for you. Dollars are not the only measure of wealth, as you gain the immeasurable value that comes from a life of integrity, the joy of improving lives and of caring for the earth. Our planet and our society need you!

As for the profiles and course listings, a few notes. The *Making A Difference Studies* listed after the profiles are a small selection of the majors offered at any individual institution. Likewise, the courses listed are only a sample, and may not reflect the most current offerings. Most often the studies listed are majors, but some minors are also listed. The vegetarian/vegan meals designation means the college claims to have nutritious vegetarian meals available in addition to the regular fare. I make no promises, however, about the caliber of the meals! Icons give you a quick picture of each college. Some colleges didn't respond to the survey - so, lack of icons shouldn't be taken as a negative indication. Most of the icon choices are accurate - but a few colleges may be a bit optimistic in their self-description - so do investigate for yourself.

An exceptional group of advisors has helped suggest colleges, and I am sincerely grateful for their input. Over the years this list has included Julian Keniry of the the National Wildlife Federation's Campus Ecology Program; Nancy Rhodes of Campus Compact; Rick Clugston of the Center for Respect of Life and Environment; Anthony Cortese of Second Nature; Robert Hackett of The Bonner Foundation; Milly Henry of New College of CA; Professor David Orr of Oberlin College; Cynthia Robinson of the Association of University Leaders for a Sustainable Future and college counselors Steven Antonoff (CO); Carol DeLucca (GA); David Denman (CA) and Martin Nemko (CA).

I have chosen to let the schools speak for themselves and write their own profiles. The absence of a school you are interested in could be due to several things: I'm unfamiliar with it; it didn't meet enough of the criteria; or it didn't respond to requests for information. In the interest of full disclosure, once a college is invited to participate in the Guide, a modest and sliding scale fee is paid. Many colleges that ask to be included are turned down.

Finally, if you're eighteen, I hope you are registered to vote. If you don't vote, don't complain about what comes down the pike. If you're not already volunteering or engaged in activism, start now! Check out activist trainings and leadership workshops too.

Both for you and the world, the choices before you are pivotal. Please use this Guide to choose a college as an important step on your way to contributing to a better world. My sincere gratitude is extended to you for joining with the many caring and often courageous people across the planet who form the original world wide web, who are working with their hearts, hands and minds to make a difference and to shape the world anew.

Miriam Weinstein, author of Making A Difference College Guide since 1992, now offers private college counseling. If you are in the San Francisco Bay Area, counseling is available in Marin County. Counseling can also be done by telephone and email if you are located elsewhere. Please contact Ms. Weinstein at mw@sageworks.net to inquire.

Affording That Education

Then of course, there's finances. Costs are not listed in this guide to encourage you not to base your decisions on cost. If you are interested in a school, please do apply to it. You should feel comfortable about talking with admissions counselors as well as the financial aid office about your financial picture. If you are low or even moderate income, take the time to learn the ins and outs of financial aid; the benefits might be more substantial than you realize. If you need aid, it is always best to apply early and complete your FAFSA early.

While the largest aid is government and college based, seek out scholarships which aren't need based. Many colleges in this guide offer large scholarships or even a "free ride" for students engaged in community service. Some offer scholarships for students majoring in specific fields such as peace studies or natural resources. The Bonner Scholars program works with specific colleges and gives funding to some students who promise to perform extra community service. There's also AmeriCorps, as described in a later essay.

One possible strategy to get more aid is to attend a college in a different state than yours that doesn't get many out-of-state students, or one that doesn't have many students from your particular state. Colleges like to say "we have students from 30 or 40 or 50 states" and they will sometimes pay extra in order to do so. A few colleges are now offering free tuition to qualified low-income students. Learn which colleges offer more generous financial aid, and consider having one or two on your "apply to" list. It pays to do your research.

It is pretty well known that financial aid packages can sometimes be negotiated. If yours isn't adequate, you might call the financial aid office and ask them very politely if some additional help might be available - but be sure to have a good reason why you are asking them. If the college is your first choice, let them know that you really do wish to go there, but without more aid it might be not be feasible. Do not do this just as a ploy to get more money. Wealthy families sometimes spend a great deal of money figuring out how to outsmart the system to get extra money for their students. I consider this rather unethical - that money should be allocated to those who need it, not those who just want it.

Be sure you are doing your part by working summer jobs and saving that money for college. The colleges will expect a higher percentage from your savings and earnings than from your parents. If finances still don't add up, one option is to attend a community college for the first two years, and then transfer into the college of your choice as a junior. In California it is well-documented that students who transfer to highly competitive UC Berkeley from community colleges actually get a higher GPA during their time there than the top students who entered Berkeley straight from high school.

If graduate school is in your plans, one way to shave expenses is to look for a 3/2 program, where you can obtain a master's degree after your fifth year. Some colleges offer these programs internally, while others do it through agreements with neighboring universities.

Whatever your family's income, don't give up too quickly on attending a particular college because of the stated sticker price - very few families pay the whole price. With school grants even an expensive private college education may be quite affordable. Whether your family is run by a struggling single mom or upper middle-class, you may be eligible for enough grant aid that will enable you to attend the college of your dreams.

RETHINKING THE MISSION OF
AMERICAN EDUCATION

JEREMY RIFKIN

The shift from the Industrial Age to the Information Age is transforming our civilization. Vast economic, social, and political changes are already underway. Preparing students for a radically different world in the 21st century requires a reaffirmation of the principles of democracy and community that have served as a beacon in the first two centuries of the American experience. Our schools, colleges and universities can play a key role in fostering a more civil society.

Corporate downsizing, the increasing automation of the manufacturing and service sectors, the shift from mass to elite workforces, growing job insecurity, the widening gap between rich and poor, continued racial tensions, escalating crime, new patterns of immigration, an aging population, and the globalization of the economy are creating a host of new uncertainties and challenges for the American economy.

At the same time, government, at every level, is being fundamentally transformed. The "welfare state" is being pared down and entitlement programs are shrinking. The social net is being streamlined and overhauled and government subsidies of various kinds are being reduced or eliminated.

The new economic and political realities stir us to look once again to America's civil society for help and guidance as we have on so many occasions in the past when our country found itself in the midst of profound change. While historians are quick to credit the market economy and democratic form of government with America's greatness, the civil society- the Third Sector- has played an equally significant role in defining the American way of life.

The nation's hospitals, social service organizations, religious institutions, fraternal orders, women's clubs, youth organizations, civil rights groups, animal welfare organizations, theaters, orchestras, art galleries, libraries, museums, civic associations, community development organizations, neighborhood advisory councils, volunteer fire departments and civilian security patrols are all institutions of the Third Sector.

Today more than 1,400,000 nonprofit organizations are serving the needs and helping fulfill the dreams of millions of Americans. The civil society is the bonding force, the social glue that unites the many diverse interests of the American people into a cohesive social identity. If there is a single defining characteristic that sums up the unique qualities of being an American, it would be our capacity to join together in civic associations to serve one another.

America's Third Sector will need to play a far more expansive role in the coming century as an arena for job creation and social service provider. The civic sector must also become a more organized social and cultural force in every community, working with, and, at times, pressuring the market and government sectors to meet the needs of workers, families and neighborhoods. Thinking of society as three sectors that work together to create a productive and caring society opens up new possibilities for reconceptualizing the social contract and the kind of education we give our young people.

Weaving a seamless web between school and community needs to be made an urgent priority if we are to meet the growing challenges of the coming century. A quiet revolution, to bring school and community closer together, has been spreading through the nation's schools and colleges over the past ten years. The effort is designed to create that seamless web. "Civil education" is based on the premise that a primary purpose of schooling is to help young people develop the skills and acquire the values necessary for civic life. Advancing the goals of a civil education requires that educators look to the non-profit sector in addition to the marketplace and government, to inform curriculum development, pedagogy, and the organization of schooling.

Civil education is gaining ground in schools around the country. Many school systems have established service learning activities which integrate service within the curriculum and/or enable students to earn credit for their involvement in neighborhood non-profit organizations, service oriented businesses, and other Third Sector enterprises. Some schools have established character education and citizen education programs to promote civic values. A growing number of schools have begun to recognize the power of connecting civil society and course curriculum. The civil society furnishes ample material for broadening and deepening the school experience across a range of academic studies. All of these initiatives are designed to create a seamless web between school and community.

At a time when teachers, parents, and communities are becoming more concerned about the growing sense of alienation, detachment, and aimlessness of the nation's students, civil education is an important development. Civil education engenders a sense of personal responsibility and accountability, fosters self esteem and leadership, and most of all, allows the feeling of empathy to grow and flourish.

Civil education can give a student a sense of place and belonging, as well as add personal meaning to his or her life. Civil education also provides a much needed alternative frame of reference for a generation increasingly immersed in the simulated worlds of the new telecommunications revolution. Television, computers, and now cyberspace, are becoming an ever more pervasive force in the lives of our students. The new Information Age media technologies offer an array of innovative teaching tools and learning environments for American students. Still, a growing number of educators worry that children growing up in front of the computer screen and TV set are at risk of being less exposed to the kind of authentic real world experiences that are such a necessary part of normal social education and youth development. Civil education, combined with the appropriate use of the new Information Age technologies, can act as an antidote to the increasingly isolated world of simulation and virtual reality young people experience.

We believe that civil education needs to be incorporated into the heart of the school experience. Learning that occurs through active student participation in service and other aspects of civil life benefits the student, as well as the community. Students learn best by doing. At the same time, weaving the rich 200-year historical legacy and values of the Third Sector into a broad range of curricula, provides a context and framework for children to understand the importance of service learning in the community and the central role that the civil society plays in the life of the country. Learning about the heroes and heroines and the many organizations, movements and causes that have helped forge America's civil society, offers historical role models for children to emulate and a positive vision to help guide their personal journeys in life. Weaving a seamless web between school and community can enhance academic performance and provide a more meaningful educational experience for American students. A civil education also benefits the community itself. Millions of young people reaching out with helping hands to friends and neighbors can enrich the civic life of communities across the country.

As we enter the Information Age, we face the very real challenge of redirecting the course of American education so that our young people will be ready to wrestle with both the demands of the new global economy and the austere new realities facing government. We need to bear in mind that the strength of the market and the effectiveness of our democratic form of government have always depended, in the final analysis, on the vitality of America's civil sector. It is the wellspring of our spirit as a people. Shifting the social paradigm from a two sector to a three sector focus and strengthening the role of the civil society, making it once again the center of American life, is essential if we are to renew our social covenant in the new century. Preparing the next generation for a life-long commitment to the civil society is, perhaps, the single most important challenge facing educators and the American K-12 and collegiate systems as we make the transition into a new era and a new economic epoch in history.

Jeremy Rifkin is the author of "*The End of Work: The Decline of the Global Labor Force and the Dawn of the Post Market Era.*" He is also co-chair of The Partnering Initiative on Education and Civil Society, whose mission is to prepare students for a lifelong commitment to the values of the civil society.

Sentiment without action is the ruin of the soul.

Edward Abbey

Bringing Wisdom Back to the New World

Matthew Fox

E.F. Schumacher, the great British economist, says "We are far too clever today to survive without wisdom." There is so much evidence at our fingertips, especially around the ecological crisis and the youth crisis that points to how we have lost touch with wisdom. I think we have essentially lost touch with wisdom because our educational systems and our political, economic, and even religious systems during this modern era, ran from wisdom into the lap of knowledge.

A number of years ago I was invited to give a series of talks at a university and I was told "You can give four talks... we'll give you the title for the first, the others you make up." I said "Okay, what's the first title?" They said, "Wisdom and the University." I have to tell you, I sweated and sweated over that talk. An hour before I was to speak I took a hot bath and thought "Maybe a revelation will come to me in the bath tub." And the revelation came, and it said, "Tell the truth." I thought "That's pretty simple." So there I was in front of an audience of about 300 faculty and students and I said, "Frankly, talking about wisdom in the university today is a bit like talking about chastity in a brothel." I tell you, the audience moved.

I wish I could say that things have changed a lot since then. But I don't feel they have. I've worked in academia for 25 years; I've kept a foot in there and a foot in the church - because I believe essentially in both. I believe in the spiritual experience that learning is, and the power when it connects to wisdom, and I also believe in the potential of religion to recover its real task which is to teach spirituality.

The university was invented in the 12th century. At that time the West was rediscovering the cosmos. What "university" meant was this: "A place to find your place in the universe." That's what it meant to go to the university, to find your place in the UNIVERSE. Today you go to university and you find your place in sociology, or art, or economics, or business or science; that's due to Newton and the modern world mindset where we've been taught that the universe itself is built of little pieces. The university today is far more indebted to the mistaken and disproved Newtonian physics than to its original inspiration which was embedded in wisdom.

Lester Brown, of the World Watch Institute, who collects data on the state of the earth says that today every living system on Earth is in decline. We're destroying 27,000 species a year. This is the greatest rate of destruction on this planet in 60 million years; the greatest destruction of species since the dinosaurs. At the rate that we are going, in 50 years, that means when you young students are grandparents there will be no species. That is the direction in which we are headed.

Now remember that the opposite of wisdom is folly, and we are headed in a direction of folly. No being would want to foul its nest in the ways in which we are fouling ours or to bring down the other species with which we are so interdependent, not only for food and clothing and shelter and shade and energy, but we are also interdependent with those species for their beauty. They feed our hearts and our souls and our music and our poetry and our dance and our ritual. To think that the path we are on in 50 years will leave us utterly lonely and incapable of survival is really something to meditate on because it is a question of wisdom.

We have been developing powers around knowledge for three-hundred years. Unfortunately, our universities are still essentially knowledge directed. I call them "knowledge factories." What we need today are wisdom schools, especially for the young who, of course, will bear the burden and are bearing the burden of the ecological destruction that is all around us.

Today, even as we speak, people in China and peasants in India are getting reruns of 'Dallas' on their television sets. This is very destructive. This is what destroys ancient cultures and rooted people. These are some of the realities of the time in which we live. It is a time for not taking for granted. We can't take healthy soil, forest air, water, ozone, for granted anymore because our civilization, so addicted to knowledge, has fled from wisdom. Knowledge is very, very powerful. If it is not tempered and contoured by greater visions, like justice, compassion, beauty, grace and thinking of the next generation and the seven generations to come - then indeed, it is dangerous. Unfortunately, many of our educational systems in the West are still very dangerous places.

So what are some of the elements of wisdom that can help us to redeem not only education but our professions as well? When you look at our work world today – when you look at law, religion, economics, and education, what you realize is we separated learning from education, we separated justice from law, we separated stewardship from commerce. And where does this separation begin? It begins at the university. What do lawyers, bankers, business people, theologians and so forth, all have in common? Most of them pass through the university. The university is like a funnel that unfortunately has damaged the heart and the conscience of our people, because it has sought knowledge at the expense of wisdom.

So, I want to talk about bringing wisdom back. One word for recovering wisdom is "cosmology." The word "cosmos" is a Greek word for "whole." We need to recover cosmology because the Newtonian era gave us knowledge with so little wisdom. We were told we lived in a machine. We were told our bodies were machines.

Our souls have shrunk during this modern era. Education and religion have often gone along with the shrinking. In the seventeenth century scientists concluded these believer types can be dangerous. They said, "We better work out some kind of truce. We'll take the universe. You religious people, you take the soul." And, that's what happened. Scientists discovered the power of the universe – atomic power and other powers. But without a conscience, without wisdom. That's why we've had the destruction and the wars – including the war against nature we've had, right up through today. Religion meanwhile, took the soul and became more introspective, rendered it punier and punier. The good news is that scientists themselves are bringing the psyche and cosmos together again. When mysticism and science come together you have an explosion of cosmology and you have new energy. And wisdom can happen again.

Wisdom is not just about knowledge, it's about love. That's what science is rediscovering, what the mystics have been telling us. We have been loved from before the beginning. There have been so many blessings that preceded our coming. Reconnecting with this blessing that is the origin of wisdom. In the 12th century when the university was invented, when cosmology and the goddess came roaring into European civilization, the theologian Adelard of Bath wrote "Were we to neglect coming to know the admirable, rational beauty of the universe in which we live, we would deserve to be cast out from it, like guests incapable of appreciating a home in which hospitality is offered to them." That is the juncture at which our species finds itself at this moment. Because knowledge alone does not teach you gratitude, reverence, a sense of the sacred -

- only wisdom teaches those things. Hildegarde of Bingen of the twelfth century wrote that, "If humanity breaks the web of justice, of creation, the web of justice that is all creation, then God's justice is to punish humanity." God is not up in the sky punishing us, but because we have part of a web of justice, if we break that relationship with the rest of creation, creation itself will wreak it's havoc on our species, which is what is happening.

When you fall in love, everything is affected, your whole way of seeing the world is affected. We need to fall in love with the forest and the soil and the water and the animals and the birds and poetry and music and the children that are to come and are to come and are to come. We have to make broader this experience of falling in love. According to biblical teaching the shortcut to wisdom is falling in love with life itself. And what a moment to do this because life itself is so jeopardized. Antoine Artaud, a French playwright who wrote in the 30's said, "It is right that from time to time, cataclysms occur that compel us to return to nature. That is to rediscover life." I can't imagine a sentence that applies more to the moment in which we live. A cataclysm is all around us; it's in the ecological disaster; it's in the despair among the young. It's in the despair among inner city people and other unemployed. It's in despair in the developing countries. It's in our prisons.

We're still clinging to models of education from modern Europe that are not working for young people today and certainly not for inner-city people. I'll tell you how to reinvent education. You reinvent it with ceremony, with ritual, with art and creativity. This is the ancient way to teach people. This is how indigenous people all over the world taught their young people for tens of thousands of years. Why? Because you can't teach cosmology through books and lectures alone. The heart has to be opened up.

We need ways of learning that open the heart up, because the heart can relate to the cosmos. Johnny Moses, a Native American from the Northwest tribes feels called as many young people do today, to spiritual leadership. He says "the essence of our medicine teaching is very simple — we must relate to everything as sacred." Compassion is the moral attribute of God, and if we can be compassionate, we're on a Godly path.

One of the great sins of our time and culture is that of couch potato-itis. It is being forced upon us by an economic system that wants to render us passive consumers, not only consumers of goods, but consumers of our time. People drag themselves home from work that is too small for their souls; they have no energy except to turn on a dial to watch other people live for them and play for them. People who live vicariously are not living. Spirituality is about living in depth, being alive. So getting back to our own creativity is the path of empowerment. Who is going to birth the God in you, the wisdom in you, if not you?

The modern age began in the fifteenth century with the invention of the printing press. That's why the modern age, including academia, has been so textually bound. That's not all negative of course, but we paid a price for it. I'm not saying we're to throw out all books, I'm saying we have to open our hearts up.

The scripture says wisdom is prophetic, she walks the streets. She's not elitist. This is why we have to take it back and pass it through hearts of compassion and values of justice. One of the lies of the modern era, and you still get it in academia, is that knowledge is value free. Don't tell me that building a nuclear bomb is value free. Don't tell me that creating machines that can tear down rain forests in a day that it takes nature 10,000 years to create is value free. Nothing humans do is value free. Nothing we give birth to is value free. We have to critique what we give birth to with a mirror of justice and of compassion. That's the test to put to our work and to our creativity.

During the modern age beauty was tossed out as a philosophical and theological category. Descartes, who is still the father of Western academia, has a whole philosophy with no philosophy of esthetics. That's why we have an ecological crisis. In the Middle Ages, when we had a cosmology, God was called Beauty.

Part of post-modernism is to incorporate what's true and good from the past, including the modern era. The modern era was intensely elitist and arrogant, as if the only way to learn was through text and books. So in the post-modern era we want to welcome knowledge and wisdom from the past, from our ancestors, including the modern era.

Lester Brown, of the World Watch Institute, says that what we need is an environment revolution, comparable to the industrial revolution of 200 years ago or the agricultural revolution of 10,000 years ago. Ten years ago he said "We have only 20 years to pull it off." Meaning today, we have 10 years left, as a species. This is why this is not a time for business as usual, religion as usual, education as usual, politics as usual. His data suggests that after 10 more years on the path we're on, we will not be able to undo the damage we are doing as a species to this planet and therefore to ourselves. He said, "I'm convinced the number one obstacle to bringing about the environmental revolution is human inertia."

Aquinas says "zeal" is the remedy for inertia. He says zeal comes from an intense experience of the beauty of things. That is so insightful. Your energy is going to come from your awareness of beauty. When you fall in love with the rain forests you will dedicate your life to defending them. Or when you fall in love with young people who are hurting you will commit to them, to that work of compassion.

Nothing is more natural than wanting to celebrate together, wanting to laugh and to sing, because when our hearts are purified we see the world this way, we are blessed by everything and everything we look upon is blessed. That experience of blessing that is at the heart of all wisdom. That is what is needed at this moment in history, in which we have 10 years left to do something. So I invite all of you to meditate on this: ask what can you do, given your gift, your talent, your know how, your connections, your role in life. What can you do to contribute to the environmental revolution to move our species from folly to wisdom?

The Celtic poet Yeats says that "education is not about filling a pail, but about lighting a fire." It is the fire that each of you is here to set on the earth. Wherever you are destined to study, to work, to relate, to be citizens, to infiltrate. Relate with persons different from yourself. Whites with blacks, blacks with whites and Asians, young with older; men with women, gays with straights; Christian with other-than-Christian; all of us with beings other than human. In this way community happens of a wider sorts. Pluralism is a moral imperative of our time. Diversity is our richness.

The only proof of good teaching, good education will be the news that three years from now and five years from now you will have not grown cynical in the struggle, but strong, that you have not let sadness overtake you; that you keep your heart and your mind green and moist and juicy; and that you are always learning; and continually in trouble. May the Spirit accompany you on your journey. Keep your passion for learning alive. May you be lit fires wherever you are, wherever you find yourselves studying and working, may the conflagration

This essay is edited from a speech given by Matthew Fox at UCLA in the 1990's. Fox, a former Dominican priest, is the founder of the University of Creation Spirituality in Oakland, California and the author of *Reinventing Work*, among others. I have changed the dates quoted by Lester Brown above to be more current.

What is Education For?

Professor David W. Orr

If humans are to flourish on this planet, education, whose dominant focus has been human culture, must clearly place culture within the larger context of nature. Here, David Orr, Professor of Environmental Studies at Oberlin College in Ohio, speaks to the myths that drive modern education and suggests a set of principles that might replace them. This essay, written in 1994, is still completely relevant today.

If today is a typical day on planet Earth, we will lose 116 square miles of rainforest or about an acre a second. We will lose another 72 square miles to encroaching deserts, the results of human mismanagement and overpopulation. We will lose 40 - 100 species, and no one knows whether the number is 40 or 100. Today the human population will increase by 250,000. And today we will add 2,700 tons of chlorofluorocarbons to the atmosphere and 15 million tons of carbon. Tonight the Earth will be a little hotter, its waters more acidic, and the fabric of life more threadbare. By the year's end the numbers are staggering: the total loss of rainforest will equal an area the size of the state of Washington; expanding deserts will equal an area the size of the state of West Virginia; and the global population will have risen by more than 90,000,000. By the year 2000 perhaps as many as 20% of the life forms on the planet in the year 1900 will be extinct.

The truth is that many things on which our future health and prosperity depend are in dire jeopardy; climate stability, the resilience and productivity of natural systems, the beauty of the natural world, and biological diversity.

It is worth noting that this is not the work of ignorant people. It is rather largely the results of work by people with B.A.s, B.S.s, M.B.A.s and Ph.D.s. Elie Wiesel recently made the same point in a speech to the Global Forum in Moscow, saying that the designers and perpetrators of Auschwitz, Dachau, and the Buchenwald were the heirs of Kant and Goethe. In most respects the Germans were the best educated people on Earth, but their education did not serve as an adequate barrier to barbarity. What was wrong with their education? In Wiesel's words: "It emphasized theories instead of values, concepts rather than human beings, abstraction rather than consciousness, answers instead of questions, ideology and efficiency rather than conscience."

I believe that the same could be said for our education. Toward the natural world it too emphasizes theories, not values, abstraction rather than consciousness, neat answers instead of questions, and technical efficiency over conscience. It is a matter of no small consequence that the only people who have lived sustainably on the planet for any length of time could not read or, like the Amish, do not make a fetish of reading. My point is simply that education is no guarantee of decency, prudence, or wisdom. This is not an argument for ignorance, but rather a statement that the world of education must now be measured against the standards of decency and human survival – the issues now looming so large before us in the decade of the 1990's and beyond. It is not education that will save us, but education of a certain kind.

What went wrong with contemporary culture and with education? We can find insight in literature including Christopher Marlowe's Faust who trades his soul for knowledge and power, Mary Shelley's Dr. Frankenstein who refuses to take responsibility for his creation, and Herman Melville's Captain Ahab who says "All my means are sane, my motive and my object mad." In these characters we encounter the essence of the modern drive to dominate nature.

Historically, Francis Bacon's proposed union between knowledge and power foreshadowed the contemporary alliance between government, business, and knowledge that has wrought so much mischief. Galileo's separation of the intellect foreshadowed the dominance of the analytical mind over that part given to creativity, humor, and wholeness. And in Descartes' epistemology one finds the roots of the radical separation of self and object. Together these three laid the foundations for modern education, foundations that now are enshrined in myths that we have come to accept without question. Let me suggest six.

First there is the myth that ignorance is a solvable problem. Ignorance is not a solvable problem; it is rather an inescapable part of the human condition. We cannot comprehend the world in its entirety. The advance of knowledge always carries with it the advance of some form of ignorance. For example, in 1929, ignorance of what chlorofluorocarbons would do to the stratospheric ozone and climate stability was of no importance, since they had not been invented. But after Thomas Midgley, Jr. discovered CFCs in 1930, what had been trivial ignorance became a life-threatening gap in human understanding of the biosphere. Not until the early 1970s did anyone think to ask "what does this substance do to what?" In 1986 we discovered that CFCs had created a hole in the ozone over the South Pole the size of the lower 48 states, and by 1990 a serious general thinning of ozone worldwide. With the discovery of CFC's, knowledge increased, but like the circumference of an expanding circle, ignorance grew as well.

A second myth is that, with enough knowledge and technology, we can manage planet Earth. Higher education has been largely shaped by the drive to extend human domination to its fullest. In this mission human intelligence may have taken the wrong road. Nonetheless, managing the planet has a nice ring to it. It appeals to our fascination with digital readouts, computers, buttons, and dials. But the complexity of Earth and its life systems can never be safely managed. The ecology of the top inch of topsoil is still largely unknown, as is its relationship to the large systems of the biosphere. What might be managed, however, is us: human desires, economies, politics, and communities. But our attention is caught by those things that avoid the hard choices implied by politics, morality, ethics, and common sense. It makes far better sense to reshape ourselves to fit a finite planet than to attempt to reshape the planet to fit our infinite wants.

A third myth is that knowledge is increasing and, by implication, so is human goodness. There is an information explosion going on, by which I mean a rapid increase in data, words, and paper. But this explosion should not be mistaken for an increase in knowledge and wisdom, which cannot be measured so easily. What can be said truthfully is that some knowledge is increasing, while other kinds of knowledge are being lost. For example, David Ehrenfeld has pointed out that biology departments no longer hire faculty in such areas as systematics, taxonomy, or ornithology. In other words, important knowledge is being lost because of the recent overemphasis on molecular biology and genetic engineering, which are more lucrative but not more important areas of inquiry. Despite all of our advances in some areas, we still do not have anything like the science of land health that Aldo Leopold called for half a century ago.

It is not just knowledge in certain areas that we're losing, but vernacular knowledge as well, by which I mean the knowledge that people have of their places. In Barry Lopez's words: "It is the chilling nature of modern society to find an ignorance of geography, local or national, as excusable as an ignorance of hand tools, and to find the commitment of people to their home places only momentarily entertaining, and finally naive... (I am) forced to the realization that something strange, if not dangerous, is afoot. Year by year the number of people with firsthand experience in the land dwindles. Rural populations continue to shift to the cities. In the wake of this loss of personal and local knowledge, the knowledge from which a real geography is derived, the knowledge on which a country must ultimately stand, has come something hard to define but I think sinister and unsettling."

The modern university does not consider this kind of knowledge worth knowing except to record it as an oddity of "'folk culture." Instead it conceived its mission as that of adding to what is called the "fund of human knowledge" through research. And what can be said of research? Historian Page Smith offers one answer: "The vast majority of so-called research turned out in the modern university is essentially worthless. It does not in the main result in greater health or happiness among the general populace or any particular segment of it. It is busywork on a vast, almost incomprehensible scale. It is dispiriting, it depresses the whole scholarly enterprise, and most important of all, it deprives the student of what he or she deserves – the thoughtful and considered attention of a teacher deeply and unequivocally committed to teaching."

In the confusion of data with knowledge is a deeper mistake that learning will make us better people. But learning, as Loren Eiseley once said, "is endless and in itself it will never make us ethical men." Ultimately, it may be the knowledge of the good that is most threatened by all of our other advances. All things considered, it is possible that we are becoming more ignorant of the things we must know to live well and sustainably on the Earth.

In thinking about the kinds of knowledge and the kinds of research that we will need to build a sustainable society, there is a distinction to be made between intelligence and cleverness. Intelligence is long term and aims toward wholeness. Cleverness is mostly short term and tends to break reality into bits and pieces. Cleverness is personified by the functionally rational technician armed with know-how and methods, but without a clue about the higher ends to which technique should be subservient. The goal of education should be to connect intelligence, with its emphasis on whole systems and the long term, with cleverness, which is being smart about details.

A fourth myth of higher education is that we can adequately restore that which we have dismantled. I am referring to the modern curriculum. We have fragmented the world into bits and pieces called disciplines, hermetically sealed from other disciplines. As a result most students graduate without any broad, integrated sense of the unity of things. The consequences for their personhood and for the planet are large. For example, we routinely produce economists who lack the most rudimentary knowledge of ecology. This explains why our national accounting systems do not subtract the costs of biotic impoverishment, soil erosion, and poisons in our air and water from gross national product. We add the price of the sale of a bushel of wheat to GNP while forgetting to subtract the three bushels of topsoil lost in its production. As a result of incomplete education, we've fooled ourselves into thinking that we're much richer than we are. The same point could be made about other hermetically sealed disciplines.

Fifth, there is a myth that the purpose of education is that of giving you the means for upward mobility and success. Thomas Merton once identified this as the "mass production of people literally unfit for anything except to take part in an elaborate and completely artificial charade."5 The plain fact is that the planet does not need more successful people. But it does desperately need more peacemakers, healers, restorers, storytellers, and lovers. It needs people who live well in their places. It needs people of moral courage willing to join the fight to make the world habitable and humane. These have little to do with success as our culture has defined it.

Finally, there is a myth that our culture represents the pinnacle of human achievement. This myth represents cultural arrogance of the worst sort, and a gross misreading of history and anthropology. Recently this view has taken the form that we won the cold war. Communism failed because it produced too little at too high a cost. But capitalism has also failed because it produces too much, shares too little, at too high a cost to our children and grandchildren. Communism failed as an aesthetic morality. Capitalism has failed because it destroys morality altogether. This is not the happy world that advertisers and politicians describe. We have built a world of sybaritic wealth for a few and Calcutta poverty for a grow-ing underclass. At its worst it is a world of crack on the streets, insensate violence, and desper-ate poverty. The fact is that we live in a disintegrating culture. In the words of Ron Miller, edi-tor of Holistic Review: "Our culture does not nourish that which is best or noblest in the human spirit. It does not cultivate vision, imagination, or aesthetic or spiritual sensitivity. It does not encourage gentleness, generosity, caring, or compassion. Increasingly in the last twen-tieth century, the economic-technocratic-statist world view has become a monstrous destroyer of what is loving and life-affirming in the human soul."

Measured against the agenda of human survival, how might we rethink education? Let me suggest six principles.

First, all education is environmental education. By what is included or excluded we teach students that they are part of or apart from the natural world. To teach economics, for exam-ple, without relevance to the laws of thermodynamics or those of ecology is to teach a fundamen-tally important ecological lesson: that physics and ecology have nothing to do with the economy. It just happens to be dead wrong. The same is true throughout all of the curriculum.

A second principle comes from the Greek concept of Paideia: the goal of education is not a mastery of subject matter, but mastery of one's person. Subject matter is simply the tool. Much as one would use a hammer and chisel to carve a block of marble, one uses ideas and knowledge to forge one's own personhood. For the most part we labor under a confusion of ends and means, that the goal of education is to stuff all kind of facts, techniques, methods, and information into the student's mind, regardless of how and with what effect it will be used. The Greeks knew better.

Third, I would like to propose that knowledge carries with it the responsibility to see that it is well used in the world. The results of a great deal of contemporary research bear resemblance to those foreshadowed by Mary Shelley: monsters of technology and its byproducts for which no one takes responsibility or is even expected to take responsibility. Whose responsibility is Love Canal? Chernobyl? Ozone depletion? The Valdez oil spill? Each of these tragedies was possible because of knowledge created for which no one was ultimately responsible. This may finally come to be seen for what I think it is: a problem of scale. Knowledge of how to do vast and risky things has far outrun our ability to responsibly use it. Some of it cannot be used responsibly, which is to say safely and to consistently good purposes.

Fourth, we cannot say that we know something until we understand the effects of this knowledge on real people and their communities. I grew up near Youngstown, Ohio, which was largely destroyed by corporate decisions to "dis-invest" in the economy of the region. In this case M.B.A.s, educated in the tools of leveraged buyouts, tax breaks, and capital mobility have done what no invading army could do – they destroyed an American city with total impunity on behalf of something called the "bottom line." But the bottom line for society includes other costs, those of unemployment, crime, alcoholism, child abuse, lost savings, and wrecked lives. In this instance what was taught in the business schools and economics departments did not include the value of good communities, or the human costs of a narrow destructive economic rationality that valued efficiency and economic abstractions above people and community.

My fifth principle has to do with the power of example over words. Students hear about global responsibility while being educated in institutions that often spend their budgets and invest their endowments in the most irresponsible things. The lessons being taught are those of hypocrisy and ultimately despair. Students learn, without anyone ever saying it, that they are helpless to overcome the frightening gap between ideals and reality. What is desperately needed are faculty and administrators who provide role models of integrity, care, thoughtfulness, and institutions capable of embodying ideals wholly and completely in all of their operations.

Finally, I would like to propose that the way learning occurs is as important as the content of particular courses. Process is important for learning. Lecture courses tend to induce passivity. Indoor classes create the illusion that learning only occurs inside four walls isolated from what students call, without apparent irony, the "real world." Dissecting frogs in biology teaches lessons about nature that no one would verbally profess. Campus architecture is crystallized pedagogy that often reinforces passivity, monologue, and artificiality. My point is simply that students that are being taught in various and subtle ways beyond the content of courses (the tacit curriculum).

If education is to be measured against the standard of sustainability, what can be done? I would like to propose four things. First, I would like to propose a dialogue in every educational institution about the substance and process of education. Are graduates better planetary citizens or are they, in Wendell Berry's words, "itinerant professional vandals?" Does the institution contribute to the development of sustainable regional economy, or in the name of efficiency, to the processes of destruction?

My second suggestion is to use campus resource flows (food, energy, water, materials, and waste) as part of curriculum. Faculty and students together might study the wells, mines, farms, feed-lots, and forests that supply the campus, as well as the dumps, smokestacks, and outfall pipes at the other end. The purpose is both pedagogic, using real things to teach stewardship, and practical, to change the way the particular institution spends its operational budget. One result would be to engage the creative energy of students in finding ways to shift the institutional buying power to support better alternatives that do less environmental damage, reduce use of toxic substances, promote energy efficiency and of solar energy, help to build a sustainable regional economy, cut long-term costs, and provide an example to other institutions. Study results should be woven into the curriculum as interdisciplinary courses, seminars, lectures, and research.

My third suggestion is to examine institutional investments. Is the endowment invested according to the Valdez Principles? Is it invested in companies doing things that the world needs done and in a responsible manner? Can some part of it be invested locally to help leverage energy efficiency and the evolution of a sustainable economy in the surrounding region? The research necessary to answer such questions might also form the basis of courses that focus on the development of sustainable local and regional economies.

Finally, every educational institution should set a goal of ecological literacy for all of its students. No student should graduate from any educational institution without a basic comprehension of: (1) the laws of thermodynamics; (2) the basic principles of ecology; (3) carrying capacity; (4) energetics; (5) least-cost, end-use analysis; (6) how to live well in a place; (7) limits of technology; (8) sustainable agriculture and forestry; (9) appropriate scale; (10) steady-state economics and (11) environmental philosophy and ethics. Collectively these imply the capacity to distinguish between health and disease, development and growth, sufficient and efficient, optimum and maximum, and "should do" from "can do."

As Aldo Leopold asked in a similar context: "If education does not teach us these things, then what is education for?"

David Orr, Professor of Environmental Studies at Oberlin College is the co-founder of the Meadowcreek Project, a nonprofit environmental center in Arkansas and author of *"Ecological Literacy: Education and the Transition to a Postmodern World."*

This essay is from his book *"Earth in Mind"* published by Island Press. Many of Professor Orr's principles were adopted in *"The Campus Blueprint for a Sustainable Future"* crafted by delegates from 111 U.S. colleges and universities at the Campus Earth Summit.

> *Until the great mass of the people shall be filled with the sense of responsibility for each other's welfare, social justice can never be attained.*
>
> Helen Keller

AmeriCorps:
Good for Your Country, Good For Your Career

Corporation for National and Community Service

If you're reading this book, chances are you want more than a quality college education. You also want to change the world – or at least make a difference. What if there was a way you could earn money for college, gain real life skills and get a leg up in the admissions process – all while solving problems and making a difference in your community?

Well, now there is. It's called AmeriCorps, the domestic Peace Corps. Created by Congress and President Clinton in 1993, AmeriCorps has offered hundreds of thousands of Americans this simple bargain: if you give a hand to your country, you'll get a hand up for your education. Just like the G.I. Bill for military service, those who serve in AmeriCorps earn money for college in exchange for serving their country. Working through national and local nonprofits, members will tutor and mentor children, build Habitat for Humanity homes, fight crime, run afterschool programs, restore parks and streams, help the Red Cross rebuild after floods and hurricanes, and do countless other things to improve our lives and bring people together.

As an AmeriCorps member, you will receive a living allowance and health insurance. After completing a year of full-time service, you'll receive an education award worth $4,725. This award can be used to pay off student loans or to finance college, graduate school or vocational training. You'll also receive limited health benefits, may qualify for child care assistance, and may get your relocation expenses covered.

At a time of rising college costs, AmeriCorps' education award is helping thousands of young Americans achieve their dream of a college degree. Equally important, AmeriCorps is helping communities across America solve their toughest social problems. We live in a time of great prosperity, but our country continues to face profound challenges that need our attention – from hunger and homelessness and environmental degradation, to city streets plagued by crime and children who can't read. At a time of shrinking government, we need citizens to do more and young people have the time, energy and talents to lead the way.

A Life-Changing Experience

You know that a college education will help you make a difference later in life. But do you want to wait? What about starting right now, before college, by giving a year of service in AmeriCorps? Not only will you learn new skills and feel the satisfaction of helping others, you will gain valuable insights to help decide what college to attend and what career to pursue.

Beyond the skills and real life experience, AmeriCorps can change your life in another more subtle way – by raising your self-confidence and aspirations. Consider the path of Marilyn Concepcion of Providence, RI. Marilyn was a high school dropout working on an assembly line. Then she joined the City Year AmeriCorps program, where she helped renovate a community center and taught English to elementary students. AmeriCorps helped Marilyn discover gifts she didn't know she had, and boosted her self-esteem. She now studying to be a pediatrician at Brown University.

At age 19, Kristen Woolf didn't know what she wanted to study in college – or how to pay for it. For Kristen, AmeriCorps was just the answer. She joined AmeriCorps and worked in an afterschool program in Austin, Texas. She enjoyed the experience so much that she signed up for another year as an AmeriCorps Leader. With nearly $10,000 in college money and two years of real- world experience, Kristen was ready to go to school. She's now studying social work at Southwest Texas State University.

After high school, some students want to take a break before plunging into full-time academics. Beyond helping others, they want an adventure, the chance to meet new people, experience new things and visit parts of the country they've never been before. All AmeriCorps programs offer this, but one in particular, the National Civilian Community Corps (NCCC) is ideally suited to this type of student.

The NCCC is a 10-month residential service program for men and women ages 18-24. It takes its inspiration from the Depression-era Civilian Conservation Corps, which put millions of young people to work restoring our natural environment. AmeriCorps NCCC retains this focus on the environment, but recognizes that our nation's challenges today are more diverse. NCCC members work in teams on a variety of projects – building trails, restoring streams and parks, building low-income housing, tutoring children, and providing disaster relief. Members live together on closed military bases and are often sent to other parts of the country to work on special projects.

With no required skills necessary, AmeriCorps NCCC teaches members what they need to get the job done. Just ask NCCC member Lisa Melkert. After renovating a Denver inner-city school and repairing a school for the deaf in Indianapolis, Lisa attended an AmeriCorps crash course on the IRS tax system. Trained and armed with a lap top, she visited local senior centers providing free tax services for low-income senior citizens. Several NCCC teams are trained by the U.S. Forest Service in forest fire suppression. One member said, "My favorite part of the NCCC so far was the time we got called out to Idaho to put out forest fires. Who ever thought I could do that?"

For parents worried about paying for college, the AmeriCorps education award can be a big help. And a growing number of colleges and universities are offering to match the $4,725 education award with their own scholarship aid. But AmeriCorps can offer more than financial help. The qualities AmeriCorps promotes – creativity, teamwork, initiative, problem-solving – are just what college admissions officers are looking for in a prospective student. Of course GPA and SAT scores are the first thing any college will look at. But increasingly colleges are looking for well-rounded students who have volunteer experience. Nearly every college and university considers preparing students to be responsible citizens as part of their mission. What better way to fulfill that mission than by selecting those who've already given a year of their life to serve their country?

A YEAR OFF -- OR ON?

AmeriCorps helps thousands of young people make a difference and figure out what they want to do before college. But it's also a very popular option for students already in college. About one-third of AmeriCorps members have a year or two of college under their belt, and are taking time off to serve their communities and explore different career paths.

There are increasing opportunities for college students to serve in AmeriCorps while they are in college. More and more universities are sponsoring AmeriCorps programs, often with part-time positions that allow students to continue taking classes while they serve. Most of these are in the area of education and childhood literacy.

History and common sense tells us the best way to make a lasting difference is to empower people to improve the conditions of their own lives. That's the key idea behind Volunteers in Service to America (VISTA), the national service program started in the 1960s now part of AmeriCorps. As an AmeriCorps VISTA member, you might help start a youth center, establish a job bank, set up a literacy program or organize a domestic violence program. Whatever you do, you'll be be helping low-income communities help themselves to create long-term sustainable change. VISTA members usually have a bachelor's degree or three years of related work experience.

In addition to AmeriCorps NCCC and VISTA, there are literally hundreds of national and local nonprofits that sponsor AmeriCorps members. They range from America's largest and most respected groups – Habitat for Humanity, American Red Cross, Boys and Girls Clubs, Big Brothers Big Sisters – to local homeless shelters, food banks and conservation corps. You can serve in your hometown or across the country; in a large city or rural hamlet; in teams or individually; whatever your interests and background, there's likely to be an AmeriCorps position right for you.

So whether you are in high school, have a few years of college, or are a college graduate, you can be a part of this national movement to get things done and bring communities together. The spirit of service runs deep in America. You can be part of that proud tradition. You'd be surprised what a year of service could do for your community, your country, and your future.

I will get things done for America –

to make our people safer, smarter and healthier.

I will bring Americans together to strengthen our communities.

Faced with apathy, I will take action.

Faced with conflict, I will seek common ground.

I will carry this commitment with me this year and beyond.

I am an AmeriCorps member, and I will get things done.

– AmeriCorps Pledge

1. 800. 942.2677   (TDD 1-800-833-3722)
www.americorps.gov/   questions@americorps.gov

Student Engagement:
The Experience of a Real Citizen

Campus Compact
Elizabeth L. Hollander

As an undergraduate in the 1960s so much was going on in the country - anti-war rallies, civil rights protests, the war on poverty - that my friends and I felt compelled to call attention to issues of neglect and injustice, and make a difference. In Philadelphia it was easy to become part of the action around campus. Some of us picketed stores with no minority employees; others started a soup kitchen; still others fought to integrate public housing. We called exercising our rights as citizens "activism"; today student community service is more prevalent on campuses.

These and other civic problems are still with us, and college students continue to use their citizenship rights to try and make a difference. What's new is that campuses are now full participants in the action. An incredible array of community service opportunities await the student who wants to feel like a citizen. Whatever issue motivates you, whatever level of commitment you bring, whatever your style and talents, the campus is a place to contribute, develop yourself, and benefit others.

The community engagement movement is breaking down walls between campuses and communities, from rural towns to urban centers; and, by working to strengthen communities, it is breathing new life into the concept of student as citizen. My organization, Campus Compact, is a leader in this effort, helping schools develop community programs that challenge, enlighten, and even inspire. We also work to integrate service into the curriculum (service-learning) and, to bring the student movement full circle, to increase students' awareness of how they can bring about policy solutions to social problems.

You can get involved through classroom work and through activities you pursue on your own time. Faculty are adding community service-learning to the curriculum because they see that when service is linked to course content, students become engaged in their own education. The American college classroom has become a powerful springboard to citizenship. I believe that students enrolled in service learning courses today are able to access the highest quality campus community service work available.

This kind of "engaged citizenship" increases a student's sense of self. First, it's an opportunity for personal development, so whatever community service you undertake can add to your sense of competence and self-confidence. Second, engaging with others through community service can grab you in satisfying ways, and become a "habit of the heart." Students often find that in selecting a community service setting that matches their interests or skills, the involvement becomes part of their identity. If you're not sure of your skills and interests, community service can teach you about yourself in surprising and satisfying ways. If you have already encountered service opportunities, you understand what this means. If community service will be new to you, an eye-opening experience awaits you. In the last academic year alone, 1.5 million undergraduates on

Campus Compact's 975 member schools were involved in community service activities, contributing an estimated $5.6 billion in service to their communities.

Another attraction of community service is that it offers students the chance for leadership experiences. Every day new programs are developed to address local needs, and students are behind much of the creativity and planning. Students are initiating food drives, designing software to help children improve their math skills, planning alternative spring breaks to help rebuild areas hit by natural disasters, and meeting with legislators about issues that matter to them. They are doing great things, and the nation is taking notice.

Campus Compact was founded by college and university presidents in 1985 to support the student service movement. The founding group saw how service activities springing up on their campuses were igniting students' passions while also promoting good will in town. The presidents also understood that when students get connected to service and community, they take on the habits of authentic citizenship. By involving themselves in projects like AmeriCorps, Learn and Serve America, and VISTA, and by voting and taking other civic actions, students can give their lives, and the lives they touch, new meaning. These students know they are contributing something tangible to the fabric of citizenship - more than just lip service about what's right for America. And this enhanced self-awareness lasts a lifetime.

As you consider what colleges best fit who you are, and who you want to become, I encourage you to look closely at the service, service-learning, and civic engagement programs available at the schools you consider. Often admissions materials include project descriptions, and the admissions staff can give you keen insights about them. Your campus visit will help in this regard, and asking questions of current students is another good strategy before you make final choices. Some schools provide specialized service scholarships, so if you already have community experience, find out if you are eligible.

Identify schools that present an interesting array of activities. If you have a passion for a particular issue like the environment, health care, or literacy, you might want to look for schools with service programs that address them. And if a school you like does not, you'd be surprised how easy it is to find faculty allies to help you create one. Next, find out who on the faculty offer service-learning courses. Colleges and universities that combine service with learning will expose you to the subtle relationships between your coursework, the social and economic problems we face together, and the institutions working to address them. Some provide for student-directed programs which will develop your leadership and organizational skills but may take time away from direct service. Others offer more time for direct service, but you will probably have less influence over the project as a whole. You will need to decide which types of activities best match the level of responsibility you seek.

Work in the community will change the way you look at the world, and give you experiences within a context you will not find anywhere else.

Good luck!

Elizabeth Hollander is the former Executive Director of Campus Compact, the only national association dedicated solely to advancing higher education's civic mission. Campus Compact is headquartered at Brown University.

Campus Compact   www.compact.org
Box 1975, Brown University
Providence, RI 02912

Environmental Literacy: A Guide to Constructing an Undergraduate Education

Thomas H. Kelly, Ph.D.
University of New Hampshire

Because all human activities are dependent upon and have repercussions within the environment, you have an opportunity to make a difference no matter what your interests. Whether you major in marketing, biology, mathematics or music and you spend your professional life in industry, government or journalism, your actions will have an environmental impact. So, remember whatever your major is, in a certain sense, it is an environmental one.

Ask yourself then, what kind of impact do you want to make? Where do you want to make it? How do you want to make it? These questions have important implications for deciding on the kind of college education you want. If you are concerned about the environment and want your education to reflect that concern and strengthen your capacity to assess, evaluate and judge where you fit into the environment, think about these questions. Independent of your ultimate career choice, what knowledge, skills and experiences do you want from your undergraduate education? If you are concerned about the Earth, yet do not wish to choose an environmental career, consider the notion of "environmental literacy."

An environmentally literate person understands the nature of the interdependence between human activities and the non-human world. With a modern education, so often career-oriented, if we are to graduate environmentally literate citizens, environmental concerns must be incorporated across the curriculum and even beyond the classroom. The prominence of the environment and an ecological perspective emphasizing systems such as the biosphere within the liberal arts education is relatively new. Many educators now seek to connect a broad range of disciplines in an effort to grasp complex, large-scale ecological problems. This is a tall order because there is a fundamental tension between the broad inclusive character of environment, and the practical significance of specialization to the job market or graduate school.

Moreover, recognition of the need to understand the social aspects of ecological problems has introduced questions of racism, equity, human rights, national sovereignty and national security into the environmental debate. These aspects of ecological problems are now widely acknowledged to be part and parcel of these issues. Internationally, the scientific, educational, and governmental communities agree that segregation of the so-called "natural sciences" from "social sciences" is a significant obstacle to environmental education. Accordingly, calls for interdisciplinary and multidisciplinary educational programs are being heard from many quarters.

Prospective undergraduates should be aware that while intuitively appealing, interdisciplinary and multidisciplinary education are interpreted differently by different schools. It is one thing to take a collection of courses from different disciplines; it is another to integrate and internalize their contents so that you can apply them to your personal and professional life.

When you are evaluating schools and deciding what kind of education you want, one consideration is the degree of disciplinary integration. Does a given program simply offer varying menus of courses from different disciplines? Or, does it offer an integrating mechanism such as a core curriculum or a culminating course or project specifically designed to aid your incorporation of the material into thinking and action? Is there a sufficient range of sciences in the curriculum to provide a graduate with a basic understanding of the materials, energy, and processes within which human activity occurs? But beware of a scientific bias in course requirements; make sure adequate study of cultural, political and economic aspects of the environment are included. How integrated are environmental perspectives with the curriculum of other majors such as international relations, chemical engineering or theater? In addition to these types of general questions, you should also frame questions specific to your interests. For example, does the university offer semester abroad programs in developing countries? To what degree does the curriculum employ field work or problem-based learning?

While a general awareness of environmental issues has been prominent since the late 1960's, colleges and universities often change slowly. Therefore you should get the most specific information you can about the school you are considering before making a choice. The institutions in this book are among the nations strongest in environmental curricula.

But of equal importance, you will be well served in your search for the best education for you, if you begin by asking questions of yourself.

Thomas H. Kelly, Ph.D. is a member of the Environmental Studies Department and Director of the Sustainability Program at the University of New Hampshire.

> *If you wait, all that happens is that you get older.*
> Leonard Nimoy

MAKING A DIFFERENCE
IN THE WORLD

INTERNATIONAL PARTNERSHIP FOR SERVICE LEARNING

HOWARD BERRY

You want to help people. You want to go abroad, or at least experience another culture in depth. You don't want to do the usual tourist thing. You want to be challenged. You want to see for yourself what this "globalization" is all about. In short, you want something different, and you want to make a difference.

One experience that responds to these concerns is service-learning. Service-learning joins study and learning with substantive community service. It has been achieving much popularity and acceptance in US colleges and universities. When held in international/ intercultural settings its value is deepened. It allows students to encounter levels of the other culture not usually possible with more traditional programs. In addition to the enhanced learning, it encourages personal development and allows students to challenge and test themselves in accomplishing tasks for the common good.

Even further, service-learning develops what Robert Bellah termed the "habits of the heart." Through the service experience students are introduced to the realities of globalization and what it means to be a citizen of their nation and of the world.

A service-learning program can be a summer, a semester, or a year, serving the needs of the hungry, the homeless, the ill or handicapped, the very young or very old. It can be teaching literacy; caring for the sick, supervising recreation for troubled teens, working in micro-economic projects. The needs and possibilities are endless.

Interestingly, the intellectual and cultural learning through the experience of responding to these issues is as equally valuable in a developed nation as in a developing country. A service-learning experience is not easy, and shouldn't be. But if you approach it with flexibility, openness, and a willingness to learn and to suspend judgment - you too will encounter the host culture in a way not possible as a tourist or a traditional study-abroad student.

Students come to international service-learning programs from a wide variety of social and religious backgrounds, academic majors, abilities, skills and goals. But there is a consistency to their choice of a service-learning experience. They want to encounter the world directly, and they want to do it in a meaningful way.

One student participated as a sophomore from a private college in New York. A Jewish-American, he worked in a Jamaican church-based community center providing holistic (physical, mental and spiritual) services to people from low income neighborhoods. At first he felt uneasy, but he soon realized "... our religious tenets shared the common principle that one who asks shall receive, and we were to assist in this process. Never before have I encountered a place where people were willing to give so much and expect nothing in return."

Students often find that their ideas about what constitutes service are challenged by the values of their host culture. Another student from a public university spent a semester in Ecuador and learned to face the differences between his notions of service and those of the community and the service agency. "The feelings and help of gringos come second in this organization. I realize now that that is how it should be."

Service learning addresses many of the complaints about higher education in this country. Concerns about its efficacy and value, doubts about the teachability of students coming into college who are alienated from the passive classroom educational process, frustration about inability to find jobs upon graduation, and lack of educational preparation for increasing globalization beset education. Educators find it difficult to teach community in a world where the traditional ideas of community no longer work.

It is here that the concept of service-learning enters. Service learning involves far more than opportunities to work while pursuing studies. It is an integrating volunteer experience, often in another culture, designed to improve one's sense of values, to provide new knowledge, and to assist in the relief of human needs.

Service-learning is based on some simple but effective and proven educational premises. That learning is easier when rooted in practical experience. Service learning programs enrich both learning and experience by providing them with meaning. By linking formal study, formal evaluation, and formal expectation with service, it becomes not an interlude in formal education but a part of it.

Volunteer work requires a willingness to put others before self, a willingness to give up something material in order to receive something spiritual in return. The right way to learn self-worth is by observing one's ability to better the self-worth of others. Living in another |culture is the best way to prepare young people for the multicultural and globalized world of today and tomorrow. Programs take place in other cultures to broaden students' horizons to the maximum, to teach them what is relative about their cultures, and to teach them to view their sense of self and their acquisition of knowledge through the values of another culture.

Students who have been through such experiences are better able to deal with the world of work, more employable, more mature, and more knowledgeable about and sensitive to the changing global world.

Lastly, when all of this has gone on, there is something left behind and that something is good. A student who participates leaves a measurable improvement in the lives of others and hence in society. International service-learning puts new life and vigor into liberal education for the 21st century, fights valuelessness and materialism, and helps students go on to live more useful lives in the new multicultural, fragile, yet infinitely absorbing world that is before us.

The late Howard Berry was President of the International Partnership for Service Learning and a major force in service learning. IPSL offers a graduate degree in International Service Learning.

www.ipsl.org

Working for a Better World
Where Science and Technology are Used
in Socially Responsible Ways

Student Pugwash USA
David Andersen

Science majors spend countless hours in laboratories, peering into microscopes, designing experiments, and cleaning petri dishes. In the midst of endless assignments and tests it is easy to lose sight of the uses of the science we are doing. Rarely do we find time to think about how science and technology should be used in socially responsible ways. With the rapid pace of scientific and technological development, however, it is important to step back, examine the work that is being done, and ask tough questions about its applications. On college, university, and high school campuses across the United States, students are thinking critically about science, technology, global affairs, and social responsibility at Student Pugwash campus chapters.

Founded in 1979, Student Pugwash USA is the US student affiliate of the Pugwash Conferences on Science and World Affairs, recipients of the 1995 Nobel Peace Prize. With the advent of the hydrogen bomb as a humbling and frightening backdrop, Albert Einstein and Bertrand Russell co-authored a manifesto urging scientists to consider the social, moral, and ethical implications of weapons of mass destruction. This manifesto led to the first Pugwash Conference, held in Pugwash, Nova Scotia in 1957. The Pugwash spirit has always implied the need for scientists to broadly consider the ethical implications of their work, beyond the challenges raised by nuclear weapons.

The mission of Student Pugwash USA is to promote the socially responsible application of science and technology in the 21st century. As a student organization, Student Pugwash USA encourages young people to examine the ethical, social, and global implications of science and technology, and to make these concerns a guiding focus of their academic and professional endeavors. Student Pugwash USA offers educational programs that are interdisciplinary, intergenerational, and international in scope, reflecting a belief that all citizens share a responsibility to ensure that science and technology are utilized for the benefit of humankind. Student Pugwash is guided by respect for diverse perspectives and, as such, does not adopt advocacy positions.

Student Pugwash USA chapters are always asking the tough questions, such as: What are the effects of science and technology on society and individuals? How can we responsibly manage science and technology? What is the role of the individual in examining these issues? What ethical questions should be considered when doing scientific research? In a given year, a single chapter of Student Pugwash USA might address issues ranging from the future of nuclear energy to the emerging trends in communications technology and from the international arms trade to the social consequences of the Human Genome Project.

They do this by organizing events such as roundtable discussions, lectures, movie nights, and panels on their campus. In addition, the national office organizes national and international conferences, and regional events. Students from all over the country pile into cars, trains, and planes to travel to these events where they are able to listen to important leaders, learn valuable leadership skills, and meet like-minded "Puggers." Often conversations last late into the night and friendships are formed that last a life time.

Student Pugwash USA's national office also has resources to help you and your chapter. This includes a Chapter Organizing Guide which explains the A to Z of starting and running a chapter; Pugwatch, the monthly chapter newsletter; and mind•full: a brainsnack for future leaders with ethical appetites, a series of issue briefs.

Asking tough questions and organizing events that address those questions adds a new level to a student's education. Instead of passively taking classes, someone involved in a Student Pugwash USA chapter takes control of his or her education. A member of Student Pugwash USA is able to influence debate on campus and encourage discussions about critical issues that otherwise might never be addressed.

In addition to the chapter program, Student Pugwash USA encourages young people to take a pledge that commits them to work for a better world. In December 1995, the Pugwash Conferences on Science and World Affairs and its then-president, Professor Joseph Rotblat, received the Nobel Peace Prize. In honor of the Nobel Peace Prize and inspired by Professor Rotblat's idea of a Hippocratic Oath for young scientists, Student Pugwash USA developed a pledge that advocates the responsible use of science and technology. The pledge campaign celebrates the work of the Pugwash Conferences and encourages students and young professionals to commit themselves to the high standards of Pugwash.

> I promise to work for a better world, where science and technology are used in socially responsible ways. I will not use my education for any purpose intended to harm human beings or the environment. Throughout my career, I will consider the ethical implications of my work before I take action. While the demands placed upon me may be great, I sign this declaration because I recognize that individual responsibility is the first step on the path to peace.

The pledge embodies our ideals, and is our way of saying that the time has come for young people to actively promote the kind of world in which they want to live. You can take the pledge at: www.spusa.org/pugwash/.

To get involved in Student Pugwash USA contact the national office in Washington, DC which can send you a Chapter Organizing Guide and talk with you about how to start a chapter on your campus. The pledge coordinator can help you initiate a pledge campaign on your campus or in your community.

David Andersen is National Chapter Coordinator for Student Pugwash.

Student Pugwash US
800. WOW-A-PUG

spusa@spusa.org
www.spusa.org

Graduation Pledge of Environmental and Social Responsibility

I, _____ pledge to explore and take into account the social and environmental consequences of any job opportunity I consider and will try to improve these aspects of any organizations for which I work.

Begun in 1987, the Graduation Pledge is intended to be taken by students and celebrated as a part of commencement ceremonies. Since its founding, dozens of schools around the country have instituted such an effort, and the Pledge has now gone international. The commitment is voluntary and allows students to determine for themselves what they consider to be socially and environmentally responsible.

Instituting the pledge gets at the heart of a good education and can benefit society as a whole. Not only does it remind students of the ethical implications of the knowledge and training they received, but it can help lead to a socially-conscious citizenry and a better world. The pledge can also serve as a focal point for further consciousness-raising around campus.

Each year more than one million American students enter the work force who might potentially influence the shape of corporate America, as well as other segments of society. Think of the impact if even a significant minority of applicants and job holders inquired about or questioned the ethical practices of their potential or current employers. And shouldn't a job represent more than just a paycheck – a place where one can feel good about his/her own assignments and the general practice of the company?

We have learned of inspiring examples concerning student commitment to the pledge after graduation. "I told my boss of the pledge and my concerns. He understood and agreed, and the company did not pursue the (chemical warfare) project." Another supporter, "Now I make an effort to teach and think about social and environmental responsibility on a daily basis." Others have turned down potential jobs they did not feel comfortable with morally.

The pledge was founded at California's Humboldt State University and has been headquartered at Manchester College since 1996.

Graduation Pledge Alliance
Manchester College
604 E. College Ave.
North Manchester, IN 46962

www.graduationpledge.org
260. 982.5346

THE CAMPUS SUSTAINABILITY MOVEMENT

ASSOCIATION FOR THE ADVANCEMENT OF SUSTAINABILITY IN HIGHER EDUCATION
CAROL BRODIE

If you have picked up this Guide, you're an individual who is looking for a college that will help you make a difference. You understand that an important part of living and working in this global society is being able to stay in harmony with your values. You want your values to be embedded in - and reflected by – the routine of your everyday life.

When you go to college, you will absorb so much information from the campus - not just in your classes, but also as you observe the administration's approach to the world. This is often taught by example - by what is done as much as what is said. If a school's walk matches its talk, including the area of social responsibility, a shared sense of community develops.

One of the movements in higher education right now is "sustainability." Simply defined, sustainability means living today so that future generations may live at least as well as we do. However, as someone once succinctly said to me: "Not until you try to do sustainability do you know what it means." On a campus it involves every aspect of governance, academics, and operations - from institutional policies and investment, to purchasing and facilities, to curriculum and outreach to the community. The way a university runs its daily business is one way to tell if the school you are looking at really walks the talk.

Much of the early focus on sustainability in higher education revolved around largely environmental issues, such as recycling, green purchasing, energy efficiency, and alternative transportation. Recently, however, the scope of higher education's sustainability consciousness has been expanding to encompass social issues such as environmental justice and social equity, issues that are embedded in most "environmental" decisions.

For example, a sustainable food system covers all aspects of society and environment. Sourcing organic foods and purchasing locally can reduce environmental impacts, increase human health, and create strong local economies. Composting can reduce the need for large landfills and their associated environmental (and social) impacts. Paying dining service employees a living wage is also part of sustainability.

Energy and climate change is another all-encompassing issue. Some universities have become leaders in the shift to a climate neutral future, by inventorying their greenhouse gas emissions (including travel) and taking actions to reduce them. Some colleges produce their own renewable energy, while others purchase up to 100% of their energy from renewable sources. Many are engaged in creative energy efficiency and alternative transportation initiatives, whether encouraging carpooling, or using biodiesel fuel or hybrid cars.

More and more campuses are building new structures utilizing green building and energy conservation techniques, and getting certified by the U.S. Green Building Council. Often these new buidings themselves are used as classroom lessons to teach about the benefits of building green.

When considering attending a college with a sustainability focus, here are some questions you should ask:

- Does it have a strong environmental studies major or a minor/certificate in sustainability studies?
- Does it have "green" policies for building and purchasing?
- Does it purchase renewable energy such as wind or solar power?
- Does the dining service provider obtain its food locally, is a large percent of its food organic?
- Does the grounds department limit the use of pesticides or avoid them completely?
- Is social responsibility a criteria for investment (and divestment)?
- Is diversity included in the institution's mission statement, and is there a diversity policy?
- Is there an expectation or requirement for civic engagement and service learning?
- Is sustainability a key part of the institution's guiding documents?
- Is there a sustainability committee that reports to a high level administrator?
- Do they have a sustainability website, or employ a sustainability coordinator?

As you look at the colleges in this Guide, you will see how each one defines itself in regards to its community and our planet. You will find that most colleges in this Guide are committed to working on our world's complex and pressing needs, both in and out of the classroom. Read the profiles and find which colleges will best support your values and goals.

Your future - and that of the world around you - will be influenced by your choice of a college. Choose wisely!

Editors tip: If you are looking for a college with strong sustainable
practices, look for the happy building icon.

Carol Brodie is a member of the Advisory Council of the Association for the Advancement of Sustainability in Higher Education. AASHE is an association of colleges and universities working to advance sustainability in higher education in the U.S. and Canada in all sectors of higher education - from governance and operations to curriculum and outreach - through education, communication, research and professional development. AASHE defines sustainability in an inclusive way, encompassing human and ecological health, social justice, secure livelihoods and a better world for all generations.

AASHE
1935 SE 24th Ave.
Portland, OR 97214

503 .222.7041
info@aashe.org

The Talloires Declaration

Association of University Leaders
for a Sustainable Future

The Association of University Leaders for a Sustainable Future is an international membership organization of academic leaders and institutions committed to the advancement of global environmental literacy and sustainability. ULSF supports members in their efforts to unite administration, faculty, staff, and students in a collaborative effort to create sustainable institutions. ULSF promotes the Talloires Declaration and maintains an international network, facilitating information exchange, providing technical support, and operating educational programs that build organizational and individual capacity to develop sustainable policies and practices.

The Talloires Declaration is an international consensus document created by a gathering of university leaders in 1990 in Talloires, France. This Declaration is a commitment to specific actions to realize higher education leadership for global environmental literacy and sustainable development. It is founded on the belief that institutions of higher learning must exercise leadership to promote and reinforce environmental responsibility by integrating the ethical, social, economic, and ecological values of environmentally sustainable development into institutional policies and practices. This leadership begins with each university's mission and expands into the community, the region, and the national and international spheres. As a signatory to the Talloires, an institution is making a commitment to providing this essential leadership and uniting with other institutions around the world in forwarding this agenda.

Talloires Declaration 10 Point Action Plan

We, the presidents, rectors, and vice chancellors of universities from all regions of the world are deeply concerned about the unprecedented scale and speed of environmental pollution and degradation, and the depletion of natural resources.

Local, regional, and global air and water pollution; accumulation and distribution of toxic wastes; destruction and depletion of forests, soil, and water; depletion of the ozone layer and emission of "green house" gases threaten the survival of humans and thousands of other living species, the integrity of the earth and its biodiversity, the security of nations, and the heritage of future generations. These environmental changes are caused by inequitable and unsustainable production and consumption patterns that aggravate poverty in many regions of the world.

We believe that urgent actions are needed to address these fundamental problems and reverse the trends. Stabilization of human population, adoption of environmentally sound industrial and agricultural technologies, reforestation, and ecological restoration are crucial elements in creating an equitable and sustainable future for all humankind in harmony with nature.

Universities have a major role in the education, research, policy formation, and information exchange necessary to make these goals possible. Thus, university leaders must initiate and support mobilization of internal and external resources so that their institutions respond to this urgent challenge.

We, therefore, agree to take the following actions:

Increase Awareness of Environmentally Sustainable Development

Use every opportunity to raise public, government, industry, foundation, and university awareness by openly addressing the urgent need to move toward an environmentally sustainable future.

Create an Institutional Culture of Sustainability

Encourage all universities to engage in education, research, policy formation, and information exchange on population, environment, and development to move toward global sustainability.

Educate for Environmentally Responsible Citizenship

Establish programs to produce expertise in environmental management, sustainable economic development, population, and related fields to ensure that all university graduates are environmentally literate and have the awareness and understanding to be ecologically responsible citizens.

Foster Environmental Literacy For All

Create programs to develop the capability of university faculty to teach environmental literacy to all undergraduate, graduate, and professional students.

Practice Institutional Ecology

Set an example of environmental responsibility by establishing institutional ecology policies and practices of resource conservation, recycling, waste reduction, and environmentally sound operations.

Involve All Stakeholders

Encourage involvement of government, foundations, and industry in supporting interdisciplinary research, education, policy formation, and information exchange in environmentally sustainable development. Expand work with community and nongovernmental organizations to assist in finding solutions to environmental problems.

Collaborate for Interdisciplinary Approaches

Convene groups of university faculty and administrators with environmental practitioners to develop interdisciplinary approaches to curricula, research initiatives, operations, and outreach activities that support an environmentally sustainable future.

Enhance Capacity of Primary and Secondary Schools

Establish partnerships with primary and secondary schools to help develop the capacity for interdisciplinary teaching about population, environment, and sustainable development.

Broaden Service and Outreach Nationally and Internationally

Work with national and international organizations to promote a worldwide university effort toward a sustainable future.

Maintain the Movement

Establish a Secretariat and a steering committee to continue this momentum, and to inform and support each other's efforts in carrying out this declaration.

University Leaders for a Sustainable Future
2100 "L" Street, NW   www.ulsf.org
Washington, DC 20037   202. 778.6133

THE COLLEGE REPORT CARD
A TOOL FOR CHOOSING FROM AMONG
YOUR TOP-CHOICE COLLEGES

MARTIN NEMKO PH.D.

Editors note: The following two sections by Dr. Nemko are general in nature, and not particularly geared to seeking a "making a difference" education. However, in a very concise manner, much invaluable guidance is offered.

DIRECTIONS

There are 47 items on the Report Card. They are the major factors that affect students' success and happiness at college. Put a checkmark next to the 5-15 factors you consider most likely to affect your success and happiness.

Make a copy of the Report Card for each college you're considering.

Over the coming months, you'll have the chance to learn how each college measures up on your 5-15 factors: by reading college guides and materials from the colleges, talking with your counselor and college students home for vacation, asking questions at college nights, phoning college personnel and students, and making a campus visit. (See "How to Test Drive a College"). A primary source of information for each item is listed alongside it. Write what you learn in the margins of each college's Report Card.

Important!!! You can get information on most of the items by phone. For example, to talk with students, call the college's switchboard (the phone numbers are available from directory assistance and have the call transferred to a residence hall front desk, the student newspaper office, or the student government office.

By spring of your senior year, you'll have a wonderful basis for choosing your college. After you've finished recording what you learned, compare the report cards, then choose your college based on your gut feeling as to which one will best promote your intellectual, social, emotional, and ethical development.

THE COLLEGE REPORT CARD
FOR_____ COLLEGE/UNIVERSITY

THE STUDENTS

1. To what extent are you comfortable with the student body: intellectually, values, role of alcohol, work/play balance, etc.

IN THE CLASSROOM

2. What percentage of the typical first years' class time is spent in classes of 30 or fewer students? (Ask students.)

3. What percentage of class time is spent in lecture vs active learning? (Ask students.)

Most educators agree that learning is often enhanced when students are active; for example, participating in discussions, case studies, field studies, hands-on activities. It's tough to achieve active learning in an auditorium. It's particularly important that first year classes be small because frosh are just getting used to college-level work. Students who might be tempted to space out or even play hooky in a large lecture class, should pay special attention to class size.

Many colleges report a misleading statistic about class size: the faculty/student ratio. This statistic typically ranges from 1:10 to 1:25, even at mega state universities, evoking images of classes of 10-25 students. The faculty/student ratio is deceptive because it often includes faculty that do research but never teach, or at least never teach undergraduates. The faculty/student ratio also includes courses that you're unlikely to take. What good is it that Medieval Horticulture has three students if Intro to Anything has 300? Hence, the previous two questions are important.

4. How easy is it to register for the classes you want; e.g., do students register by telephone? Are enough sections of classes offered? (Ask students)

5. If you are attending a large school, are there special programs that enable you to get into smaller classes: e.g., honors programs, college within-a-college, living-learning centers? How are students selected for these programs? (Read college guides and admissions material.)

6. What percent of your instructors would you describe as inspirational? (Ask students.)

7. What letter grade would you give to the average instructor? (Ask students.)

8. Does the college make available to students a booklet summarizing student evaluations of faculty? (Ask students.)

Such a booklet makes it much easier to find good instructors. Also, its presence suggests that the college is more concerned about student rights as a consumer than it is about covering up professors' failings.

9. In a typical introductory social science or humanities course, how many pages of writing are typically assigned? In an advanced class? (Ask students.)

10. Does feedback on written work typically include detailed suggestions for improvement or just a letter grade with a few words of feedback? (Ask students.)

11. Must all assignments be done individually, or are there sufficient opportunities to do team projects? (Ask students.)

12. Is the institution strong in your major area of interest?

13. If you might want a self-designed major, is this a strong point at the school or an infrequently made exception. (See catalog, ask students)

14. Are there mechanisms for integrating different disciplines: interdisciplinary seminars, team teaching, internships, capstone classes? (See catalog, ask admissions)

INTELLECTUAL LIFE OUTSIDE THE CLASSROOM

15. Describe and evaluate the advising you've received. (Ask students.)

16. How easy is it to get to work on a faculty member's research project? (Ask students and faculty in your prospective major.)

Working under a professor's wing is an excellent opportunity for active learning, also when students become part of the research effort, they feel more like a member of the campus community.

17. To what extent do the viewpoints expressed on campus represent a true diversity of perspectives rather than, for example, just the liberal view or just the conservative stance? (Ask students and faculty.)

18. How frequently do faculty invite students to share a meal? (Ask students.)

19. How much does the typical student study between Friday dinner and Sunday dinner? (Read college guides, ask students)

20. Do faculty live in student residence halls? Does it encourage good faculty-student interaction? (Call a residence hall front desk.)

The remaining questions in this section can probably best be answered via a phone call or a visit to the academic affairs office.

21. How does the institution assess a prospective faculty member's ability to teach?

Ideally, undergraduate institutions should require prospective undergraduate faculty members to submit a teaching portfolio consisting of videotapes of undergraduate classes, student evaluations, syllabi, and conduct a demonstration class at the freshman level. Many colleges only require prospective faculty to do a demonstration of a graduate level seminar in their research area. That says little about their ability to teach undergraduates.

22. Recognizing that this will vary from department to department, how likely is it that a good teacher who publishes little will get tenure?

23. On your most recent student satisfaction survey, what was the average rating for academic life? For out-of-classroom life?

This is the equivalent of asking hundreds of students how they like their college. If they say that the institution doesn't conduct student satisfaction surveys, you've learned that the institution doesn't care enough to assess student satisfaction.

24. How much money per student is spent annually on helping faculty to improve their teaching? (not to include money for research-related sabbaticals and conventions.)

Colleges frequently espouse the importance of good teaching. The answer to this question lets you know if a college puts its money where its mouth is.

25. What is done to ensure that students receive high quality advising?

For example, does faculty get special training in how to advise students? Does advising count in faculty promotion decisions? Can students and advisors, via computer, see what courses the student has taken and yet must take?

Co-Curricular Life

26. Does the new-student orientation program extend beyond the traditional 1-3 days? (Ask students, consult admissions brochure, and/or catalog.)

27. What percentage of freshmen, sophomores, juniors, and seniors can obtain on-campus housing? This affects campus community. (Consult admissions material, ask admissions or housing office.)

28. Describe residence hall life. How close is it to the living-learning environment described in admission brochures? (Ask students.)

29. How attractive is student housing? (Ask students. Tour facilities.)

30. How well did you like your freshman roommate? This item assesses the quality of the college's roommate-matching procedure. (Ask students.)

31. Is the school's location a plus or minus. Why? (Read college guides, ask students.)

32. How many crimes were committed on or near campus last year? Ask admissions reps for the "crime pamphlet." (Each school is required to provide one.)

33. What is the quality of life for special constituencies; e.g., gay, adult, minority, or hand-icapped students? (Read admission materials, ask students, phone the office that serves that constituency.)

34. How strong is the sense of community and school spirit among the students? (Read college guides, ask students.)

35. In the dining hall, do students primarily eat in homogeneous groups: for example international, racial groups, etc. (Ask students, observe first-hand.)

36. How extensive are the opportunities for community service? What percentage of students participate in it? (Ask students, the career center, service office.)

The 'Real' World

37. How extensive are the internship opportunities?

Internships embody active learning, allow students to bridge theory and practice, try out a career without penalty, and make job connections. (Ask students, contact career center.)

38. How good are career planning and placement services? (Ask upperclass students)

Most colleges offer some career planning and placement, but the best ones offer critiques of videotaped mock interviews, the SIGI or Discover computer career guidance systems, video-interviewing with distant employees, extensive counseling, many job listings, on-campus employee interviews, and connections with alumni. (Ask students and personnel at the career center.)

39. In your field, what percentage of students get jobs or into graduate school? What percentage go into service-oriented careers? (Ask students, faculty in your prospective major, ask at the career center.)

Overall Indicators of the Institution s Quality

40. What percentage of incoming freshmen return for the sophomore year? (Consult college guides, ask admissions rep or call the office of institutional research.)

41. What percentage of students graduate within four years? Five years? (Consult college guides, ask admissions rep, or call the office of institutional research.)

Graduation rate depends in part on student quality: often the better the students, the higher the college's graduation rate. But take note if two institutions with similar S.A.T. averages have very different graduation rates. The one with a higher graduation rate will generally have more satisfied students.

42. What should I know about the college that wouldn't appear in print? (Ask everyone.)

43. What's the best and worst thing about this college? (Ask everyone.)

44. In what ways is this college different from_____College? Ask about a similar institution that you're considering. (Ask admissions rep, students, perhaps faculty.)

45. What sorts of students are the perfect fit for this school? A poor fit? (Read college guides, ask everyone.)

46. What is the total cost of attending this college, taking into account your likely financial aid package? (Ask the financial aid office.)

47. What other information about the school could affect your decision? E.G., beauty of campus, food, a graduation requirement you object to, percent of students of your religious or ethnic group. (Consult catalog, college guides, ask admissions rep.)

How To Test Drive A College

College A or College B? A visit is the best key to deciding. You wouldn't even buy a jalopy without popping the hood and test-driving it. With a college, you're spending thousands of dollars and four or even six years of your life, so better take it for a good spin. Trouble is, many students make a worse decision after a visit than they would have made without one. A college can feel so overwhelming that many students come away with little more than, "The campus was beautiful and the tour guide was nice."

Here's how to put a college through its paces

Preparing

Plan to visit when school is in session. Visiting a college when it isn't in session is like test-driving a car with the engine off.

Call ahead. Ask the admissions office if you can spend the night in a residence hall, perhaps with a student in your prospective major. If you think it might help, make an appointment for an interview. Get directions to campus, a campus map, and where to park. Also find out when and from where tours are given.

Reread the college guides. If you're just about to visit, that seemingly boring profile of Sonoma State may become fascinating. It can also raise questions, like, "The book describes Sonoma's Hutchins School of Liberal Studies as excellent. Is it?"

Review the questions on the College Report Card.

The Visit

Write what you learn on the College Report Card. Especially if you're visiting more than one college, the differences between them can blur.

Here are the stops on my campus tour. If you're with parents, split up, at least for part of the time. Not only can you see more, but it's easier to ask questions like, "What's the social life like?"

The Official Tour

Take the tour mainly to orient you to campus geography, not to help you pick your college. Tour guides are almost always enthusiastic unless, of course, they're in a bad mood. The tour guide, however, is usually a knowledgeable student, so while walking to the next point of interest, you may want to ask some questions.

Grab Students

I know it's scary, but grab approachable students in the plaza or student union and ask a question. Most love to talk about their school. You might start with, "Hi, I'm considering coming to this school. Are you happy here? What would you change about the school? What should I know about it that might not appear in print?"

In addition to students at random, consider dropping by a residence hall and talking with the student at the front desk. Or pay a visit to the student government or student newspaper office. Folks there know a lot about life on campus. While you're at the newspaper office, pick up a few copies of the student newspaper. What sorts of stories make the front page? What's in the letters -to the editor? Activists should query activists on campus. Volunteers visit the volunteer office.

The key is: never leave a campus without talking with at least five people that the admissions director did not put in front of you. Don't just speak with who's paid by the school, speak with who's paying the school. Like at high school, some people love the school and others hate it, but talk with ten people, and you'll get the picture.

A Dining Hall and/or the Student Union

Sample the food. Tasty nuggets or chicken tetrachloride? Are you a vegetarian? See if there's more than salad bar and cheese-drenched veggies. While you're in the dining hall (or in the student union), eavesdrop on discussions. Can you see yourself happily involved in such conversations?

Most colleges claim to celebrate diversity. The dining hall is a great place to assess the reality because, there, integration is voluntary. Do people of different races break bread together?

Bulletin boards are windows to the soul of a college. Is the most frequent flyer, "Noted scholar speaks", "Political action rally", or "Semi-formal ball"?

Sit In On a Class

Best choices are a class in your prospective major, a required class, or in a special class you're planning to enroll in, for example, an honors class.

At the break, or at the end of the class, stop a group of students and ask them questions. If it's a class in your prospective major, ask students how they like the major and what you should know about the major that might not appear in the catalog.

How to Visit 10 Classes in Half an Hour

Rather than follow the standard advice to "sit in on a class" which only lets you know about one class, ask a student for the name of a building with many undergraduate classes. Walk down its halls and peek into open doors. What percentage of classes are alive and interactive? In what percentage is the professor droning on like a high schooler reciting the pledge of allegiance with the students looking as bored as career bureaucrats two days from retirement?

Some students say that they are too shy to peek into or sit in on classes, but it's worth conquering the shyness. Shouldn't you look at a sample of classes before committing to four years worth?

A Night in the Dorm

It's an uncomfortable thought. "I'm a dippy high school kid. I'll feel weird spending a whole night with college students." Luckily, it usually ends up being fun as well as informative. A bunch of students will probably cluster around you, dying to reveal the inside dirt. You'll also learn what the students are like: Too studious? Too raunchy? Too radical? Too preppy? At 10:30 P.M. on a weeknight, is the atmosphere "Animal House," an academic sweatshop, or a good balance?

Are the accommodations plush or spartan? One prospective student found a dorm crawling with roaches. You won't get that information on the official tour.

Beware of Bias

We've already mentioned the peril of an overzealous tour guide. Here are other sources of bias in a college visit:

TIMING

You visited a college on Thursday at noon. That's when many colleges are at their best. Students are buzzing around amid folks hawking hand-crafted jewelry or urging you to join their clubs or causes, all perhaps accompanied by a rock band. But if you were to arrive at 4:30, even the most dynamic college won't seem as exciting.

WEATHER

No matter how great the college, rain can't help but dampen enthusiasm for it.

THE CAMPUS

Chant this 10,000 times: "Better good teachers in wooden buildings than wooden teachers in good buildings." As mentioned earlier, it's so easy to be overwhelmed by ivy-covered buildings, lush lawns, and chiming bell towers. A beautiful campus is nice, but don't let it overwhelm other factors. Colleges begin to melt together after a while, however, so you might want to take photos of each campus.

AFTER THE VISIT

Finish recording what you've learned on the College Report Card immediately after leaving campus. Especially if you've visited a number of colleges, it's easy to confuse key features of one with another: "Was it North Carolina - Asheville or St. John's that had great vegetarian food?"

Probably, additional questions about each college will come to mind after you leave. Write them down and send them to your college interviewer as part of a thank you note which expresses your appreciation for the time spent and the advice you received.

THE DECISION

After you get home, ask yourself four questions:
- Would I be happy living and learning with these types of students for four years?
- Would I be happy being instructed by these professors for four years?
- Would I be happy living in this environment for four years?
- Will this college help me achieve my goals?

If it's yes to all four, you may have found your new home.

Congratulations!

Martin Nemko, Ph.D., co-author of 'Cool Careers for Dummies" and author of "You're Gonna Love This College Guide" is an Oakland, California based consultant to families and colleges on undergraduate education.

www.martynemko.com

MAKING A DIFFERENCE CAREERS

African-American Studies   See Ethnic Studies

Agricultural Engineering   Design systems and strategies that preserve and protect water and soil resources, regarding various engineering aspects of food and fiber production. Work in developing countries helping with appropriate technology for increasing food production and quality while using human and natural resources responsibly.

Agroecology   (The study of sustainable agriculture - or organic farming') Graduates are in demand in farming, agribusiness, teaching, research and government.

American Studies   Graduates find work as journalists, lawyers, government workers, teachers, business people, historical preservationists and museum workers.

Anthropology   Majors find work in federal, state, and local government, law, medicine, urban planning, business, and museums. They often go on to graduate work in anthropology as well for a career in teaching.

Atmospheric Science   See Meteorology

Child Development   Careers as adoption counselors, child development specialists, educational consultants, working with handicapped children, hospital childlife specialists and go to graduate work for Marriage & Family Counselor degrees. They work in crisis centers, hospitals, and private and public agencies at the local and national level.

Civil Engineering   Conceive, plan, design, construct and operate dams, bridges, aqueducts, water and sewage treatment plants, flood control works and urban development programs. Employed by governmental agencies, engineering contractors, consulting firms and in the areas of teaching, research, materials testing and administration.

Community Health   Work as school health educators, community health educators, family planning educators, environmental health specialists, occupational safety specialists, public health investigators, consumer safety investigators and OSHA inspectors.

Economics   Prepares students for careers both nationally and internationally in business labor, government, public service or law.

Entomology   (Study of insects) Work in the area of Integrated Pest Management, an essential part of organic farming. They work to understand the role of insects in the natural world and how they interact with man. They seek safe and effective solutions to insect problems in urban environments and agriculture.

Environmental Education   Can lead to work in park and natural preserve administration, aquarium management, environmental advocacy organizations, nature writing, photography and documentation, teaching in elementary and secondary schools, and government work for environmental agencies.

Environmental Engineering   Work in the areas of control of air & water pollution, industrial hygiene, noise & vibration control, and solid & hazardous waste management. Graduates find work in industry, consulting firms, and public agencies concerned with air and water pollution control and water treatment.

Environmental and Forest Biology   Careers as animal ecologists, aquatic biologists, botanists, conservation biologists, consulting biologists, environmental assessment specialists, environmental conservation officers, fisheries biologists, natural resource specialists, ornithologists, park naturalists, plant and wetlands ecologists, public health specialists, sanctuary managers, soil conservationists, toxicologists, waterfowl biologists, wildlife biologists, game biologists and entomologists.

Environmental Health   Work for state governments enforcing and administering laws governing water, food, and air contamination, noise, land use planning, occupational health hazards, and animal vectors of disease.

Environmental Studies   A myriad of careers from community resource development, cultural impact analysis, to environmental lobbyist, interpretive naturalist, park managers, to wilderness survival instructors. Work as pollution analysts, environmental journalists, air quality aides, transportation planners, environmental affairs directors, recycling co-ordinators, environmental educators, energy conservation specialists and legislative researchers.

Environmental Toxicology   Those not going on to graduate study find work with government agencies, universities, industry research and consulting firms in the areas of residue analysis, environmental monitoring, forensic toxicology, animal toxicology, environmental health and safety and pest control.

Ethnic Studies   Work in community service organizations concerned with opportunities and problems of ethnic and racial groups. They work as affirmative action officers, Equal Opportunity representatives, human relations specialists, ombudsmen, urban specialists, diversity directors, educational specialists and lobbyists. Preparation for graduate work in the social sciences, law and humanities, and for work in municipal, state and federal government.

Fisheries   Work in management, law enforcement and public information phases of fisheries work with national and international agencies as well as regional, state and local government. Opportunities with private industry interested in conservation, hydropower companies, and recreation business. Careers in research, administration or teaching.

Forest Engineering   Work in the areas of water resources (including water supply for urban areas and ground water aquifer protection) pollution abatement and hazardous waste management. Design and plan collection systems to store and transport water, timber and energy structures, pollution abatement systems, and energy management. Careers as energy efficiency specialists, environmental engineers, hydrologists, water rights engineers and ground water investigator.

Forestry Graduates find work as foresters, arborists, environmental consultants, forest ecologists, urban foresters, land use specialists, forest economists, interpretive naturalists, consultants, environmental scientists, outdoor recreation, environmental conservation officers, policy makers, forest protection work, including fire, insect and disease control. Managerial work planning timber crop rotations, and evaluating the economics of alternative forest management plans.

Forest Ranger Graduates find work as county park rangers, environmental conservation officers, forest firefighters, forest rangers, forestry aides, survey party chiefs, engineer's aides, and forestry technicians.

Fuel Science Graduates find work seeking to provide reliable energy sources without adverse environmental effects. They are employed by industry, government and utilities, as well as continuing on to graduate school.

Geology Seek new resources, while insuring the most environmentally responsible means of doing so, ensure preservation of land and water quality, formulate plans for restoration of degraded lands. Career opportunities include industry, government and education. Many continue on to graduate school in urban planning, engineering, environmental studies etc.

Geography Careers with environmental and resource management, location and resource decision-making, urban and regional planning and policy questions, and transportation in government, private, non-profit and international agencies.

Gerontology Human service positions with the elderly or preparation for grad school.

Human Services Work in advocacy, program development, management, direct service and case management in child-welfare agencies, drug and alcohol programs, crisis intervention, group homes for adolescents, community action and emergency housing programs, parole and probation. May provide needs assessment, stabilization and supportive task-oriented short term counseling.

International Agriculture Development Helping to solve hunger problems in Third World countries working at the local level with government, private business, church or philanthropic organizations. Suitable for students with or without agricultural background.

Labor and Industrial Relations Graduates find employment in business, government, and labor organizations as labor relations specialists, personnel and human resource specialists, researchers, organizers, consultants and professionals in mediation and arbitration. The degree is also good preparation for graduate or law school.

Landscape Architects Work as city planners, coastal specialists, coastal zone resource specialists, community planners, environmental and land-use planners, land designers, landscape architects and contractors, regional, site and transportation planners.

Landscape Horticulture   See Urban Forestry

Land Use Planners   Work with state or federal regulatory agencies, regional planning commissions, consulting firms and municipalities.

Marine Biologists   Find careers in marine research, education and administration in marine industries and aquaculture, as well as further graduate study and research.

Medical Anthropology   (The study of the relationship between culture and health - a growing discipline for persons involved with the health needs of ethnically diverse populations.) Employment areas include local, state, federal and voluntary health agencies, and preparation for graduate programs.

Meteorology   (Study of the atmosphere) This field is important in environmental, energy, agricultural, oceanic and hydrological sciences. Graduates find careers with industry, private consulting firms, government, or continue on to graduate school.

Native American Studies   Graduates teach social sciences, work in tribal governments and communities, and prepare for graduate work in anthropology, history, sociology, or professional training in law or business.

Natural Resources Planning & Interpretation   Soil conservationist, environmental journalist, natural resources librarian, park ranger, rural county planner, environmental education leader, naturalist, hydrologist, information specialist.

Natural Resources Management   Graduates work as public affairs specialists, soil technicians, wildlife biologist/managers, plant curators, park ranger/managers, environmental planners, city planners, soil conservation planners, shellfish biologists, naturalists and hazardous materials technicians. (See fisheries, forestry, wildlife...)

Natural Resource Sciences   Careers in professional areas with a holistic perspective on resource management and research. Work at major public and private land management and wildlife organizations as foresters, range conservationists, wildlife biologists, park managers, information specialists, game managers, consultants, researchers and in developing countries.

Oceanography   Work as oceanographers, marine biologists, research assistants, aquatic biologists, water pollution technicians, earth scientists and environmental specialists.

Outdoor Education & Interpretation   Careers in designing and administering recreation programs, guiding groups in wilderness adventures, counseling and working with diverse populations (troubled youth, handicapped people, senior citizens). Work with state, federal, private recreation departments, environmental education centers, camps, schools, groups such as Outward Bound.

Paper & Science Engineering   Careers in recycling, paper making, waste treatment, hazardous waste management, oil spill prevention, environmental monitoring.

Peace & Conflict   Careers in arms control and public policy, third world development and human rights, the faith community, Peace Corps, the United Nations, domestic social and economic justice, civil rights, mediation and conflict resolution. Preparation for law, journalism, education, government and communications.

Political Science   (The study of predicting, explaining, and evaluating political behavior, beliefs etc.) Graduates find socially relevant careers in public service, political analysis and teaching. They attend graduate school in areas such as law, teaching, social work, journalism, public administration and public policy.

Public Administration   Work in administrative positions, personnel, budgeting and public relations, and in policy areas from health and human services and environmental protection to defense, criminal justice, transportation and taxation. City and town management, regional planning commissions, state budget office and administrative positions in education, national and international agencies.

Public Health   Careers as program analysts, mid-level administrators, technical staff persons, department heads in all areas of the health services delivery, and in the regulations field that require policy development, implementation, and evaluation.

Range Management / Resource Science   Careers as range conservationists, range managers, natural resource specialists, environmental specialists, soil scientists, park rangers, biological technicians and agricultural inspectors.

Science, Technology and Values   See Technology and Society

Sociology   Consultants to business and government, as social change agents (such as community organizers,) politicians, educators and diplomats. Careers as urban planners, youth counselors, employment counselors, public opinion analysts, social ecologists, industrial sociologists, correctional counselors, probation officers, health services consultants and personnel management specialists.

Social Work   Work in areas of health care, services to the elderly, community practice, rehabilitation, youth work, mental health, services to children and families, substance abuse, residential treatment, the developmentally disabled and employment services. They work in nursing homes, public schools, and probation offices.

Soil Science   Conservation planning, wetland identification and delineation, land reclamation, sediment and erosion control, land use planning, site evaluations, waste management, soil fertility management, computer modeling of nutrient and pesticide movement, and with international institutions and organizations.

Technology and Society   Employment is found in private industry, consulting companies, environmental foundations, government in the areas of policy analysis and formulation, planning, risk analysis and environmental impact assessment.

Urban Forestry & Landscape Horticulture   prepares students for careers in planning and managing vegetation and natural resources in or near urban communities, and for direct involvement in resource management or for specialized supporting roles in areas such as urban planning and environmental education. Urban forests include areas along streets and in parks, private lands, greenbelts, and open spaces. Urban foresters help communities plan, design, or protect urban and peri-urban forests; supervise tree selection and planting; and design insect control/disease protection and plant health care programs.

Wildlife Studies   Wildlife biologist, wildlife and wildlife refuge manager, fish & game warden, conservation officer, forestry technician, park ranger, soil scientists, naturalist, environmental planner, agricultural inspector, preserve manager, fisheries technician, and studying rare and endangered species. Work with state and federal environmental agencies and groups such as Audubon Society and The Nature Conservancy.

Women's Studies   An asset to careers in such fields as education, social service, government, business, law, the ministry, journalism, counseling, health and child care. More specialized work is found in battered women's shelters, rape counseling services and in displaced homemaker centers. Graduates also work as women's health care specialists, political advocates, psychologists and teachers.

MAKING A DIFFERENCE COLLEGES

ICON KEY

Next to the names of many of the colleges, you'll find the following icons. Some of the colleges don't have icons - usually because the school didn't update their information. Generally icons haven't been added for large universities.

As the choice of icons comes from the colleges, be aware that they might interpret things differently than you or I. Even with a wide range of interpretation, I'd give the icons over a 90% accuracy rating.

 Strong concerns for social justice, often coupled with service-learning.

 Very environmentally focused - often at more alternative college or a college of natural resources / forestry...

 Strong focus on peace - includes colleges affiliated with the traditional "peace" churches - Quaker, Mennonite, Brethren.

 Interdisciplinary classes/majors. A critical component of a making-a-difference education. Always found at alternative colleges, now widely accepted.

 Innovative. Can mean lots of different things! Once again, a virtual certainty at alternative colleges formed in the 1960's.

 Field studies. Varies from travel programs to colleges with many classes in the field. A component of experiential education.

 This smiling building means a "green campus" - how the campus is managed (local produce, recycling, energy conservation...) and/or green dorms.

 Get to the heart of the matter with service-learning. Another component of experiential education combining studies with service. Growing nationwide.

 Roll up your sleeves, this is a work college - all students work at the college in exchange for lower costs.

 Lots of activism on campus (not always tree-hugging.)

 For you outdoorsy folks - skiing, kayaking, biking, hiking, rock climbing... often organized on campus.

 For those of you who'd like to grow your own (food, that is) - organic gardens on campus.

ANTIOCH COLLEGE

600 Students   Yellow Springs, Ohio

Antioch College was founded in 1852 by educational reformer Horace Mann as a pioneering experiment in education which offered the first "separate but equal" curriculum to both men and women and stressed that there should be no bars for race, sex, or creed. Today, Antioch continues to dedicate itself to the ideas of equality, "whole-person" education, and community service.

Antioch students are expected to reach beyond conventional learning. They are encouraged to become courageous practitioners, intelligent experimenters, and creative thinkers. Both the faculty and the students strive towards the common goals of refinement and testing of ideas through experience, and of extensive student participation to mold both the campus and the community. All majors at Antioch are self-designed.

Antioch is committed to internationalization and to peace. Antioch encourages its students to have a balanced respect for all of life (for one's self, for others, for society, and for the Earth). Empowered by their education, students are encouraged to empower others.

To accomplish its mission of enhancing classroom education with hands-on experience, Antioch has one of the most challenging cooperative education programs in the nation. In their second and third years, students alternate terms of study on campus with terms of work off campus in one of Antioch's established Co-op Communities.

Examples of positions open to students in the Co-op Communities include working in the Wild Spirit Wolf Sanctuary, the Santa Fe Art Institute, Shaw Environmental, The Center for Economic Justice, or the Los Alamos Study Group in Northern New Mexico to working with Congresswoman Eleanor Homes Norton, the Alternative Press Center, City at Peace, International Association of Chiefs of Police, the Substance Abuse and Mental Health Services Administration, or in law offices in Washington, DC.

The variety of experience this provides is substantial. The Co-op Faculty maintains a network of employers who hire students on a regular basis. Advisers assist students in choosing and evaluating their co-ops, as well as dealing with unexpected problems.

During the study terms, students take part in an academic program which relies on utilizing the strengths of each individual, a willingness to both speak and listen critically, and an international, multi-cultural focus. Professors apply their lessons to "the real world" by bringing politics, world events, and students' co-op experiences into discussions. Classes are evaluated not by grades, but with written evaluations. The performance of each individual in class is assessed both by the professor and the student.

At Antioch College, all students design their own majors in conjunction with faculty mentors. Recent self-designed majors include Botany, Environment and Culture; Bioenergy; Sustainability, Environment and Information Systems; Law and Society; Community Organization & Multi-Cultural Societies and Social Justice. Fields of study from which students design their major include:

Africana Studies	Buddhist Studies
Anthropology	Environmental Studies
International Relations	Gender Studies
Entrepreneurship	Peace Studies

World Law	Political Science
Sociology	Women's Studies
Political Science	Philosophy

Of special note is Antioch's first year Core Program, in which students are immersed into the liberal arts through Core Program Learning Communities, team taught interdisciplinary courses. One example is "Citizenship: Politics, Law and Justice in America," with aspects from political science and international relations, history, and art. This course is a study of the historical development of American social, political and economic organizations, rights and responsibilities associated with being an American citizen, contemporary institutions, power relationships, and policies that impact our lives, and the politics of public art, including questions of propaganda and how art influences culture and citizenship.

Antioch recognizes that an important part of today's education involves the ability to live and work in the multinational and multicultural society of the 21st Century. In order that students learn about the geography, customs, and traditions of other peoples, the school mandates a cross-cultural experience (either inside or outside of the U.S.) Students can take advantage of the Antioch Education Abroad program, which has included Buddhist Studies programs in Bodh Gaya, India, a Comparative Women's Studies Term in Europe.

Another integral part of Antioch campus life is Community Government. Decision-making councils consist of students, faculty, and administrators. The councils consider the many views of the community regarding administrative policy, academic programs, curriculum, budget allocations, tenure, new programs, quality of campus life and matters such as publication standards and social activities.

A wide variety of independent groups such as UNIDAD, Third World Alliance, and Women's Center, exist on the Yellow Springs campus. With the community as small as it is, everybody knows, works, and studies with everybody else. The College nurtures close-knit relationships between students, faculty, and administration. Because of this, a common sense of responsibility for the campus prevails. This responsibility manifests itself in a recycling program, a student-authored sexual offense policy, an organic garden, and more.

The College's history of experimentation, its commitment to questioning traditional values and practices, and its willingness to act on its beliefs have had a profound impact on generations of Antioch students. Their achievements represent the living legacy of the Antioch educational experience. Antioch students approach their education, as well as their lives following graduation, with a serious resolve to tackle important issues, question the status quo, and work toward constructive change. Antioch's success carrying out its basic educational mission ‹ empowering students to make a worthwhile difference ‹ is its proudest and most enduring tradition.

Glen Helen, the College's 1000 acre nature preserve, located right across from campus, often serves as a laboratory for science-related courses. It also offers opportunities for hiking, horse-back riding, cross-country skiing, canoeing, rock-climbing, rappelling and solitude.

With its Little Art Theater, health food stores, cafes, bookstores, a town library, the village of Yellow Springs is a safe haven where students can find the essentials. The town offers an array of restaurants and off-beat shops, as well as seasonal street fairs. Antioch alumni, staff, and faculty account for a sizable percentage of the village's population of 3,600 people.

Making a Difference Studies

Core Program Learning Communities

- **American Identities: Exploring Visual and Cultural Narratives** with literature, photography, and anthropology. This course will explore visual and cultural narratives of peoples who originally inhabited or migrated to the Americas. Students and faculty will investigate questions of identity, authenticity, relationship to community, race and nation, and the complexities involved in self-representation and representation by others.

- **Sense of Place** with economics, environmental studies, and mathematics. With attention to the virtual and visceral aspects of communities and globalization, this course will investigate what it means to have a "sense of place" with our contemporary world. Students will explore the notion of sense of place by investigating such issues as trade and monetary exchange, environmental destruction and ethics, art making and aesthetic appreciation, and the world of work.

There are no "majors" at Antioch, so the lists below represents classes you can take from a few study areas.

Environmental Studies

Biogeochemistry

Wildlife Ecology

Earth's Surface Environments

The Marine Environment

Water and Pollution

Environmental Movements and Social Change

Environmental Botany

Environmental Journalism

Wildlife Ecology

Plants & People

International Relations and Peace Studies

Preventing War and Making Peace

Women; Peace; and World Community

Ecology; Peace and Global Security

Lives of Commitment in a Complex World

Human Rights and Responsibilities

Human Rights and Responsibilities

Nonviolence: History; Theory; Action

Nonviolence: History; Theory; Action.

International Law and Justice

Preventing War and Making Peace

Social and Behavioral Sciences

Management of Non-Profit Organizations

Fascism

Environmental Economics

Politics and Change in the Middle East

Minority Group Relations

The Economics of Developing Countries

Women in Cross-Cultural Perspective

Political Change: Non-Western Societies

Sex, Gender and Identity

Development, Sociology and Social Policy

Brazilian Ecosystems (in Brazil) the protection & management of biodiversity

Portugese

Brazilian Natural Resource Management

Ecology and Biodiversity of Brazil

Field Research and Independent Study

Buddhist Studies in India and Japan

Buddhist Philosophy

Contemporary Buddhist Culture

Beginning Hindi Language

Japanese Buddhist Culture

History of South Asian Buddhism

Buddhist Meditation Traditions

Beginning Tibetan Language

Philosophies & Development of Buddhism in Japan

Apply by 3/1

• Field Studies • Co-op Education • Interdisciplinary Classes • Self-Designed Majors
• Optional SAT's • Service Learning • Vegetarian/Vegan Meals

Office of Admissions
Antioch College
Yellow Springs, OH 45387

800. 543.9436
admissions@antioch-college.edu
www.antioch-college.edu

AUDUBON EXPEDITION INSTITUTE

LESLEY UNIVERSITY
100 Students   Cambridge, Mass

Audubon Expedition Institute (AEI)at Lesley University is a traveling undergraduate and graduate program based in Belfast, Maine and Cambridge, MA. For thirty years AEI has nurtured inspired, compassionate and creative environmental leaders and activists. AEI offers two traveling programs, a BS in Environmental Studies and an MS in Environmental Education and welcomes interim year and dual enrollment students. AEI also offers an MS in Ecological Teaching and Learning for informal and formal educators with field and online components.

AEI immerses students in the issues behind textbooks and the media through direct experience. Students are asked to challenge their intellect and assumptions through real life experiences addressing subjects such as biodiversity, geology and natural history. They also learn first hand about issues such as environmental justice, sustainable economics, conflict resolution, ethics and environmental psychology. Students meet the people who are part of the solution. AEI has developed an extensive network of professionals and specialists throughout North America who teach, inspire and share with our students their experiences, perspectives, and wisdom. Some of the people you'll visit include grassroots activists, government officials, lobbyists, professional environmentalists, industry leaders, laborers, scientists, and authors. AEI offers a powerful education for students who are serious about protecting the environment, and exposes students to a broad network of career possibilities and people working within these fields.

AEI students also learn from the land itself. Dorms in the traveling programs are replaced with sleeping out under the stars, traveling on a specially equipped bus and part of each semester is spent in the backcountry. Your teachers include fjords, coral reefs, ancient forests, barrier islands, desert canyons, Pacific Rim volcanoes, and alpine valleys. The program offers an opportunity to actively experience nature and people as parts of a whole. The Institute's program fosters a thorough understanding of the world of plant, animal, air, earth, and spirit - the world where community, relationships, and life are of primary importance. While connecting with the land and water students see, first hand, environmental impacts on these areas. You visit places such as oil fields and mineral mines, nuclear waste repositories, hydro-electric dams, clear cut forests, paper pulp mills, and inner-cities.

Students learn from each other. Each learning community consists of up to twenty students. Students of all ages join AEI's learning communities, resulting in a rich mixture of experience and insight. Three AEI faculty facilitate the learning community and its activities, guiding students as they take charge of their education as self-directed learners and become proficient at participatory decision-making.

Participation in AEI's undergraduate degree in Environmental Studies is an exciting opportunity for a student to broaden his or her experience while preparing for careers in education, public policy, conservation, small and non-profit business, industry, science, or environmental work. The environment becomes your educator as you immerse yourself in the study of culture and nature. Students develop skills in such diverse subjects as ecology, geology, English, psychology, history, and anthropology, and meld the sciences with the humanities to bring a holistic overview to each student's journey in education. The faculty members guide students in becoming effective communicators and expanding their ability to think critically about environmental issues. Each student's vision is cultivated through direct contact with diverse cultural groups, studies in nature, idea exchanges among students and faculty, and critical reflection on expedition experiences.

Each student is encouraged to cultivate individual spiritual growth. Developing a spiritual relationship with the environment is of primary importance in understanding the inherent connections between people, nature, and culture. AEI encourages a lifestyle that leads to the integration of humanity and nature. By providing ethical, philosophical, and practical skills development in ecological studies, AEI prepares you for a life of service as a global citizen. AEI invites students to consider that their physical, emotional, intellectual, and spiritual well-being can lead to global health. The Institute encourages students to approach their relationship to the Earth with the care and reciprocity that allows all persons to seek their fullest potential.

Because students enter AEI with varying levels of knowledge, skill and expertise in the various areas of study, AEI uses a self-referencing assessment system. This system assesses achievement in relation to each individual's skill level and growth, rather than using a predetermined norm. A key to the AEI assessment process is differentiating between simply experiencing something and defining the learning and application gained from a given experience.

The Bachelor of Science degree in Environmental Studies includes four semesters on the bus or three bus semesters and a sustainable practices semester on an organic farm in Maine. The final two years are an individually designed course of study that could include one or two Quest semesters (described below), study abroad, or courses at the Lesley University campus. A student advisor assists each student in developing a personalized program of study.

Quest is a student-designed, junior or senior year personal expedition to seek educational and career settings that complement the expedition experience. Quest may take the form of an internship, an apprenticeship, an independent study project, or a combination of these during the third year.

Students may wish to participate in Audubon Expedition Institute programs immediately following high school as a post-graduate year instead of taking a year off before college. Credits taken with AEI can generally be applied towards a student's undergraduate degree. Many students come as sophomores or juniors in order to enhance their classroom experiences and have no difficulty transferring credit from Lesley University.

Audubon Expedition Institute also offers a Master of Science in Environmental Education and a Master of Science in Ecological Teaching and Learning.

The Audubon Expedition Institute is on the progressive edge of both environmental education and philosophy. Its mission is to offer higher education that fosters ecological awareness and personal and societal transformation through immersion in a variety of environments and cultures, critical reflection, and experiential learning communities. As learners, you awaken to a deeper sense of participation within the web of life and engage in lifelong ecological and social justice and responsible global citizenship. As W. B. Yeats once wrote, "Education is not the filling of a pail, but the lighting of a fire." This belief permeates every aspect of the AEI program.

MAKING A DIFFERENCE STUDIES

Most recently AEI has been traveling in the Pacific Northwest, Alaska, Hawaii, Southwest, Adirondacks/Southern Appalachians and the Atlantic Coast.

SOUTHWEST SEMESTER:

Generations have grown up in the Southwest Desert region not knowing what the ecosystems looked like just one hundred years ago. Students learn to understand some of the massive changes to the landscape that have occurred since the time of European settlement and earlier. We explore a sky island in a sea of desert landscape. By simply traveling up in elevation a few thousand feet we experience the curious phenomenon of altitudinal zonation as we travel through the magnificent geological wonders and the unusual diversity of vegetation that exists in the Chiricahua Mountains. Investigate ranching and water issues and explore past and present native cultures such as the Anasazi and Navajo. Immersion in the desert allows for study of desert ecology, migratory bird routes and the vivid geology of the canyons and mesas. Learn first hand about issues such as the Navajo/Hopi land dispute, the damming of the Colorado River, and land management. Be prepared to have the desert enchant you and shape your thoughts with both its semi-harsh living conditions and its tender beauty. Experience living among cat tracks the size of your fist and perhaps be afforded the uncommon meeting with a mountain lion. Coyotes, jackrabbits, javalina, coatimundi, saguaro cacti, and cottonwood trees all become well-known friends. Travel spectacular wilderness areas such as the canyon country surrounding the Escalante region. Visit larger urban areas to get a sense of how a city such as Phoenix can exist in a region that only receives twelve or less inches of precipitation per year. People we might interact with include: radical environmental leader, grassland scientist, cattle rancher, archeologist, park ranger, Border Patrol, and Navajo chanter.

FIRST YEAR COURSES (32 CREDITS)

Environmental Literature

Natural History and Ecology

The Individual in Culture and Society

Learning Community as Personal & Social Change

Outdoor Living Skills

Regional Environmental Issues

Special Topics in Regional Ecology

Community Leadership and Ecological Citizenship

Outdoor Leadership

Environmental Policy and Practices

Writing as an Ecological Citizen

Human Ecology throughout History.

- **Community Leadership and Ecological Citizenship** Students learn to define and develop community ethics and accountability, and explore leadership roles such as facilitator and mediator. They investigate theoretical and practical applications of group development theory and decision-making. Focus is placed upon ways an environmental leader can work towards helping others become more ecologically sensitive citizens.

SECOND YEAR COURSES

Applied Ecology

Eco-Philosophy

Practicum in Environmental Education

Special Topic in Ecology

Human Diversity

Methods of Independent Learning & Self-Directed Study

- **Eco-Philosophy** Blending philosophy with communication, this course empowers students to refine and articulate environmental values and ethics. Environmental literature is examined, seeking new paradigms for understanding the interaction of human and natural worlds. Students work together to bring these ideas into the learning community. Throughout the course, students create a personal journal synthesizing and expanding their own ecological philosophy as they reflect on resource issues, ethical problems and ways of perceiving the world.

THIRD YEAR QUEST COURSES

Voice of Nature   Environment As Educator
Survey of Personal Growth   Internship in Environmental Education

- **Faculty Bio** Hank Colletto (M.S. Environmental Education, Lesley University, MA 1984, B.S. Environmental Studies, University of Maine/Fort Kent, ME 1982, A.A. Environmental Science, Berkshire Community College) Hank developed an intimate connection with the more-than-human- world at an early age. Organic gardening, environmental activism, and living out of doors were a mainstay of his formative years. Following his formal education Hank lived in an intentional community land trust where he taught himself to build a super-insulated, earth-bermed, solar heated home, an experience that served as the foundation from which he obtained work in the field of energy. In addition to teaching on the bus Hank teaches a sustainable practices AEI semester on the 152 acre Ravenwood Collective where he has been developing sustainable systems for agriculture, transportation and building. Hank's deep commitment to living a simple life together with his dedication to experiential, self-directed learning offer students the opportunity to explore how each of us can put our principles into practice.

- **Faculty Bio** Larkspur Morton (Ph.D. Animal Behavior, University of California, Davis, M.S. Animal Behavior, University of California, Davis, B.A. Biology, Hamline University, Saint Paul, MI) As a recipient of a National Science Award for the Integration of Research and Education Larkspur taught Biology, Ornithology and Biodiversity as a postdoctoral fellow at Colby College. She has presented at the Wildlife Colloquium at the University of Maine in Orono as well as organizing and facilitating workshops on teaching and learning for her colleagues. Larkspur is an environmental activist and traveler interested in Latin American culture and history, Zen Buddhist philosophy and practice and folk and world music. She has held leadership positions with Minnesota Public Interest Research group, thru-hiked the Appalachian trail, spent time in Peru and Bolivia and speaks Spanish.

Apply by: Fall Semester & Full Year - Early Decision 1/1, Preferred Admissions 3/1
Spring Semester - Early Decision 9/1, Preferred Admissions 11/1
Average Age: 19

• Team Teaching • Individualized Majors • Exclusive Seminar Format
• Service-Learning • Student Environmental Audits • Vegetarian Meals • Graduate Program
• Required Community Service

Audubon Expedition Institute   617. 349.8489
Lesley University   800. 999.1959 ext. 8489
29 Everett Street   info@lesley.edu
Cambridge, MA 02138   www.getonthebus.org

BELOIT COLLEGE

1,150 Students   Beloit, Wisconsin

Experiential learning, interdisciplinary thought and global understanding are the hallmarks of a Beloit education. Since its founding over 150 years ago, Beloit prepares students to be at home in the world of ideas and to be active participants in changing contemporary times. It is on this beautiful 75-acre campus - reminiscent of its New England heritage - that students combine rigorous academics with internships, research opportunities, community service and global engagement in order to become responsible headers in the 21st century.

The concept of service is so important at Beloit that it has now made community service an integral part of the First-Year Initiatives (FYI) Program, Beloit's first-semester seminar and orientation program for new students. On "move in" day, FYI immediately links new students with an experienced professor and a group of peers. Together the class determines their community service project. The professor also serves as academic advisor and mentor until the student declares a major.

For many, FYI is just the beginning of volunteerism. Beloit students have traveled to, among other places, Guatemala, the Netherlands, Alaska and even Beloit, Alabama, doing such projects as researching acid rain, teaching, inventorying Bald Eagle populations and building schools.

In fact, Beloit College provides grant funding for community service projects. First-year students vie for Venture Grants of up to $1,500 to fund community research projects of their choosing. Similarly, the Beloit is America Program funds innovative community internships that engage students in meaningful service projects in the city of Beloit. Beloit students' commitment to social change is evident when they graduate, too: the College is consistently ranked in the top 20 colleges/universities for producing Peace Corps volunteers.

At Beloit, students share their learning experience with peers from 49 states and 56 nations. It's just as likely that your roommate will be from New York, Oregon, or Missouri, as it is that they'll be from Finland, Zaire, or Wisconsin. What they all share, however, is this practical idealism, a deep respect for individuality, and a commitment to making diversity work.

With more than 100 clubs and organizations, you can find your cultural and social niche at Beloit - or organize a new club that suits your fancy. Students can "invent themselves" because there is no lengthy list of requirements, no rigid formula for choosing a major, no mold in which you're expected to fit. Students are encouraged to build a larger program of study by exploring social interests through an interdisciplinary minor, a second major, internships, and study abroad opportunities. There are literally hundreds of directions to go at Beloit - and Beloit is committed to providing students the resources that will allow them to make the critical and productive connections between thought and action in all aspects of their lives.

Making a Difference Studies

Environmental Geology

Department is a member of the distinguished Keck Geology Consortium, providing majors with outstanding opportunities to participate in summer research activities in US and overseas.

Enviro Geology and Geologic Hazards
Sedimentology
Natural History
Foundations of Economic Analysis
Geologic Field Methods

Mineralogy and Crystallography
Hydrology
Challenge of Global Change
Marine Biology
Field Excursion Seminar

Biology: Environmental, Behavioral, Medical, Molecular Biology

Botany
Behavioral Ecology
Comparative Physiology
Microbiology
Biological Issues

Environmental Biology
Population Biology
Zoology
Molecular Biology and Biotechnology
Developmental Biology

Philosophy and Religion

Biomedical Ethics
Personal Freedom and Responsibility
Violence and Non-Violence
Hebrew Scriptures
Islam

Business Ethics
Philosophy of Science
Logic
Oriental Philosophy
20th Century Theology

Government and International Relations

Women and Politics
Civil Liberties
Communist & Post-Communist Systems
Parties and Groups in American Politics
American Presidency

Principles of Government and Politics
The Politics of Developing Countries
Politics of Advanced Industrial Democracies
Theories of International Relations
American State Gov't. and Politics

- **International Organization & Law**   Political foundations of int'l. institutions and law. Transformation of UN, growth of specialized agencies and contemporary legal framework. Int'l. peace & security, arms control, economic development, social welfare & human rights in int'l. organizations.

Interdisciplinary Studies

Individually developed majors have included Women, Environment and Change; Choreography of the Universe; Set-design for Educational TV & African Studies.

Energy Alternatives
Liberal Education and Entrepreneurship
Sense of Place: Regionalism in America
Circumstances of Agriculture in US
Photographic Images as Recorders of History and Social Change

Town and City in the Third World
Mass Communication in a Modern Society
Women, Feminism and Science
Cultural Resource Management

Sociology   Women's Studies   Health Care Studies
Apply by 1/15

- All Seminar Format   • Self-Designed Majors   • Required Community Service
- Interdisciplinary Classes   • Theme Housing   • Field Studies   • Vegetarian & Vegan Meals

Admissions Office
Beloit College
700 College Street
Beloit, WI 53511-5595

608. 363.2500
800. 923.5648
www.beloit.edu
admiss@beloit.edu

BEMIDJI STATE UNIVERSITY

4,400 Undergraduates   Bemidji, Minnesota

On the shores of Lake Bemidji in Minnesota's northern lakes and forests region, Bemidji State University focuses on preparing students to be active, responsible world citizens. All students study global, environmental and civic stewardship as part of their liberal arts requirements. To prepare for careers, students choose from over 65 majors and pre-professional programs.

Freshmen explore values, ethics, and a commitment to service through our First-Year Experience program, which serves as a semester-long, campus-wide orientation. All students participate in the "Responsible Men, Responsible Women" program where they learn the actions needed to become principled leaders. Bemidji State is student-centered with small class sizes, a low student/faculty ratio, and individual faculty advising.

Student talents are strengthened outside the classroom too. Bemidji State's Outdoor Program Center is the nation's most active, sponsoring over 1000 activities and trips each year. Bemidji State also stresses service learning and much of that service is in the environmental area. In fact, the World Wildlife Federation recognized Bemidji State as a nationally leading school in more categories than any other Minnesota university. Students also find service opportunities through 85 student organizations. These organizations range from a nationally award-winning Habitat for Humanity chapter to an Accounting Club that helps the elderly prepare their income taxes. Bemidji State was one of the first Minnesota state universities to officially recognize volunteerism with a Student Development Transcript that documents their service activities.

Helping build a sense of community, the residential life program includes a single-parent housing and Open Borders, a multi-cultural dormitory community. In Open Borders, students from different cultures live and learn together through social and educational experiences. This same community-building spirit is reflected in the American Indian Resource Center. The center is a cultural and educational hub for the campus and surrounding communities, including three Native American reservations. International students are an active part of campus, annually hosting an international festival to share their heritages with the campus community. For first-hand international experiences, students participate in an ever-expanding study abroad program. Bemidji's program is one of the state system's most active, and offers annual trips and exchanges to destinations such as Iceland, China, South Africa, Western Europe, Hawaii, Australia and Malaysia.

Interdisciplinary learning is the cornerstone of the School of Integrative Studies. The school offers the university's Honors Program and programs in Indian Studies, Women's Studies, and International Studies. These programs broaden students' understanding of cultural and intellectual traditions through interdisciplinary courses and projects.

In a learning environment that promotes personal responsibility, global thinking, and life-long education, students experience a combination of the lake, the learning, and the life that is uniquely Bemidji State University. Founded on a sound liberal education, Bemidji State programs educate students so that they may live as responsible, productive, and free citizens in a global society.

Making a Difference Studies

Aquatic Biology
Prepares students for careers involving water quality and natural resource management.

Limnology

Organic Evolution

Water Analysis

Aquatic Biology Internship

Fisheries Management

Aquatic Plants

General Ecology

Intro and Advanced Laboratory & Field Projects

Environmental Studies
Defines and solves environmental problems caused by human actions.

Environmental Conservation

Ecosystem Studies

Environmental Economics

Risk Assessment and Auditing

Environmental Internship or Senior Thesis

Environmental Politics

Waste Management

Society and Environment

Air Pollution Technology

Community Health
Addresses the intellectual, occupational, social, emotional, physical and spiritual aspects of well being.

A Lifestyle for Wellness

Health and Drugs in Society

Family Violence

Group Processes

Community Health Epidemiology

Nutrition

Personal and Consumer Health

Health Practicum and Internship

Psychology and Applied Psychology
Exploring the science of behavior, cognition and affect.

Learning and Cognition

Family Systems

Psychological Measurement

Abnormal Psychology

Personality Theories

Human Sexuality

Counseling and Crisis Techniques

Lifespan Development

Death and Culture

Psychology Internship

Social Work
Focuses on improving the quality of life for individuals, groups and communities.

Intercultural Communication

Social Welfare Policy

Family Dynamics and Intervention

Generalist Practice Experiences

Social Work Field Experiences and Internship

Social Work and the Law

Dependency: Prevention and Intervention

Behavior in the Social Environment

Chemical Dependency: Prevention & Intervention

Space Studies
Explores space as a natural extension of human inquiry through a natural science foundation and an interdisciplinary emphasis.

Introduction to Planetary Science

Geographic Information Systems

Introduction to Oceanography

History of Space Exploration and Studies Environments

Aerial Photography

Mineralogy and Petrology

Advanced Planetology

Psych. of Living in Isolated & Confined Environments

Indian Studies

Addresses the heritage, culture and diversity of Native Americans.

Native North Americans
American Indian Lands
American Indian Literature
Tribal Government
Federal Indian Law

History of the Ojibwe
First Nations of Canada
Elementary Ojibwe
The American Indian: Social Work Perspective
Senior Thesis in Indian Studies

Women's Studies

Issues of race, class, religious preference, sexual identity and gender as influences on women's lives.

Women's Issues
Feminist Theories and Practice
Women and Diversity
The Politics of Women's Health

Family Violence
Women in World Literature
Women and Philosophy
Practicum in Women's Studies

International Studies

Promotes awareness, appreciation and knowledge of the global community.

The Global Economy
World Regional Geography
Introduction to International Relations
Cultural Anthropology
Economic Geography

Comparative International Study Project
International Law and Organizations
Religion in the Modern World
International Communication
International Experience

Regional & Land-Use Planning, Geographic Info Systems, Park & Recreation Planning

Focuses on geographical analysis, techniques and applications at the regional, national and global levels within emphasis areas.

Land Use Analysis and Planning
Urban Geography
Site Analysis and Planning
American Indian Lands
Data Modeling and Design
Weather and Climate

Regional Planning Methods
Geographic Information Systems
Geography and Planning of Outdoor Recreation
Public Administration
Conservation Biology
Intro to Environmental Ed. & Interpretation

Applied Public Policy (Minor)

Focuses on a sophisticated understanding of the laws, codes, social service programs and regulations affecting daily lives

State and Local Politics
Public Economics
Benefit Cost Analysis
Environmental Economics
Labor Economics

Introduction to American Politics
Markets and Resource Allocation
Public Administration
Society and the Environment
Global Resource Politics

Environmental Engineering Science   Environmental Mgm't.   Environmental Chemistry
Wetlands Ecology   Outdoor Education   Wilderness Mgm't. & Outdoor Rec. Planning
Chemical Dependency   Criminalistics   Religious Studies   Social-Anthro   Pre-professional

Rolling Admissions   In-State Tuition for All Students
•Team Teaching   • Interdisciplinary Classes   • Service Learning   • Theme Housing
65% of classes have fewer than 20 students and only 4% of classes have more than 50 students

Admissions Office
Bemidji State University
Bemidji, MN 56601

1. 877. BEMIDJI
800. 475.2001 (Information)
admissions@bemidjistate.edu
www.bemidjistate.edu

BEREA COLLEGE
1500 Students   Berea, Kentucky

Founded in 1855 as the first interracial and co-educational college in the South, Berea College promotes understanding and kinship among all people, service to communities in Appalachia and beyond, and sustainable living practices which set an example of new ways to conserve our limited natural resources. Berea builds upon a distinctive history of 150 years of learning, labor and service, and find new ways to apply it's mission to contemporary times, and holds to its founding motto "God has made of one blood all peoples of the earth." The utilitarian and the practical, the scientific and the spiritual, have always been part of Berea's heritage."

Berea nurtures intellectual, physical, aesthetic, emotional and spiritual potentials and with those the power to make meaningful commitments and translate them into action. Berea commits itself to provide an educational opportunity primarily for students from Appalachia, black and white, who have great promise and limited economic resources. Financial need is a requirement for admission. Berea believes the following:

•   To assert the kinship of all people and to provide interracial education with a particular emphasis on understanding and equality among blacks and whites;

•   To create a democratic community dedicated to education and equality

•   To encourage a way of life characterized by plain living, pride in labor well done, zest for learning, and concern for the welfare of others.

The Sustainability and Environmental Studies (SENS) Program is an important part of Berea College's efforts to develop a sustainable campus. SENS links the formal curriculum of the classroom to the many opportunities for experiential learning- learning by doing- that come from participation in the creation and operation of a College that "walks the walk" regarding sustainability. By conveying to all members of the Berea community an understanding of the severity of threats such as global climate change, social disruption, and economic globalization, and by exploring alternative visions of a sustainable future, the SENS Program seeks to both teach and foster sustainability at scales from local to global.

Berea's cultural studies requirements insure that each student will gain an understanding of aspects of other cultures; a recognition of, and sensitivity to, similarities and differences in cultures; and an expanded perspective on a pluralistic world.

Each student performs some of the labor required in maintaining the institution, thus gaining an appreciation of the worth and dignity of all the labor needed in a common enterprise and to acquire some useful skill. This makes Berea available to students who are unable to meet college expenses, but have the ability and character to use a liberal education for responsible service to society. Through the fellowship of meaningful work, an atmosphere of democratic social living prevents social and economic distinctions and instills an awareness of social responsibility. Student industries including weaving, woodcraft and wrought iron are sold in a student run gift shop and hotel.

The Berea College Ecovillage is an ecologically-sustainable residential and learning complex. Rigorous performance goals include: reduction of energy and water use by 75%; treatment of sewage and wastewater on-site to swimmable quality, and recycling, reusing or composting at least 50% of waste. The Ecovillage incorporates a wide range of "green design" including passive solar heating, photovoltaic panels and wind-powered electrical generators. Roof-top capture of rainwater contributes to landscape irrigation and production of fruits and vegetables.

MAKING A DIFFERENCE STUDIES

GENERAL STUDIES

Community Building

Freedom and Justice: The Third World

Housing: American Dream or Nightmare

Politics of Food

Immigrants and Minorities

Sacred Earth, Sacred Relationships

Health Decisions: Justice and Autonomy

Women, Society and Mental Health

Technology, Culture, Belief

Community and Spirituality

Values in Conflict

Labor, Learning and Leisure

- **One Blood, All Nations: Cultural Diversity & Environmentalism**   Tensions between advocacy for cultural diversity and environmentalism, especially the environmental concept of a global commons. Achieve a deeper understanding of the issues contained within the concepts of kinship of all people and a way of life characterized by plain living; deeper understanding of the relatedness of these concepts; and understand how these concepts generate questions of freedom and justice.

BLACK STUDIES

Introduction to Afro-American Studies

Slavery & Afro-American Culture

Afro-American Music: An Overview

Black Emancipation & Reform in the U.S.

Critical Issues of Black Americans in the Twentieth Century

Afro-American Literature

Contemporary Afro-American Experience

Race in America

Sub-Saharan Black African Art

AGRICULTURE AND NATURAL RESOURCES IN SUSTAINABLE SYSTEMS

Develops broadly educated graduates and prepare them for modern and sustainable careers in the production of food and fiber, natural resource management, veterinary medicine and related fields.

Science and Society's Food Supply

Agricutural Economics

Bees and Beekeeping

Intro to Global Agriculture

Soil and Water Conservation

Animal Science

SUSTAINABILITY & ENVIRONMENTAL STUDIES (Minor)

Natural building workshops in cordwall, living roof, earthbag construction and cob.

Agroecology

Sustainable Appalachian Communities

Sustainability and Environmental Studies

Ecological Architecture

Intro to Ecological Design

Experiential Learning Project

APPALACHIAN CULTURE (Minor)

Appalachian Literature

Appalachian Problems and Institutions

Appalachian Music

Appalachian Culture

Health in Appalachia

Appalachian Crafts

- **Community Analysis: The Appalachian Case**   History, demography, social structure and forces promoting social change in Appalachian rural communities. Sociological approach to understanding the concept of community, its various systems, institutions and groups. Community problem-analysis orientation. American, European & Third-World communities examined.

WOMEN'S STUDIES   CHILD /FAMILY STUDIES   SOCIOLOGY

Rolling Admissions   Suggest Early Application by November 30

Student Body: 80% from Southern Appalachia, 12% Minority, 7% International

All tuition costs are met by the college

• Green Campus   • Field Studies   • Co-op Work Study   • Study Abroad   • Interdisciplinary

Office of Admissions

Berea College

CPO 2220

859. 986.3500

www.berea.edu

admissions@berea.edu

BROWN UNIVERSITY

6,000 Undergraduates   Providence, Rhode Island

Very few centers of higher education can honestly claim to offer their students the breadth and depth of a university's resources, and the intimate experience of an undergraduate liberal arts college. Brown offers this rare balance. Recently implemented "University Courses" emphasize synthesis rather than survey, and focus on the methods, concepts, and values employed in understanding a particular topic or issue. Using a single discipline or interdisciplinary approach, they introduce students to distinctive ways of thinking, constructing, communicating, and discovering knowledge. This emphasis has spawned unusual interdepartmental concentrations and programs. Biomedical researchers have worked with the departments of Philosophy and Religion to create a concentration in Biomedical Ethics. The Health and Society concentration pulls together the fields of human biology, community health, economics, and the social and behavioral sciences to examine health care systems and address policy issues at the local, national, and international levels.

The Environmental Change Initiative is an interdisciplinary research and education program linking faculty and students from a number of departments and centers at Brown University. The initiative allows faculty, postdoctoral fellows, graduate students and undergraduates to use an interdisciplinary team approach to tackle significant problems in environmental change.

Working at organizing workshops, courses, and fostering research and graduate training, our efforts build on relationships among Brown's other strong academic units and affiliated institutions such as the Marine Biological Laboratory. Brown takes advantage of the wealth of knowledge and resources of its partner units, including: the Departments of Geological Sciences, Ecology and Evolutionary Biology, Sociology, Economics, as well as the Center for Environmental Studies, the Marine Biological Laboratory, the Watson Institute for International Studies and the Population Studies Center. Brown is also making headway in greening its campus operations.

Brown University's historical strength in multidisciplinary research and scholarship is opening new possibilities. Collaborations between faculty and undergraduates in research and course development have resulted in research on the impact of TV advertising on election campaigns, developing models of predator-prey interactions in marine ecosystems, collaborated with engineering professors to build a "clean air" automobile and worked at a missionary hospital in Kenya.

Former Brown President Gregorian noted "more than ever, we need to recover a sense of the wholeness of human life and to understand the human condition.... We need to admit questions of values to the arena of discussion and debate. The social implications of a political system, the ethical consequences of a scientific technique, and the human significance of our responsibilities should have a place in classrooms and dormitories. To deny that place is to relinquish any claims or any attempt to link thought and action, knowing and doing."

Brown's emphasis on civic and social responsibility, and on bridging the gap between academia and the world beyond, provides opportunities to integrate community work with academic and career goals. The Center for Public Service coordinates activities with academic programs, including Public Policy, Health and Society, Urban Studies and Environmental Studies. The Taubman Center for Public Policy is working with the city of Providence to develop a comprehensive antipoverty program, and the Feinstein World Hunger Program tackles the issue of starvation amid plenty.

Making a Difference Studies

Public Policy and American Institutions

Health Economics
Woman and Public Policy
Public Policy and Higher Education
Social Welfare Policy
The Price System and Resource Allocation

Environmental Regulation
Liberalism Beyond Justice
Law and Public Policy
Housing & Community Development Policy
Civil Liberties, Moral, Political, Legal Approaches

Development Studies: Global Security, global Environment, Political Economy

Fundamentally concerned with understanding how processes of change impact the distribution of wealth and opportunity both within and between nations.

Population Growth and the Environment
Problems in International Environmental Policy
Nuclear Weapons: Technology and Policy
Women & Health Care
Burden of Disease in Developing Countries

Sociological Perspectives: Mexico - U.S.Migration
Globalization and Social Conflict
Shaping of World Views
International Health: Anthropological Perspectives
Islam and Politics in the Modern World

Community Health

Culture and Health
Ideology of Development
AIDS in International Perspective
International Environmental Issues
Red, White & Black in the Americas
Comparative Policy and Politics: East Asia

Environmental Health and Policy
Epidemiology of Violence and its Consequences
Nutritional Problems in the Developing World
Social Change in Modern India
Third World Political & Economic Issues
Cost vs. Care: The Dilemma for American Medicine

International Relations: tracks in global security, political economy & development, politics, culture and Identity, global environment

Examines a range of issues including diplomacy, war, and peace; poverty, inequality, and development; trade, globalization, and economic conflict; human rights and humanitarianism; the production and role of culture and political identities; and the environment and global public health.

Int'l. Political Economy of Development
Chinese Democracy Movement
The Environmental State
Corporations and Global Cities
Self Determination and Secession

Conflict & Cooperation in International Politics
Human Rights & Justice after Political Transitions
Ethnographic Perspectives on Poverty & Progress
Health, Hunger & the Household: Developing Countries
Ethnic Politics and Conflict

Sociology

Economic Development & Social Change
Industrialization, Democracy and Dictatorship
Social Inequality
War and the Military
Environmental Sociology

American Heritage: Racism & Democracy
Population Growth and the Environment
Race, Class and Ethnicity: Modern World
Women in Socialist & Developing Countries
Social Structures & Personal Development

Gender Studies   Environmental Studies   Urban Studies   Africana Studies

Education   Ethnic Studies   Public Policy   Geological Sciences   Marine Biology

Apply by 1/1

Admission Office
Brown University
Providence, RI 02912

401. 863.9300
www.brown.edu
admission_undergraduate@brown.edu

BRYN MAWR COLLEGE

1350 Students   Bryn Mawr, Pennsylvania

Bryn Mawr is a liberal arts college in both the modern and traditional senses. Its curriculum is modern in offering a full range of subjects in the arts, sciences, and social sciences, but the College is also traditional in its commitment to the original sense of "liberal arts" — the studies of a free person.

Bryn Mawr believes in a broad education which prepares students to be free to question or advocate any idea without fear. This kind of education results in graduates who are determined to change society. Among Bryn Mawr graduates are the former domestic policy adviser to Vice President Albert Gore; the deputy director of the U.S. Office of Management and Budget; the medical director of the only women's health clinic in Nairobi; federal judges, children's legal advocates, teachers at every level, and a much higher than usual percentage of women who are in positions to improve society — in this country and around the world.

Stemming from the College's Quaker roots, Bryn Mawr's commitment to understanding the world, engaging with it, and transforming it for the better has been longstanding. The Praxis Program is Bryn Mawr's community-based learning program, created to enhance liberal arts education with practical experiences in field settings beyond the campus. The Community Service Office strives to spark life-long commitment to service, activism and advocacy by helping students connect their academic and extracurricular work to principles of social justice.

Individual responsibility with a concern for the community are prime traits of Bryn Mawr students. The college believes that the pleasure of knowledge is insufficient if that knowledge does not lead to social action. Too many people act without knowing and too many highly educated people won't act on behalf of others. Bryn Mawr seeks students who wish to use their education, not merely for personal enrichment but to be fully contributing, responsible citizens of the world. Mary Sefranek is a good example of Bryn Mawr's philosophy in action. She was one of twenty USA Today All Academic Team winners for, among her many accomplishments, the work she has done with a middle School in Philadelphia. Mary created a special program for this low-income, primarily Hispanic public school, including co-ordinating teams of Bryn Mawr student tutors and field trips.

The unusually high percentage of foreign students means everyone learns first-hand about real world problems. Bryn Mawr is among a handful of private colleges which give financial aid to foreign students. A CBS Sunday Morning News show featured four Bryn Mawr students in a segment called "Women of the Revolution." Students from Kuwait, the People's Republic of China, Rumania, and South Africa talked about their hopes that their Bryn Mawr educations would be put to use for their people at home.

The Minority Coalition, an organization representing all of the minority student organizations, enables minority students to work together to increase the number of minority students and faculty, and to develop curricular and extra-curricular programs dealing with United States minority groups and non-Western peoples and cultures.

Making a Difference Studies

Peace and Conflict Studies

Draws upon Bryn Mawr's interest in war, conflict, peacemaking, and social justice, as well as associated fields of anthropology, economics, history, political science, social psychology and sociology. Theoretical understanding of bargaining, internal causes of conflict, cooperative and competitive strategies of negotiation, intergroup relations and the role of institutions in conflict management

Peace and Globalization

Social Inequality

History and Principles of Quakerism

Ethnic Group Politics

Conflict and Conflict Management: A Cross-Cultural Approach

Indigenous Movements of MesoAmerica

Cultural and Ethnic Conflict

Human Rights, Conflict & Transitional Justice

Great Powers and the Near East

Growth and Structure of Cities

Interdisciplinary major challenges students to understand the relationship of spatial organization and the built environment to politics, economics, culture and society.

Urban Culture and Society

Ancient Greek Cities and Sanctuaries

Latin American Urban Development

Taming the Modern Corporation

Topics in History of Modern Planning

Environment and Society: History, Place & Problems

The Form of the City

Comparative Urbanism

Urban Culture and Society

Introduction to Architectural and Urban Design

Ethnic Group Politics

Anthropology

Sex, Culture and Society

African Ethology: Urban Problems

Nutritional Anthropology

Psychological Anthropology

Traditional and Pre-Industrial Technology

Medical Anthropology

Language in Social Context

Human Ecology

Conflict & Inequality in Latin America

Ethnography of South Asia

Gender and Sexuality Studies

Beauty and Sexuality

Patterns in Feminist Spirituality

Social Inequality

Psychobiology of Sexual Differences

Women in Contemporary Society: Third World Women

Ethics

Topics in European Women's/Gender History

Women in Early Christianity

Gender, Class and Culture

Political Science

Politics of Ethnic, Racial & National Groups

New European Social Movements

Developmental Ethics

International Politics

Israel and the Palestinians: History, Politics, Negotiation and Conflict

Politics and the Mass Media in US

Comparative Public Policy

African & Caribbean Perspectives in World Politics

Citizenship and Migration

Environmental Studies   Geology   Cross Registration with Haverford College

Apply by 1/15

Student Body: 16% Asian American, Other Minority 15%, International 8%

• Team Teaching • Self-Designed Majors • Interdisciplinary Classes • Service Learning • Vegetarian Meals

Office of Admissions
Bryn Mawr College
Bryn Mawr, PA 19010

610. 526.5000
www.brynmawr.edu
admissions@brynmawr.edu

U. of California at Santa Cruz

13,600 Undergraduates   Santa Cruz, CA

UC Santa Cruz has a unique residential college system. Every undergraduate student affiliates with one of ten colleges while they participate in a campus wide academic program. Although students take classes in any number of colleges throughout the campus, core courses within each college provide a common academic base.

Off-campus internships are an integral part of programs in Community Studies, Economics, Environmental Studies, Health Sciences, Latin American and Latino studies, Psychology, and Teacher Education. And unlike most schools in the UC system, UCSC is committed to undergraduate teaching.

Adlai Stevenson College's theme, "Self and Society", emphasizes the goals of both self-understanding and active participation in one's community. Stevenson students major in a wide array of fields - humanities, social sciences, natural sciences, the arts, and engineering.

The theme of College Eight, "Environment and Society", embodies a concern for environmental issues within a social, political, scientific and humanistic context. The core course "Environment and Society", examines education, identity, nature, community, livelihood, and livability at local and national levels as contemporary global transformations affect them.

Kresge College is a center of innovative interdisciplinary, social, and cross-cultural programs, where diverse groups come together with the vision of communication across boundaries in an effort to spearhead social change. It was founded to reconnect the intellectual life of the classroom with everyday spiritual, psychological, and emotional concerns.

College Nine's intellectual theme is international and global perspectives. Its mission is to empower students to achieve educational success in the context of a diverse learning community that encourages critical thinking and ethical development. Students are provided with opportunities to develop critical thinking, leadership skills, and cultural competency. Through these experiences, our aim is for College Nine students to become conscientious global citizens with an appreciation of our interconnected world.

College Ten's theme is Social Justice and Community. Special attention is paid to those who are denied opportunities afforded to more privileged members of society. Issues include racism, sexism, poverty, greed, ethnic hatreds, violence against gays, and environmental threats. Community involvement is emphasized as a means of addressing social injustices.

The Center for Agroecology & Sustainable Food Systems is a research, education, and public service program dedicated to increasing ecological sustainability and social justice in the food and agriculture system. The 2-acre Alan Chadwick Garden and the 25-acre farm are managed using organic production methods and serve as research, teaching, and training facilities for students, staff, and faculty. The farm includes research plots, raised-bed gardens, row crops, orchards and a solar green house. It's live-in Apprenticeship Program is open to non-students.

About 400 acres of campus wildlands are designated as a Natural Reserve which contains redwood forest, springs, a stream, vernal pools, a madrone/Douglas fir forest with plenty of opportunities for hiking, bicycling, surfing, sailing and scuba diving. A 4,000 acre reserve on the Big Sur coast that acts as a teaching and research facility includes undisturbed watershed containing numerous terrestrial and aquatic habitats.

Making a Difference Studies

Environmental Studies: Agroecology, Environmental Policy, Conservation Biology, Political Economy

Political Economy and the Environment
Nature Literature
Integrated Pest Management
Environmental Law and Policy
Tropical Ecology
Energy Resource Assessment and Policy

Rain Forests Future
Political Ecology & Social Change
Sustainable Development
Environment, Culture and Perception
Environmental Assessment
Pol. Econ. of Sustainable Agric. in Latin America

Marine Biology

UCSC is situated within five miles of Monterey Bay and its great diversity of coastal marine ecosystems; nature reserves; state, federal, and private marine research institutions. Combined with the Long Marine Laboratory, UCSC is exceptional for the study of marine biology, coastal conservation and management.

Kelp Forest Ecology
Ecological Field Methods
Biological Oceanography
Marine Botany
Marine Ecology

Intertidal Organisms
Biology of Marine Mammals
Ecology of Reefs, Mangroves, and Sea Grasses
The Marine Environment
Biology of Marine Mammals

Community Studies

Students actively committed to social change work on a full-time basis and designs their curriculum around a 6 month field study or internship with a community organization or agency.

Social Documentation
Theory and Practice of Economic Justice
Introduction to Community Activism
In the Eye of 9/11
Feminist Organizing/Global Realities

Chicanos and Social Change
Walmart Nation
Youth and Social Movements
Theory & Practice of Resistance & Social Movement
Workers & Community in Industrializing Amer.

Global Economics

Economic Development
International Finance
Global Corporations and National States
International Political Economy
Development and Underdevelopment

International Trade
Resource Allocation and Market Structure
Latin American Economies
Rural Mexico in Crisis
The Economies of East and Southeast Asia

Sociology

Sociology combines the elements of a search for social order with a vision of a just, free, and egalitarian society a vision that may require fundamental social change.

Famine & Hunger
Development, Inequality, and Ecology
Global Transformation
Death & Dying

Social Justice
Sociology of Health and Medicine
Inequality & Identity
Sociology of Environmental Politics

Education   Earth Sciences   Latin American Studies   Economics   Ocean Sciences
World Literature & Cultural Studies   Women's Studies   Anthropology

Apply by 11/30

• Interdisciplinary Majors   • Individualized Majors   • Field Studies   • Vegetarian Meals

Office of Admissions
University of CA, Santa Cruz
Santa Cruz, CA 95064

831. 459.5779
www.ucsc.edu
admissions@ucsc.edu

CALIFORNIA UNIVERSITY OF PA.

5,900 Undergraduates   California, Pennsylvania

California University of Pennsylvania, a comprehensive regional institution of higher education and a member of the Pennsylvania State System of Higher Education, is a diverse, caring and scholarly learning community dedicated to excellence in the liberal arts, science and technology, and professional studies that is devoted to building character and careers, broadly defined. California University is located in a picturesque, safe rural community just 35 miles south of Pittsburgh.

The University is inspired by its core values of integrity, civility, and responsibility and is guided by its bill of rights and responsibilities: the right to safety and security, the responsibility to ensure the safety and security of others; the right to be treated with respect, the responsibility to treat others with respect; the right to expect the best, the responsibility to give our best; the right to be treated fairly, the responsibility to treat others fairly.

To advance its ultimate mission of building the character and careers of students, the University focuses its efforts on three goals: student achievement and success, institutional excellence and community service. These interrelated ends are facilitated by high quality faculty, students, programs, and facilities.

California University encourages students to take part in the life of the university and the wider community as well. A number of programs provide an opportunity for students to learn and to grow both in and out of the classroom. Students can participate in a campus chapter of Habitat for Humanity and work on various builds throughout the county. One on-campus activity involved living and sleeping for several days in cardboard boxes in the center of campus to draw attention to the need for adequate housing.

The University maintains a relationship with the Center in the Woods, a nearby senior center and housing complex. The Center offer hands-on experience for students from a variety of disciplines including gerontology, social work, pre-physical therapy, communication disorders, and even journalism and public relations. Many students volunteer at the Center, working with the adult day program, assisting persons with Alzheimer's disease or delivering meals on wheels.

Caring for and preserving the environment for future generations is a priority for many academic programs, as well as a special grant-funded program, Partners for Fish and Wildlife Conservation. The program involves faculty, students and staff through research, internships, and other activities with the goal of restoring farmlands and watersheds.

The University has a commitment to service learning, and many courses have a service learning component. Service takes many forms at the university from fundraising for charities to working with the Special Olympics. Martin Luther King Day is celebrated by a day of service to the surrounding communities. Students volunteer at local organizations, community centers, educational facilities, churches and elsewhere.

The Stephen Covey course on The Seven Habits of Highly Effective People, available to all students, faculty and staff, is offered at various times throughout the year.

In 1995, the Character Education Institute was founded to foster critical discussion of ethical issues in the academic curriculum, and to promote the timeless ideals of responsibility and respect. Institute activities promote the core values espoused in the US Constitution such as honesty, human worth and dignity, justice, due process and equality of opportunity.

MAKING A DIFFERENCE STUDIES

ENVIRONMENTAL STUDIES

Introduction to Environmental Science
Introduction to Environmental Geology
General Botany
Earth Resources
Wetlands Ecology

Principles of Biology
General Zoology
Wildlife Management Techniques
Introduction to Public Policy
Development & Mgm't. of Leisure Enterprises

ENVIRONMENTAL RESOURCES

Introduction to Geology
Meteorology
General Botany
Remote Sensing
Conservation of Biological Resources

Hydrology
Groundwater Hydrology
Advanced Environmental Geology
Site Planning and Design
Ecology

ENVIRONMENTAL CONSERVATION

Principles of Biology
Ecology
Plant Ecology
Mammalogy
Wetlands Ecology

General Chemistry
Design and Analysis
Ornithology
Water Pollution Biology
Animal Population Dynamics

FISHERIES AND WILDLIFE BIOLOGY

Wildlife and Fisheries Management Techniques
Design and Analysis
Ichthyology
Water Pollution Biology
Principles of Wildlife Management

Plant Taxonomy
Ornithology
Geographic Information Systems
Land Use Analysis
Animal Population Dynamics

GERONTOLOGY

Introduction to Gerontology
Introduction to Social Work
Aging Policies and Services
Social Work with the Aging
Mental Health and Aging

Aging in American Society
Biology of Aging
Emergency Medical Technician
Adult Development and Aging
Grief and Bereavement

CRIMINAL JUSTICE

Criminal Law
Problems in Policing
Police Organization and Management
Sociology of Substance Use and Abuse
Sociology of Deviance

Law, Justice, and Family
Ethics
Crimes Against Children
Terrorism
Juvenile Justice System

SOCIAL WORK   WATER RESOURCES   METEOROLOGY   EARLY CHILDHOOD ED   GEOGRAPHY

PUBLIC ADMIN.   ANTHROPOLOGY   SPECIAL ED: COMMUNITY SERVICES/COMMUNITY LIVING A.A.

Apply by 8/15

• Team Teaching • Field Studies • Self-Designed Majors   • Student Enviro Audits •
• Service Learning • Interdisciplinary Classes • Life Experience Credit • Theme Housing
• Required Community Service • Distance Learning   Vegetarian & Vegan Meals

Director of Admissions
California University of PA
250 University Ave.

724. 938.4404
www.cup.edu
inquiry@cup.edu

CARLETON COLLEGE

1950 Students   Northfield, Minnesota

Carleton is one of the nation's most respected small liberal arts colleges, unusual for its location in the Midwest. Its vital intellectual community draws students from all states and 20 other countries. Co-educational since its founding, Carleton has a long history of encouraging original thought and a sense of intellectual adventure through rigorous study of traditional academic disciplines.

One such program appealing to students interested in environmental studies is the Environment and Technology concentration which explores the threats posed to natural ecosystems by patterns of human development. The concentration is integrated and multi-disciplinary and draws faculty from many departments including economics, geology, English, sociology, philosophy, fine arts, and biology.

Carleton's setting is distinct, with an 800-acre arboretum bordering the campus. The "Arb", as it is called by students, consists of a variety of habitats including floodplain forest, wetlands, prairie, and a pine plantation. Used for both research and recreation, the arboretum is growing in size as land that was previously used for farmland is being restored to its natural state.

Students at Carleton have a long history of activism, involving themselves in over 100 organizations on campus. Acting in the Community Together, or ACT, is one of the most popular. Through this umbrella volunteer organization, students administer over thirty separate community-based programs. Some of those programs include: Bread Basket, Habitat for Humanity, Sundays at Clare House (an AIDS hospice), ESL Tutoring, WomanSafe Center, and Adopt-a-River.

Carleton encourages students to engage in honest discussions of issues of difference whether based on gender, race, ethnicity, socio-economic background, or political viewpoint. One example of this encouragement is the College's "Common Reading" which takes place during new student orientation. Before new students arrive at Carleton, they are asked to read a particular book. Recent choices have been *The Color of Water* by James McBride and *The Spirit Catches You and You Fall Down* by Anne Fadiman. When they arrive on campus students meet with faculty and staff in their homes to discuss the book.

Another example is the "Recognition and Affirmation of Difference" requirement. To fulfill this requirement students must take a course centrally concerned with another culture; with a country, art or tradition from outside Europe and the US; or with issues of gender, class, race or ethnicity.

With over two thirds of its students participating in off-campus studies, Carleton operates one of the largest study abroad programs on any college campus. In an average year, Carleton students partake in 100 different programs. Whether it be Mali, Costa Rica, or China, Carleton students gain not only an unusual academic experience, but also an invaluable personal one.

MAKING A DIFFERENCE STUDIES

BIOLOGY

Global Change Biology
Biology of Conservation
Ecosystem Ecology
Population Ecology
Field Investigation in Tropical Rainforest Ecology (in Costa Rica)

Sustainable Agriculture
Marine Biology
Sexed Bodies/Sexed Science?
Biology Field Studies: Australia & New Zealand

ENVIRONMENT AND TECHNOLOGY STUDIES

Envisioning Landscapes
Intro to Environmental Geology
Philosophy of the Arts
Principles of Environmental Chemistry
American Nature Writing
Environment Justice from North Carolina to India

Field Drawing
Wilderness in America
Environmental Ethics
Technology in American History
Animals: Mind, Morals and Nature

SOCIOLOGY / ANTHROPOLOGY

Population & Food in the Global System
Ecology, Economy and Culture
Myth, Ritual, and Symbolism
Anthropology and Indigenous Rights
Work& Occupations in Contemporary Society
Actors & Issues in Contemporary Third World 'Development'

Human Evolution and Prehistory
Middle Eastern Social Theory
Anthropology of Health & Illness
Ethnography of Reproduction

POLITICAL SCIENCE

Civil Rights: Martin and Malcolm
Urban Politics
Global Resurgence of Democracy
Ethnic Conflict
Justice Among Nations
Chinese Economy in Transition (in Beijing)

National Policymaking
Chicana Politics and Public Policy
Energy and the Environment
American Environment Thought
The American Farm
Feminist and American Separatist Movements

- **Poverty and Public Policy** Relationship between race, class, gender and poverty in the U.S. Analyze growth of underclass and homelessness as well as policy strategies for reducing poverty.

ECONOMICS

Economics of Inequality
Water and Western Economic Develop
Economics of Developing Countries
Contemporary Economics of East Asia
Economics of Natural Resources and the Environment

Labor Economics
Public Interest in Private Economic Behavior
Urban Economics
Economic Transitions in Europe

EDUCATIONAL STUDIES CONCENTRATION   CROSS CULTURAL STUDIES CONCENTRATION

WOMEN'S & GENDER STUDIES   AFRICAN/AFRICAN-AMERICAN STUDIES

Apply by 1/15   Early Admissions: 11/15

Average Class Size: 17 students

• Team Teaching   • Interdisciplinary Classes   • Theme Housing   • Vegetarian Meals

Dean of Admissions
Carleton College
100 S. College St.
Northfield, MN 55057

507. 646.4190
800. 995.2275
www.carleton.edu
admission@acs.carleton.edu

CENTER FOR GLOBAL EDUCATION

100 Students   A program of Augsburg College, MI

The Center for Global Education at Augsburg College offers six undergraduate academic programs abroad for students from colleges and universities throughout the U.S. and Canada. These unique study programs: bring you face-to-face with people struggling for justice; give you hands-on opportunities to meet and discuss current issues with people at the grassroots level; expand your worldview and challenge your perceptions about global justice and human liberation; and provide you with a life-changing experience and the foundation for a job that can make a difference in the world.

These six programs are currently available for sophomores, juniors and seniors at any college or university in the U.S. or Canada. These programs enjoy nation-wide recognition as first-class study abroad experiences that integrate solid academic work with real-life experiences. The Center has consortial arrangements with many colleges and universities, allowing you to participate in the programs without changing schools.

What makes the Center's study abroad programs unique?

- Experiential Education: You Integrate solid academic work with real-life experiences. You learn not only from books, but also by living fully in the midst of the society you are studying, encountering the people and culture inside and outside the walls of a classroom.

- Diverse Guest Lecturers: Learn directly from local people involved in some of the most important issues of our time -- policy-makers and business leaders; human rights advocates and community organizers; members of women's organizations and union workers; the poor and marginalized.

- Living/Learning Community: Reflect on your learning experience in a community of students interested in similar issues.

- Family Stay: Spend several days to several weeks living with local families and participate in their daily life and activities.

- Regional Travel: Broaden your perspective on the cultural history and current social and political struggles in the region through group travel experiences.

Programs in Mexico and Central America require one previous college-level course in Spanish or its equivalent. Students from over 200 colleges and universities in the U.S. and Canada have participated in the Center's academic programs abroad. The Center also coordinates numerous one- to three-week programs in Mexico, Central America, and Southern Africa.

What have previous students said about the programs?

"A person who is sincere about ... questioning himself/herself has everything to gain from this experience. It has deepened my understanding and widened my perspective on the world immeasurably. A wonderful, deeply gratifying experience."

"This was an adventure in empowerment -- being confronted with so many other realities made me look so much more critically into my own. Thanks!"

"My experience in Mexico with this program will always be remembered in a positive light and it has influenced the directions I have pursued professionally. Thanks for running the program and giving such a great experience to so many."

MAKING A DIFFERENCE STUDIES

MEXICO/CENTRAL AMERICA

CROSSING BORDERS: GENDER & SOCIAL CHANGE IN MESOAMERICA (Fall Semester) Engage in gender analysis of key social, economic, political, and cultural issues; explore the interconnectedness of race, class, and gender; and learn first-hand from both women and men who are involved in struggles for sustainable development and social change. Based in Cuernavaca, Mexico with travel to Chiapas and Guatemala. Orientation at US/Mexico border.

Intensive Spanish

Latin America Liberation Theologies

Latin American Literature - 20th Century Voices

Women, Gender & Social Change in Latin America

SOCIAL & ENVIRONMENTAL JUSTICE IN LATIN AMERICA (Spring Semester) Explore socio-economic and political issues with a focus on the impact of environmental policies on the lives of women and men from varying economic classes and ethnic groups in Mexico and Central America. Based in Cuernavaca, Mexico with travel to El Salvador and Guatemala.

Environmental Politics

Comparative Social Policy

Environmental Theology and Ethics

International Social Welfare: Mexico

GUATEMALA, EL SALVADOR & NICARAGUA

SUSTAINABLE DEVELOPMENT & SOCIAL CHANGE IN CENTRAL AMERICA (Fall & Spring) Explore the life and culture of the people of Guatemala, El Salvador. and Nicaragua. Improve Spanish language skills while living with families in Guatemalan highlands. Study the role of the Church and social injustice in El Salvador. Examine economic development and the impact of social change movements in Nicaragua.

Latin American Liberation Theologies

Spanish Conversation and Composition

Cultural Conflict and Change in Latin America

Sustainable Economic Development

NAMIBIA/SOUTH AFRICA

NATION BUILDING, GLOBALIZATION & DECOLONIZING THE MIND: SOUTHERN AFRICAN PERSPECTIVES (Fall and Spring Semesters) Learn from Namibia and South Africa as they struggle to build nationhood and deal with the legacies of apartheid and colonialism; the challenges posed by rapid globalization; under-and unequal development; and the long-term process of decolonizing the mind. Based in Windhoek, Namibia with travel to South Africa.

The Development Process

Sustainable Economic Development

Internship

The Church and Social Change

Namibia and South Africa: A Historical Perspective

Political and Social Change in Namibia: A Comparative Perspective

Social Stratification: Gender, Class and Ethnicity

Contemporary Social Movements in Central Amer.

Environmental Theology and Ethics

Women in Comparative Politics

Apply by 10/15 for Spring Semesters, 4/1 for Fall Semester
Average Group Size: 20 students
• Team Teaching   • Service-Learning   • Interdisciplinary Classes   • Vegetarian Meals
• Financial aid from your institution usually applies   • Scholarships Available

Center for Global Education
Augsburg College
2211 Riverside Avenue
Minneapolis, MN 55454

800. 299.8889
globaled@augsburg.edu
www.augsburg.edu/global/

CLARK UNIVERSITY

2,250 Undergraduates   Worcester, MA

Typical Clark University students don't like to be called typical. They enjoy challenging convention and seeking out people who are different than themselves. These characteristics fit well in an academic community long distinguished for its pioneering research and concern for significant social issues.

Clark's culture prompts students to venture beyond the classroom and into the community, across cultures and even across the globe. In the university's own neighborhood, Main South, students are an important part of the University Park Partnership, a university-led revitalization effort that is improving the quality of life for residents and setting the standard for effective urban renewal. Students act as tutors for the neighborhood high school, help give free music lessons to local children, and include young students in academic and artistic projects. Student groups also excel in identifying the places in the city that need their help the most, whether it be at local soup kitchens, nursing homes, or elementary schools.

To encourage more students with a commitment to service to join the Clark community, the university offers Making a Difference Scholarships. These 20 scholarships, each worth $11,000 per year, are awarded to students who have demonstrated commitment to their community. In addition, Making a Difference Scholars are offered a $2,500 stipend to support projects they undertake with the University Park Partnership during the summer following their sophomore or junior years.

Clark students look beyond the local community as well. Campus culture is heavily influenced by the large percentage of international students—10 percent of undergraduate students come from more than 90 countries. That means at least one person in an average classroom, probably more, comes from another country and brings a different point of view to class discussions and projects. This sharing of cultures is also reflected in the diverse social opportunities offered on campus. One of the most popular events on campus is the international buffet, a smorgasbord of delicious food from around the world cooked by members of the International Students Association.

Faculty research involves every part of the world. In classrooms and laboratories, professors try out new ideas and recount their firsthand experience in, for example, measuring Chernobyl's radioactive fallout in Europe, or helping villagers use resources more effectively to produce food in Kenya, Somalia and Zimbabwe.

Clark was one of the first universities to offer an undergraduate major in the interdisciplinary field of Environmental Science and Policy. E.S.&P. is for students who hope to find solutions to complex societal problems such as environmental protection, energy policy, technological hazards and risk analysis. The International Development and Social Change program focuses on ways in which individuals can identify effective local action in the context of global change.

Other uniquely Clark projects, such as a cogeneration plant that recycles energy and a yearly non-profit career fair, reflect the university's commitment to encouraging students to make a difference in their world.

Making a Difference Studies

Urban Development and Social Change

Urban Economics

U.S. Urban History and Landscape

Urban Ecology

Utopian Visions

Population, Environment and Development

People, Power & Conflict in U.S. Cities

Immigrants & the City: The World Comes to Worcester

Modernism, Postmodernism and the City

Architecture and Democracy

Urban Transportation

- Complexities of Urban Schooling Addresses the social and academic questions that surround urban education using linguistic, sociological and psychological perspectives.

Cultural / Humanistic Geography

The End of America: Los Angeles

Culture, Place and Environment

Gender and Environment

Feminism, Nature and Culture

Divided Cities, Connected Lives

Keeping of Animals: Patterns of Use and Abuse

Before and After Columbus: Ancient Middle America and Impact of the Conquest

Regional / International Development / Political Economy

International Political Economy

Management of Arid Lands

Political Econ. of Third World Underdevelopment

GIS and Local Planning

Geography of the Global Economy

African Environments & Geographical Implications

Environmental Science and Policy

Science, Uncertainty and Decisions

Energy and the Campus

Management of Environmental Pollutants

Environmental Ethics

Tools for Quantitative Policy Analysis

The Earth Transformed

Cancer: Science and Society

Environmental Toxicology

Limits of the Earth

Societal Analysis & Evaluation of Enviro. Hazards

Environmental / Resource Management

Earth Systems Science

Environmental Ethics

Environmental Policy and Management

Forest and Wilderness: Values and Uses

Ecological Systems

Biosphere - Atmosphere Interactions

Land Degradation

Physical Geography of Human Systems

Biogeography

Tropical Ecology

Earth Science and Development

Urban Ecology: Cities as Ecosystems

Environment and Disasters

Watershed Ecology

Land Degradation

Physical Environment of Arid Lands

Oceanic Islands: Geology and Ecology

Agriculture and Grazing

**Government Philosophy Sociology Psychology Screen Studies Geography
Environmental Studies Women's Studies Race & Ethnic Relations Peace Biology**

Apply by 1/15 Early Admission 11/1

More than 70% of classes have less than 20 students

- Service Learning • Interdisciplinary Classes • Field Studies • Team Teaching • Self-Designed Majors
- Socially Responsible Investing • Green Campus • Special Interest House: "Global Environment House"

Dean of Admissions

Clark University

Admissions Office

950 Main St.

Worcester, MA 01610

508. 793.7431

admissions@clark.edu

www.clarku.edu

COLLEGE OF ENVIRONMENTAL SCIENCE & FORESTRY
STATE UNIVERSITY OF N.Y.
1,600 Students   Syracuse, NY

When the rest of the country celebrated the first Earth Day in 1970, it finally caught up with the SUNY College of Environmental Science and Forestry. Since 1911, SUNY-ESF has been preparing scientists, resource managers, designers and engineers to nurture the planet by teaching scientific principles and applications that support the sustainable use of natural resources. Students at ESF share an interest in the environment and in the science, design and engineering required to conserve resources and to improve their world. The college is a leader in the discovery of new knowledge and tools to deal with environmental challenges, and the latest faculty research is aimed at bioprocessing willow trees to produce ethanol.

ESF serves society through instruction, research, and public service related to: understanding the world's ecosystems; developing, managing, and using renewable resources; improving outdoor environments ranging from forests to urban landscapes; and enhancing environmental quality and biodiversity.

As society becomes increasingly concerned about global warming, invasive species, alternative energy needs, and other critical environmental issues, the faculty and students of the ESF family have timing in their favor. Modern society, with its compelling demands from industry and government, needs people who think objectively and constructively, and who act creatively and responsibly. ESF faculty and students are committed to resolving environmental hazards, learning how to avoid future problems, and offering policy alternatives. Student involvement with societal issues is enhanced through a very active community service program and more than 60 service learning courses.

Academic programs at ESF share a foundation of natural science, a dedication to wise use of natural resources, and a focus on career preparation. The faculty's cutting-edge research becomes part of the classroom experience, and the classroom also merges with the world beyond campus. Each program features internships, field study, research projects or cooperative education to provide students with career-related experience. The college's highly rated Landscape Architecture program requires a full semester of off-campus study, with students often choosing to complete design projects at international locations.

Students participate in hands-on and laboratory work at the main campus in Syracuse, and on 25,000 additional acres of ESF property located throughout New York State. The largest regional campus is located on the 15,000-acre Huntington Wildlife Forest in Newcomb.

Faculty, undergraduates, and visiting scientists use the facility for general research and work related to forest management. The Wanakena campus in the Adirondacks is the site of the ESF Ranger School, where the college offers degree programs in Surveying Technology and Forest Technology.

A final unique aspect of ESF is its longstanding partnership with neighboring Syracuse University, where students can take classes to further explore their academic interests, join student organizations, and enjoy all the social advantages of a large university community.

Making A Difference Studies

ESF offers 22 undergraduate programs and 26 graduate programs focused on the environment.

Environmental & Forest Biology

Aquatic and Fisheries Science

Conservation Biology

Natural History & Interpretation

Biotechnology

Environmental Biology

Wildlife Science

Forest Health

Principles of Animal Behavior

Bioprocess Engineering

Program seeks to train engineers who will work in the emerging bioprocessing and biofuels industry to produce ethanol and related chemical products from renewable resources.

Bioseparations

Engineering Design Economics

Plant Biotechnology

Chemical Ecology

Bioprocess Kinetics

Co-op Experience in BPE

Environmental Studies

Environmental Geology

Environmental Impact Analysis

Nature and Popular Culture

Environmental Law and Policy

Environmental Psychology

Government and the Environment

Water Use and Reuse

Environmental Studies Internship

Landscape Architecture

Intro to Landscape Architecture

Comprehensive Land Planning

Computer Graphic

Structures and Materials

Planting Design and Practice

Landscape Architecture Design Studio

Writing for Environmental Professionals

Off-Campus Design Thesis

Natural Resource Management

Environmental Economics

Field Dendrology and Ecology

Outdoor Recreation Management

Geographic Information Systems

Introductory Soils

Natural Resources Administration Law

Watershed Hydrology

Soil and Water Conservation Policy

Forest Engineering

Water Pollution Engineering

Harvest Systems Analysis

Soil Mechanics and Foundations

Introduction to Remote Sensing

Forest Ecology and Silviculture

Forest Engineering Planning and Design

Forest Technology (Ranger School) AAS Degree

Forest Entomology

Forest Roads

Fire Management

Structure & Growth of Trees

Computer Applications

Aerial Photogrammetry

Forest Pathology

Personnel Management

Forest Recreation

Elements of Wildlife Ecology

Apply by 1/15   Early Action: 11/15

• Field Studies   • Service Learning   • Interdisciplinary Classes   • Team Teaching   • Green Campus

• Third-world Service-Learning   • Student Environmental Audits   • Vegetarian & Vegan Meals

Director of Admissions   315. 470.6600

SUNY College of Environmental Science & Forestry   800. 777.7ESF

1 Forestry Drive   www.esf.edu

Syracuse, NY 13210-2779   esfinfo@esf.edu

COLLEGE OF THE ATLANTIC

280 Students   Bar Harbor, Maine

College of the Atlantic offers a curriculum with a conscience. Classes are geared to understanding the relationships between humans and our environments - and doing something to improve those relationships: in policy, art, science and a multitude of fields that defy categorization. At COA, this effort is known as Human Ecology - the sole major offered. Having one major means that classes are interdisciplinary, relationships are emphasized and students are encouraged to go to the source, doing their own creative thinking. Ultimately, all students fashion their own course of study, combining classes in all fields with a dose of independent work, off-campus internships and a capstone project. Students come to COA for a coherent, rigorous, individualized education. Students also come hoping to make a difference in this world.

Making a difference requires nurturing, which is why the COA community is intentionally small. Courses are focused on discussions which frequently extend beyond classes to lunches, dinners and chance meetings on campus - in addition to scheduled office meetings. With a student body numbering just under 300, close friendships among students and between students and faculty are the norm.

COA classes engage in real activities. In 2006, an advanced class prepared students to attend the third Biosafety Protocol negotiations (MOP3) of the Convention on Biological Diversity in Curitiba, Brazil, by reading international law along with environmental science texts. A more introductory class was titled, "Practical Activism." In science, students don't just study genetics, they will do genetic research, taking advantage of the proximity of two scientific laboratories, The Jackson Laboratory and the Mount Desert Island Biological Laboratory. In literature classes, students are as likely to submit poetry or short stories as analytic papers. One ongoing class is bringing several students through completion of their first novel.

Students receive individual evaluations of their work in addition to (optional) grades. The atmosphere is supportive and friendly while maintaining a high degree of scholarship and academic rigor. Currently, 65% of students attend graduate programs, including COA's own master's of philosophy in human ecology.

The hands-on nature of COA doesn't stop in classes. Students are part of most decisions made on campus. Most committees and all search committees must have student membership. Essential campus decisions, as well as updates of all committees, are brought to a weekly All-College Meeting, attended by all members of the community - students, faculty and staff.

Students are also active in the surrounding community. Service opportunities include social and educational programs such as Habitat for Humanity, AIDS education outreach and environmentally-related activities in neighboring Acadia National Park. Recently, students have become extremely active in the youth environmental movement, at both the delegate level to United Nations committees and at the youth activist level, through such organizations as SustainUS. There is an active artistic community; exhibitions as well as theatrical productions have received critical acclaim.

Although small, COA is not provincial. Students hail from all parts of the world. Currently, international students represent 17% of the student population, from Afghanistan to Zimbabwe. While some 20% of students are from Maine, the rest come from across the nation. Significant international experience is often part of the COA education.

The campus itself is situated on the ocean, at the edge of Acadia National Park. The stunning beauty of the natural surroundings offers a unique setting and sparks a deep and lasting affection for outdoor activities and in which to pursue learning. Here are located the college's dorms and academic buildings, as well as the Ethel H. Blum Gallery and the George B. Dorr Museum of Natural History, featuring environmental displays created by COA students, designed to raise awareness of ecological issues.

The College is also the home of Allied Whale, an internationally-recognized marine mammal research center. Additional COA resources include two island lighthouse field research stations and Beech Hill Farm, a 77-acre organic farm, which serves as a source of the College's food and as a learning lab for students interested in agricultural issues and practices.

Students living on campus have a choice of one more traditional, though environmentally sensitive dorm, and four former summer cottages. Fundraising is now ongoing for a new campus residence which will be a hallmark of sustainability among college campuses.

Internships are a required facet of the program at COA. Students have worked at the Marlborough Sounds Dolphin Project, Student Global AIDS Campaign, Sundance Film Institute, Acadia National Park, Bimini Biological Field Station, Canadian Wildlife Foundation, Consumer Energy Council, Friends of the Earth, New Alchemy Institute, World Peace Camp and the Solar Energy Research Institute as well as in art galleries and publishing houses around the nation.

To introduce students both to outdoor recreational activities and to one another, the College coordinates optional outdoor orientation trips for entering students. Staff members and older students lead these trips which sharpen outdoor skills and encourage the development of friendships. Recent trips have included canoeing the Allagash, hiking along the Appalachian Trail to Katahdin, sea kayaking and rock climbing.

The College's location enables students to participate in many outdoor activities. Nearby Acadia National Park has more than 50 miles of carriage paths and 100 miles of open trails. Students regularly jog and bike, hike and rock climb, windsurf, canoe, and sailon the island lakes and in Frenchman Bay, In the winter, they cross-country ski, snowshoe and skate.

The College itself is located in the town of Bar Harbor on Mount Desert Island, Maine, connected to the mainland by a causeway. Living on MDI introduces one to a preservation ethic-an ethic that encourages people to develop a sense of history and to value the buildings, gardens, parks, and open space in their community. COA's curriculum and the political-social climate of the island encourage students to join with residents in developing land-use policies to insure the islands uniqueness will be preserved.

Ultimately, College of the Atlantic seeks to nurture in its students a conservation ethic, environmental concern and social activism enabling them to visualize and contribute to a more sustainable, just and balanced world.

Making a Difference Studies

Environmental Sciences

Animal Behavior
Biology of Fishes
Ecological Physiology
Chaos and Complex Systems
Entomology
Ornithology
Plant Taxonomy

Biology I and II
Bio-Organic Chemistry
Conservation of Endangered Species
Marine Ecology
Women in Science.
Plants and Humanity

- **Marine Mammals** Biology of whales, porpoises and seals, concentrating on species that frequent New England waters, but also including other species or habitats. Study of skeletal anatomy, prey species, visits to harbor seal ledges, observe gray seals and whale watching.

Human Studies

Aesthetics of Violence
Chinese Philosophy
Critiquing the Global Economy
Environmental Law

American Culture: Race, Class & Gender
Critical Theory to Feminist Theory
Environmental Journalism
History of American Reform Movements

Humans in Nature

International Environmental Law
Issues in Regional Resource Management
Literature of Third World Women
Philosophy of Nature

International Peace In Theory and Practice
Literature and Ecology
Outdoor Education and Leadership
Technology and Culture

Arts and Design

Animation
Environmental Design
Graphic Design for Activists
Photography I and II
Projects in Theater Workshop

Digital Photography and Printing
Film Studies
Jazz, Rock and Blues
Primitive Art
Women in the Visual Arts

Teacher Certification K-12

Approximately 20 percent of COA graduates are engaged in graduate studies or employed in the field as naturalists, environmental educators, and classroom teachers.

Educational Pyschology
Intercutural Education
Learning Theory
Qualitative Research in Schools

Experiential Education
Intro to Philosophy of Education
Curriculum & Instruction in Secondary Schools
Mainstreaming the Exceptional Child

Apply by 2/15   Early Admission: 12/1   Transfer: 4/1
Average Size First Year Classroom: 12

- Interdisciplinary Classes   • Team Teaching   • Organic Gardens   • Eco Dorm   • Self-Designed Majors
- All Seminar Format   • Field Studies   • Optional SAT's   • Socially Responsible Investing
- Required Community Service   • Vegetarian & Vegan Meals   • Green Campus   • Graduate Programs

Office of Admission
College of the Atlantic
105 Eden St.
Bar Harbor, ME 04609

207. 288.5105
800. 528.0025
inquiry@coa.edu
www.coa.edu

University of Colorado at Boulder

25,850 Undergraduates   Boulder, Colorado

As the flagship institution of the four-campus University of Colorado system, CU-Boulder has a long tradition of teaching environmental and social responsibility to students. The campus has an international reputation for environmental education and research programs, which can be pursued through several avenues.

Environmental studies – a bachelor's degree program in place for more than 40 years – features a comprehensive curricula in the basic sciences, economics, ethics, and policy that prepares students to make a difference in the real world. Academic tracks in environmental sciences, and in society and policy allows undergraduates to specialize in areas ranging from environmental and natural resources to decision-making, planning, and public policy.

The University also offers a unique environmental studies program for undergraduates that offers course work and seminars within a residence hall setting. Courses in biology, economics, expository writing, geography, geology, mathematics and political science meet core requirements and are taught in classes of about 25 students.

All the environmental programs on campus are buoyed by outstanding faculty, some of whom are affiliated with internationally known campus institutes like the Cooperative Institute for Research in Environmental Science and the Institute of Artic and Alpine Research. The Mountain Research Station, located about 45 minutes from campus, features a long-term ecological study site and hosts students and faculty from around the world.

The long tradition of volunteer service on campus is underscored by the fact that CU-Boulder ranks second in the nation in the number of volunteers recruited by the Peace Corps. A total of 300 students have gone on to Peace Corps service over the past seven years, helping people in developing countries to help themselves.

CU's International and National Volunteer Service Training (INVST) program combines academic training and fieldwork in how to start and run volunteer service organizations. During junior and senior years the 16-credit-hour INVST program features courses in global and community development, human ecology and social change. Participating students also learn about bookkeeping, office management, program evaluation techniques and how to gain access to global computing networks.

Students can also participate in the Farrand Program, an academic program set in a residence hall that emphasizes humanities studies. In addition to surveying western art and culture, the program offers contemporary subjects – like global ecology, film and ethics — that are taught by some of the finest University faculty. The program also provides a number of community outreach opportunities.

The University of Colorado at Boulder has launched a Renewable and Sustainable Energy Initiative to coordinate the university's already extensive campus resources devoted to energy coursework and research, mobilizing resources to underscore CU-Boulder's leadership in energy innovation. Campus studies of economically viable solar photon conversion systems, hydrogen production from water and solar irradiation, biofuels development, identification of legal barriers to the use of new energy sources, public attitudes about energy and other topics reflect the depth of energy programs at CU-Boulder.

Making a Difference Studies

Environmental Studies

Conservation Biology
The Environment and Public Policy
Landscape Ecology
Environmental Economics

Conservation Trends
Forest Geography
Water Resource & Management of Western US
Energy & Environmental Policy

Atmospheric and Oceanic Sciences (minor)

Weather and the Atmosphere
Weather and the Atmosphere Laboratory
Air Chemistry and Pollution
Oceanography
Desert Meteorology

Atmosphere, Ocean, and Climate
Analysis of Climate and Weather Observations
Principles of Climate
Introduction to Atmospheric Dynamics
Policy Implications of Climate Controversies

Farrand Residential Academic Program

Ethics of Ambition
Understanding Privilege and Oppression
The Individual and the Community
Farrand Service-Learning Practicum
Future of the Spaceship Earth

Community Service: Personal Growth & Public Good
Gandhi's Satyagraha: Love in Action
Nonviolence for Everyday: Meditation
Banned Books and the First Amendment
Exploring Good and Evil through Film

International Affairs

Political Geography
International Conflict in a Nuclear Age
Alternative World Futures
Power: Anthropology of Politics

American Foreign Policy
International Relations
Comparative Politics: Dev. Political Systems
Cross-Cultural Aspects of Socioeconomic Devlp't.

Sociology: Population & Health; Sex & Gender; Environment & Society

Sociology of Gender, Health and Aging
Women of Color: Chicanas in U.S. Society
Population Studies: Fertility and Mortality
Nonviolence & Ethics of Social Action

Women, Development and Fertility
Social Conflict and Social Values
Violence Against Women and Girls
Ethics & Social Issues in U.S. Health & Medicine

Anthropology

Hopi & Navajo, Cultures in Conflict
The Maya
North American Indian Acculturation
Medical Anthropology

Amazonian Tribal Peoples
Ethnography of Mexico & Central America
Africa: Peoples and Societies in Change
Culture and Power

Ethnic Studies

Racist Ideology in American Life
Race, Class, and Gender
Culture, Racism & Alienation in America
Race, Class, and Pollution Politics

Multicultural Leadership
Immigrant Women in the Global Economy
Culture, Racism, and Alienation in America
People of Color and Social Movement Struggles

International & National Voluntary Service Training Certificate

Democratic & Nonviolent Social Movements
Critical Thinking in Development

Facilitating Peaceful Community Change
Global Development

Kinesiology   Peace & Conflict   Philosophy   Women's Studies   Enviro Engineering

Apply by 1/15

• Self-Designed Majors   • Environmental Housing   • Service-Learning

Office of Admissions
U of Colorado at Boulder
Boulder, CO 80309-0030

303. 492.0030
www.colorado.edu
apply@colorado.edu

CONNECTICUT COLLEGE

1,700 Students   New London, Connecticut

Connecticut College is known for its innovative programs and tradition of academic excellence. Dating back to its founding in 1911, it also has a long history of teaching students how to effect social and environmental change. Today, service learning and volunteerism are hallmarks of campus culture and students contribute an average of 26,000 hours per year at locations from local classrooms to soup kitchens and prisons. The College's international studies programs have expanded the possible locations for volunteerism and internships to include the global arena, and more than 150 alumni have served in the Peace Corps. With its strong environmental studies program, the College has hundreds of "green alumni" who are making a difference as environmental activists.

The Holleran Center for Community Action and Public Policy is a multidisciplinary academic center dedicated to teaching, research, and community collaborations that foster active citizenship and community leadership in a multicultural democratic society. The Center builds community partnerships, explores public policy, and supports faculty and students interested in the complex issues facing communities. The Certificate Program in Community Action (PICA offers students a unique opportunity to combine course work and community-based experiences to complement any major. Students engage in a wide variety of community projects and research, exploring the balance of individuals' needs, community needs and citizens' responsibilities. Recent PICA projects have included art therapy with children in Washington D.C., activist anthropology in Belize, Central America, and working with minority juveniles and the court system in New Haven, CT.

Connecticut College's tradition of environmental activism dates back to the establishment of the Connecticut College Arboretum in 1931. Encompassing more than 750 acres, the Arboretum's natural areas have nurtured generations of faculty and students in ecology, environmental teaching and field research. The College's coastal location also provides access to the marine environment. In 1969 the College established one of the nation's first environmental science majors, Human Ecology, now called Environmental Studies.

The Goodwin-Niering Center for Conservation Biology and Environmental Studies (CCBES) is an interdisciplinary program that draws on the expertise and interests of faculty and students to address contemporary ecological challenges. CCBES strives to integrate all areas of learning to deal with the issues of sustainability and the natural environment. CCBES's certificate program allows students to supplement their liberal arts experience with environmental topics and awareness. Recent internships include the commercialization of tropical medicinal plants with the Malaysia-MIT Biotechnology Partnership and environmental research and policy at the Oregon Environmental Council.

The Center supports and facilitates many campus-wide environmental programs and activities. The Environmental Model Committee oversees campus sustainability programs including recycling, and energy and resource conservation. Student-run organizations include the Renewable Energy Club, Students Against Violence to the Environment, and Students Educating for Animal Liberation.

The Center for International Studies and the Liberal Arts certificate program allows students to internationalize any major and pursue a unique immersion in internationalism.

MAKING A DIFFERENCE STUDIES

PROGRAM IN COMMUNITY ACTION (PICA)

The PICA certificate is awarded to students who supplement a major with a set of requirements organized around a senior integrative project that addresses a specific community issue.

Participation and Leadership
Public Policy and Social Ethics
Deliverance Narratives: Tolerance, Intolerance, & the Intolerable

The Good Society
Deliverance Narratives: Literacy & Liberation

SERVICE-LEARNING COURSES

Integration of volunteer service with traditional coursework so that learning is enhanced by service

Urban and Regional Economics
School and Society
The Pluralism Project
Service-Learning for Mathematics
Hispanic Family: Culture & Community Proyecto Comunidad

Language, Thought, Development & Imagination
Feminist Theory: Women in the Polity
Practicum in Community Settings
Foundations of Social/Cultural Identity in US

ENVIRONMENTAL STUDIES

An interdisciplinary program that combines natural science and social science while examining local, regional, national and international environmental problems in a holistic manner.

Intro to Environmental Geology
River Hydrology and Hydraulics
International Environmental Cooperation
Law, Science and the Environment
Indigenous Use of Tropical Rainforests
International Environmental Cooperation

Ethnobotany
Field Work in Environmental Education
Environmental River Restoration
Intro. to Geographic Information Systems
Enviro Activism: Political Impact Around The Globe
Environmental Justice in Global Perspective

GENDER AND WOMEN'S STUDIES

An interdisciplinary transnational study that examines the nuanced historical processes through which women and men live out gender; the set of practices that shape it; and the concrete processes and political movements through which inequalities are transformed.

Family, Kinship, & Gender
Sex, Love and Friendship in Antiquity
Sex and Status in South Asia
Gender & National Identity in Russian Culture
Feminist Theory in the United States
Intro to Gender & Women's Studies: A Transnational Feminist Approach
Transnational Women's Movements: Five Continents, Seven Seas

Anthropology of Sex & Gender
Contemporary African-American Fiction by Women
Trans: Gender/Region/Nation: Southern Literature
Women in Judaism, Christianity and Islam
Women and World Politics

SOCIOLOGY & URBAN STUDIES

Sociological Approaches to Social Problems
Sociology of Development
Ethnic and Race Relations
Family Analysis and Life Styles
Analysis of Research on Sex and Gender
Inequality

Sociology of Education
Sociological Analysis of Jewry
Deviant Behavior and Social Control
Methods of Social Research and Analysis
Industrialization, Dictatorship and Democracy
Human Nature and the Social Order

Apply by 1/1   Early Decision 11/15, 1/1

• Team Teaching • Individualized Majors • Service-Learning (35 courses) • Third World Service-Learning
• Theme Housing • Interdisciplinary Classes • Vegetarian & Vegan Meals • Optional SAT's • Green Campus

Director of Admission & Fin. Aid   860.439.2200
Connecticut College   admission@conncoll.edu
270 Mohegan Avenue   www.connecticutcollege.edu
New London, CT 06320

CORNELL UNIVERSITY
SCHOOL OF LABOR & INDUSTRIAL RELATIONS

700 Undergraduates   Ithaca, New York

Is the Cornell School of Labor and Industrial Relations the right place for you? Ask yourself this: are you a problem solver? The peacemaker among classmates? The person everyone turns to when there's a mix-up, impasse, or disaster? If contemporary affairs, psychology, sociology, history, economics, and government are the classes that send intellectual sparks flying for you; if you are active in student government, political campaigns, peer mediation, mock trials, debate, or conflict resolution; if you think you might like to apply the social sciences to solving human problems–think about Cornell's School of Industrial and Labor Relations, The field of industrial and labor relations focuses on some of the most important issues in the workplace: protecting jobs, increasing productivity, computerization, worker participation, labor law, international labor relations, expanding and declining labor markets, and new methods of decision making in business and government.

In the years following the Great Depression and during World War II, leaders in business, industry, labor, government,and education recognized the growing need for a new kind of school–a place where people could become skilled at dealing with the volatile issues of the changing American workplace. They also recognized that Cornell's double heritage–its creative synthesis of the rigorous intellectual tradition of the Ivy League and the democratic spirit of the great state schools–made this university the ideal home for such a college. In the autumn of 1945 Cornell's School of Industrial and Labor Relations admitted its first students. It was the only institution of its kind anywhere.

Today the ILR school remains the nation's only institution of higher education offering a full four-year undergraduate program in industrial and labor relations; in addition it offers several graduate degree programs. The faculty–specializing in personnel and human resource management, labor law and history, and social statistics–is the largest concentration of distinguished scholars in the field of industrial and labor relations.

Research at the ILR school focuses on some of the most important issues in the workplace: protecting jobs, increasing productivity, computerization, worker participation, expanding and declining labor markets, and new methods of decision making in the human resources field. You'll choose electives not only from ILR but from over 4,000 courses in Cornell's seven undergraduate colleges. You'll prepare for a career in business, law, finance, the union movement, public policy, political activism and other fields as well.

A rich array of centers and institutes and affiliated programs that find their home at ILR include: the Institute of Collective Bargaining, Institute for Workplace Studies, Union Leadership Institute, Institute for Labor Market Policies, Institute for Women and Work, Workers' Compensation Managed Care Pilot Program and the New York State/Cornell AFL-CIO Union Leadership Institute. The Institute on Conflict Resolution's mission is to educate practitioners, users, teachers, and students of the field of conflict resolution through research; collection and dissemination of information; public and private assistance; graduate and undergraduate curriculum development; and, training programs.

MAKING A DIFFERENCE STUDIES

COLLECTIVE BARGAINING LABOR LAW AND LABOR HISTORY

Labor & Employment Law	Collective Bargaining
Negotiation& Dispute Resolution	U.S. Labor History: The Twentieth Century
Contemporary Trade Union Movement	History of American Workers - 1960-90's
Strangers And Citizens: Immigration & Labor In US History	

HUMAN RESOURCE STUDIES

Human Resource Management	Workplace Diversity: Stepping Into 21st Century
HR Econ & Public Policy	Career Develpmt:Theory & Practice
Training And Development	Globalization Of Services
Human Resources Management Simulation	Immigration & American Labor Force
Career Develpmt:Theory & Practice	Globalization Of Services
International HRM	Employee Relations & Diversity

LABOR ECONOMICS

The institutional arrangements, terms, and conditions under which workers supply their labor and under which firms demand their labor. Faculty are especially concerned with understanding the workings of labor markets and the effects of various public policies. Topics include: analysis of the labor force, employment and unemployment, wages and related terms of employment, income distribution, income security programs, health and safety in industry, retirement, pensions and social security, economic aspects of collective bargaining, and economic demography.

Economic Wages & Employment	Economic Security
Develop Of Economic Institutions	Personnel Economics For Managers
Women In The Economy	Science, Technology and the American Economy

- **Diversity in the Workplace** Issues of diversity and discrimination in corporate, union, and legal environments. The purpose is to understand, analyze, and discuss the experience of being part of a culturally and ethnically diverse workplace. Examples of topics include: subtle forms of prejudice and discrimination, how employing organizations are responding to the changing composition (demographics) of the workplace, mentoring programs, the role of networking opportunities for minorities and women, how unions are changing in response to increasingly diverse workforces, and unique issues or problems faced by other disadvantaged groups (e.g., disabled, gays and lesbians).

INTERNATIONAL & COMPARATIVE LABOR

Latin American Labor History	Workers' Rights as Human Rights
International Labor Law	International Human Resource Management
The Globalization at Work	Working in the New Economy: Sociology of Work
Immigration and the American Labor Force	Comparative Human Resource Management
Politics of the Global North	Int'l. Human Resource Policies & Institutions
The Political Economy of Mexico	Comparative Labor Movements in Latin America

ORGANIZATIONAL BEHAVIOR   INTERNATIONAL & COMPARATIVE LABOR   SOCIAL STATISTICS

To apply to ILR, apply to Cornell University, indicating that you wish to attend
the School of Industrial Labor and Relations.

Apply by 1/1   Early Decision: 11/1

Undergraduate Admissions Office	607. 255.5241, 607. 255.6693 (ILR)
Cornell University	admissions.cornell.edu/apply/
410 Thurston Avenue	www.cornell.edu
Ithaca, NY 14850-2488	www.ilr.cornell.edu

Cornell U. School of Labor and Industrial Relations 89

EARLHAM COLLEGE

1,175 Students   Richmond, Indiana

Earlham is a distinctive teaching and learning community in which students build an education that is principled, humane, global, and rigorous. Founded by Friends (Quakers) in 1846, Earlham continues as a non-sectarian college firmly rooted in the values and practices of Friends. At the heart of Earlham are commitments: to upholding the value and dignity of every person; to personal integrity and academic honesty of the highest degree; to open inquiry in a safe, but challenging, atmosphere; to increasing harmony in the world, both among humanity and between humanity and the natural environment.

Earlham's mission is to provide an undergraduate education shaped by the distinctive perspectives of the Quakers. Earlham emphasizes: pursuit of truth; lack of coercion, respect for the consciences of others; openness to new truth and therefore the willingness to search; and application of what is known to improving our world.

The College strives to educate morally sensitive leaders for future generations. Therefore Earlham stresses global education, peaceful resolution of conflict, equality of persons, and high moral standards of personal conduct. Earlham seeks a diversity of students and faculty, requiring a heightened sensitivity in the way we listen and speak to others. Earlham values individual freedom, but not at the expense of respect for those who are different or whose ideas we find disagreeable.

Earlham values social justice and peaceful resolution of conflicts. Students and faculty have many opportunities to work for justice and to give of themselves in service. Following the example of early Friends, Earlham seeks not only to avoid violence, but to remove its causes. Students, staff, and faculty share in governing the College through a system of joint committees. As much as possible, Earlham tries to reach decisions by consensus, by arriving at what Friends call a 'sense of the meeting' that is shared by all involved.

About a quarter of students major in interdisciplinary programs, including Peace and Global Studies, Human Development and Social Relations, Latin American Studies, African and African American Studies and Women's Studies. All students benefit from a curriculum that threads interdisciplinary experience through every student's education.

Earlham recognizes a responsibility for enabling students to grow in their knowledge and appreciation of American cultures, but also for challenging students through encounter with world cultures not familiar to them. The Bolling Center houses Earlham's innovative, value-grounded curriculum, emphasizing Interdisciplinary Programs; Global Reach; Experiential Learning; Collaborative Projects and Networked Information Resources.

Students often design their own majors such as Outdoor Education, Social Thought, and Museum Studies. Many students collaborate with professors on research and creative projects such as focusing on the search for a cure for leukemia; responses of the American peace movement to Middle Eastern conflict; or seminars on women, social movements and temperance. Students frequently participate in field study research, whether in Puerto Rico, Kenya, the Galapagos, Indiana, or in Quaker Libraries.

Student life at Earlham is enriched by a 600-acre back campus of ponds, woods, and meadows which serves as a biological field station, the site of the College's observatory and farm, and a place where students may wander, run, or ride horses.

MAKING A DIFFERENCE STUDIES

CONSERVATION BIOLOGY

Ecological Biology

Ornithology

Population and Community Ecology

Biological Diversity

Field Botany

Tropical Biology Interterm

Field Biology Training Program at Manomet Bird Observatory, Massachusetts

ENVIRONMENTAL CHEMISTRY

Techniques of Water Analysis

Chemical Dynamics

Instrumental Analysis

Organic Chemistry

Environmental Chemistry

Biochemistry

Quantum Chemistry

Chemistry in Societal Context

PEACE AND GLOBAL STUDIES

Culture and Conflict

Politics of Global Problems

Conflict Resolution

Christian Ethics & Modern Moral Problems

Moral Education

Introduction to Philosophy: Food Ethics

Methods of Peacemaking

Theories of International Relations

Religious Responses to War and Violence

Technology and Arms Control

HUMAN DEVELOPMENT AND SOCIAL RELATIONS

Theories of Human Development

Persons and Systems

Social Science and Human Values

Field Study

Social Relations

Human Biology

Comparative Cultures

Institutions and Inequality

Frontiers of Psychological Inquiry

Counseling & Psychotherapy

BUSINESS AND NONPROFIT MANAGEMENT

Moral and ethical choices about how to interact with workers, and how to use the Earth's resources.

Nonprofit Organization and Leadership

Leadership in Dealing with Differences

Programming and Problem-Solving

Public Administration

Intercultural Communication

Conflict Resolution

Health, Medicine and Society

Nonprofits in Civil Society

Industrial Organization and Public Policy

Political & Econ. Development of Pacific Rim

INTERNATIONAL STUDIES

Combines experiential learning with a multidisciplinary approach to the study of international politics, economics, history, development and underdevelopment.

Introduction to Comparative Politics

Issues Before the United Nations

Theories of International Relations

International Trade

Introduction to International Relations

Introduction to Macroeconomics

International Law

Economic Development

AFRICAN/AFRICAN-AMERICAN STUDIES   ENVIRONMENTAL GEOLOGY   WOMEN'S STUDIES

EDUCATION   INTERNATIONAL STUDIES   LATIN AMERICAN STUDIES   JEWISH STUDIES

Apply by 2/15   Early Decision by 12/1

• Team Teaching   • Individualized Majors   • Service-Learning   • Field Studies   • Organic Gardens

• Theme Housing   • Interdisciplinary Classes   • Vegetarian Meals   • Energy Conservation

Director of Admissions
Earlham College
Richmond, IN 47374

800. 327.5426
admission@earlham.edu
www.earlham.edu

EASTERN MENNONITE U

1,000 Students   Harrisonburg, Virginia

Eastern Mennonite University places outstanding academics into the context of global awareness and active Christian involvement. The university's unique Global Village Curriculum builds on the belief that we are all interdependent in ways which can affect the survival or destruction of civilization. Eastern Mennonite educates students to use their talents to promote human transformation by working for peace, by creating just social structures, and by aiding access to basic human resources for life and dignity.

This educational perspective is rooted in the 450 year old Anabaptist-Mennonite tradition. The Anabaptist Christian community challenges students to pursue their life calling through scholarly inquiry, artistic creation, guided practice, and life-changing cross-cultural encounter. EMU invites each person to witness faithfully, serve compassionately, and walk boldly in the way of nonviolence and peace. Students are encouraged to embrace this faith heritage while their own convictions and experiences and those of other religious heritages are respected. EMU seeks to deepen students' faith and life in Christ, while also encouraging them to critique their own faith tradition in wholesome ways.

EMU educates students to live in a global context. The cornerstone of this approach to learning is Eastern Mennonite's Cross- Cultural Program, one of the strongest programs in international and cross-cultural education in the country. EMU students study in a wide range of international and domestic locations such as Central America, the Middle East, Europe, China, Japan, Russia, Africa, Mexico, Los Angeles, New Orleans and American Indian reservations. On these cross-cultural study tours students receive an education that reaches far beyond the classroom. The larger world serves as a laboratory for testing and refining knowledge, no matter what a student's major. EMU students have life-changing experiences which broaden their world view and give them expanded possibilities after graduation.

On campus, Eastern Mennonite is a vibrant community bringing together students from a rich variety of cultural and religious backgrounds. A large majority of faculty have lived and served abroad. This international perspective enters the classroom, as do the perspectives of the 14% of students who are international or American multiethnic. With about 1,000 students, EMU is a good size - large enough for a full range of quality programs and activities, but small enough so students are not lost in the crowd. Personal relationships with professors are part of every student's experience.

Strategies for Trauma Awareness and Resilience (STAR) Program is a unique approach to trauma healing that connects personal transformation with organizational, societal and global wellbeing. STAR participants come from the United States and many international settings that experience different levels of conflict and trauma. STAR activities honor multifaith participation and the important interaction of those from diverse backgrounds in the US and around the world

In addition to the college's strong theater, athletic, and music programs, students participate in a wide array of extracurricular clubs and events. These include community service opportunities coordinated by student organizations. Students quickly discover that at Eastern Mennonite success is measured not only by what they achieve after graduation, but how they have developed along the way. Development of the whole person is the goal at Eastern Mennonite University.

Making a Difference Studies

Biology & Environmental Science

Environmental Science
Conservation Ecology
Food and Population
Advanced Ecology and Field Biology

Plant Pest Management
Soil Science
Biology as Inquiry
Conservation Ecology

- **Agroecology** Explores agricultural ecosystems, especially in food deficit countries. Physical, biological, social & economic bases of agroecology examined using a variety of sources and case studies. Appreciate traditional agricultural rationality, investigate effects of modifications of existing agroecosystems.

International Business (Interdisciplinary Approach)

International Conflict and Peacemaking
Economic Development
International Business

International Marketing
Sociology of Development

- **Peace & Justice in Global Context** Religion, theology, economic perspectives, int'l. organization, models for social change (development, revolution etc.) and missionary activity in the creation, maintenance & change of social systems. Civil religion, Third World Theology, economic organization, and development as related to peace and justice.

Justice, Peace and Conflict

Exploring the Peacebuilding Arts
Biblical Theology of Peace and Justice
Mediation and Conflict Transformation
Peace and Justice in the American Context

Peace and Justice in Global Context
Developing & Sustaining the Peacebuilder
Justice and Compassion
History and Philosophy of Nonviolence

Applied Sociology: Community Development, Enviro. Conservation, Int'l. Development

Human Behavior & Social Problems
Sociology of Int'l. Development
Anthropology and Social Change
Economic Development.
Sociological Theories for Social Change

Transformative Approaches to Justice & Peace
Peace and Justice in Global Context
Social Policy Analysis
International Conflict and Peacemaking
Social Movements, Racism and Terrorism

Camping, Recreation & Outdoor Ministries

Outdoor Education
Outdoor Living Skills
Backpacking
Adventure, Initiatives & Ropes Course
Human Services Skills

Fdns. of Christian Camping & Outdoor Ministry
Technical Rock Climbing
Introduction to Youth Ministry
Recreation Programming: Design & Implementation
Sophomore Recreation Practicum

Visual and Communication Arts: Journalism, Photography, Art, Communication

Students are pushed to go beyond the aesthetic to consider community and global aspects of their work, and to be transformers of cultural and community landscapes. Seeks to nurture a profound appreciation for the spiritual, emotive and poetic aspects of human existence.

Mass Communication and Culture.
Film and Culture

Documentary Production
Visual Communication Theory

Strategies for Trauma Awareness and Resilience

Rolling Applications   Transfer Apply by 8/1   Student Body 55% Mennonite

• Team Teaching • Field Studies • Service Learning • Self-Designed Majors • Required Community Service
• Vegetarian & Vegan Meals • Socially Responsible Investments • Non-smoking, Non-drinking Campus

Director of Admissions
Eastern Mennonite University
Harrisonburg, VA 22802

800. 368.2665
admiss@emu.edu
www.emu.edu

EcoVersity

Santa Fe, New Mexico

EcoVersity is a work in progress. Ecoversity holds a vision of place-based education for sustainability. While working on a larger vision for an accredited bachelor's degree program, they offer wonderful workshops around Santa Fe.

An education at EcoVersity is bioregional in scale, enabling your senses and feelings to inform intellect and intuition. Such a view is holistic and grounded in sensory knowledge of landscape, climate, flora and fauna. EcoVersity's practice is rooted in studying land-based traditions, values and awareness. It affirms the importance of honoring local knowledge, science and wisdom, in addition to Western thought and science. Sophisticated cultural traditions inform contemporary adaptations such as Permaculture, organic gardening, natural building, herbal medicine and similar ecological practices. Engaging in place-specific projects develops tools for transforming alienated cultures by engaging in ecological and holistic ways of living, thinking, and acting.

EcoVersity's 11-acre campus serves as a demonstration site and a community building center for the promotion of "hands-on" learning and sustainable living. The Earth Based Vocation Certificate Program is a 10-week long intensive program in integrated practical and theoretical skills of sustainable living, that leads to lifestyle and career change, Earth-Based Vocations includes studies of permaculture design, natural building, renewable energies, water harvesting, and community action. The Certificate is designed for students seeking to join the fast growing field of professionals who are developing whole system approaches for the design of human environments.

EcoVersity offers a Permaculture Certificate program. With its ethically informed process of design, and holistic approach to problem solving, permaculture empowers people with tools to achieve self-reliance. It teaches sustainability in all realms of human endeavor. It is an underlying core component of the sustainability training at EcoVersity.

The philosophy within permaculture is one of working with rather than against nature, and of protracted and thoughtful observation rather than premature and thoughtless action. Permaculture design techniques encourage land use which integrates principles of ecology and applies lessons from nature. It teaches us to create settings and construct ecosystems which have the diversity, stability, and the resilience of natural ecosystems.

Students may enroll in a 2-Week Intensive or a Weekend Program. The participants of either program meet an informal classroom setting for a combination of lectures, discussion, slide shows and field trips. Participants are encouraged to keep a journal reflecting their experiences in addition to the classroom notebook.

Today, more than ever before, a wealth of opportunities are available for training with such practical visionaries, both here and abroad. Most skilled practitioners of sustainable living, however, are not to be found in classrooms or on the faculties of our colleges and universities. One must look for them on farms, in the field, in forests, or in the wilderness. They may be deeply engaged in community development, or working for change with small, non-profit organizations. They may be involved in such projects as alternative technology, community gardens, eco-forestry, conservation biology and environmental education.

Making a Difference Studies

Earth Based Vocation Certificate

The program consists of two components: In-Residence Training, and Roving Scholars practicum and mentorship. The first part of the program takes place on campus, and is an intensive curriculum of classroom and hands-on learning activities. The second part of the program is a self-directed internship or practicum. Students have an option of taking it in the field of their choice, by continuing learning at EcoVersity or a learning center of their choice, or by entering real world and gaining practical experience, learning by doing. Each and every Roving Scholars arrangement is unique, and will depend on a student's imagination, interests and financial resources.

The focus of the natural building segment is on current natural building technologies, including natural building and ecological design and roots in cultural traditions and regional aesthetics. Students learn how the natural building design process develops solutions that reflect place and ecological conditions. Natural designs are informed by ecological accounting, mimic natural patterns, and acknowledge sacred geometry. Students learn to incorporate voluntary simplicity, appropriate technologies, and develop regenerative design strategies to create truly sustainable (green) buildings.

Natural Building

Renewable Energy

Seminar for Earth-Based Vocations

Sustainable Forestry

Land & Garden

Community Arts & Activism

Ecological Design

Permaculture Design

Permaculture Design Certificate

Principles of Natural Systems

Design Methodologies

Large Scale Land Restoration Techniques

Grey Water Recycling

Cultivated Ecologies

Urban Environment Permaculture

Naka-Ima - Honesty in Group Dynamics

Reading the Land & Analyzing Site Elements

Water Harvesting Techniques

Irrigation Strategies

Energy Conservation Technologies

Wildlife Management and Biological Pest Control

Invisible Structures: EcoVillages, Credit Unions, Community Supported Agriculture, Strategies for an Alternative Nation

Community Classes   Held on an ongoing basis around Santa Fe

Herbal Arts

Alternative Fuels and Transportation

Natural Building

Strategies for an Alternative Nation

Backyard Animals

Sustainable Energy

Bee Keeping

• Organic Gardens • Green Campus   • Field Studies • Work Trades   • Internships

EcoVersity

2639 Agua Fria

Santa Fe, NM 87505

505. 424.9797

www.ecoversity.org

admissions@ecoversity.org

EUGENE LANG COLLEGE

NEW SCHOOL UNIVERSITY

950 Undergraduates   New York, New York

In the midst of one of the nation's most vibrant cities lies a small, personable, and innovative liberal arts college. Eugene Lang College is the undergraduate division of New School University, a major urban university founded in 1919 and known for its progressive stance on social justice issues. The college offers unique courses in the social sciences, humanities, and the arts. Eugene Lang College is located in the heart of Greenwich Village in New York City and fosters independence, originality, and a sense of spirit in learning. The College strives to create and sustain an educational environment in which every aspect of the academic community reflects the multicultural city and the international world in which we live, work, and learn.

Eugene Lang College is the undergraduate division of New School University. It offers a distinctive liberal arts education with an interdisciplinary focus designed for engaged and independent-minded students. The College is a vital intellectual community which aims to foster in its students a critical self-consciousness about the process and purpose of knowing. Students at Lang College are encouraged to participate in the creation and direction of their education.

The curriculum of Eugene Lang is special. It is open and flexible. Under the guidance of an academic advisor, students design their own programs of study. The program is creative and forward thinking. Many Lang courses explore topics that cross traditional academic boundaries and approach classic texts and traditional subjects from new perspectives. The curriculum is diverse and inclusive; Lang courses include works, voices, perspectives, and ways of knowing different peoples and different cultures.

Classes are challenging and demanding and are taught in small classes (20 students maximum) with an emphasis on reading primary texts, and the use of writing and revision as a way of learning. These hallmarks of the Lang educational program mean that students work hard and feel responsible for active participation in their classes. Most classes are conducted in seminar format. Seminars permit the most direct engagement of students with the material and the opportunity for close relationships with faculty.

Eugene Lang College offers students 13 areas of concentration within the liberal arts curriculum which allow them to make connections between varied modes of thought and different approaches to topics and ideas. A student's particular course of study within a concentration consists of 8 to 10 courses which lead to a relatively advanced knowledge of an area of study. As a freshman, you will choose from specially designed seminars that will introduce you to new fields of inquiry and lay the foundation for more advanced work in a particular field. Upper-level students create an interdisciplinary course of study within one of the following 13 concentrations:

- Cultural Studies
- Arts in Context
- Theater
- Philosophy

- Education Studies
- Literature
- Writing
- Psychology

- Religious Studies
- Urban Studies
- Science, Technology, & Society / Quantitative Reasoning
- Social & Historical Inquiry (Sociology, Political Science, History, Economics)
- Dance

At Eugene Lang, the 'Historical Social Inquiry' study area brings together a wide range of courses from such disciplines as history, political science, economics, anthropology, and sociology. 'The 'Urban Studies' concentration brings a multi-disciplinary focus to bear on the history, development, politics and problems of contemporary urban life. Urban Studies is specially designed for students who seek a more direct pathway to additional training and careers in the area of public policy. The concentration makes the city an object of study and uses New York City as an educational laboratory and resource. It unites theoretical inquiry with field experience, academic internship, and urban research.

For highly motivated students, Eugene Lang College offers several combined degree programs with other divisions of the University. Students may accelerate their progress toward a master's degree by combining their undergraduate work at Lang with study at one of the University's graduate divisions. These opportunities include the B.A. / M.A. program with The New School and the Graduate Faculty of Political and Social Science, and the B.A/M.S. program with the Robert J. Milano Graduate School of Management and Urban Policy.

Internships are central to undergraduate liberal education. Students earn college credit while contributing to the wider community and gaining a variety of skills available through hands-on work experience. The internship program takes students into every corner of NYC, and includes such organizations as: Newsweek Magazine, The World Policy Institute, MTV/VH1, The National Organization For Women, SPIN Magazine, The Urban League and Saturday Night Live.

Whatever path a Lang student chooses, no matter what the concentration, it will involve issues and perspectives of different peoples and different cultures, including those historically underrepresented in academic study. Eugene Lang has school-wide efforts (including hiring practices) to promote sensitivity and understanding about racial, religious and gender differences.

In addition to the courses offered through Eugene Lang, students may take advantage of the educational opportunities available among the University's vast curricular resources represented by The New School, the Graduate Faculty of Political and Social Science, the Robert J. Milano Graduate School of Management and Urban Policy, Parsons School of Design, Mannes College of Music, and the Jazz & Contemporary Music Program.

Making a Difference Studies

First Year Studies

Ethnicity and Multicultural America

Introduction to Indo-Tibetan Buddhism

Reading Race, Writing Law

Spiritual Autobiography

Genes: The Code of Codes

Philosophy of the Sexes and Racism

Spacetime Physics from Newton to Einstein

Voyage Out: Women Write Travel

- **Is the "Good Life" Possible? Philosophy and Literature in Dialogue**   What does it mean to live the "Good Life"? How has literature attempted to answer this question? How has philosophy attempted to answer it? Is there a difference in approaches? Read from Plato, Augustine, Kant and Nietzsche discussing what the Good Life is, and how one might lead it. Also read works of literature each of which portrays an individual who reflects upon and struggles with his failure to have been a good person.

- **The Unthinkable Thought**   Imagine the moment when the apple fell on Newton's head, or Galileo saw the earth going around the Sun, or Watson and Crick stumbled over the double helix. Each of these moments produced an "Unthinkable Thought," which created a revolutionary new "paradigm" of reality, changing both science and our lives for all time. Review and discuss how science has evolved not by dispassionate logic, but by the passionate pursuit of these new "paradigms". Look at the origins and social implications of the paradigms of astronomy, the atom, motion, relativity, new sociology...

- **Faculty Bio:** Sara Ruddick Ph.D. (Harvard) Sara Ruddick has taught at New School University, New York University and Haverford College. She is a consultant for Union Graduate School, on the editorial board of Peace and Justice, and a member of Network for Women in Development. Professor Ruddick received a Ford Foundation Grant for Faculty and Curricular Development in Women's Studies

Upper Level Studies

Introduction to Anthropologies

Economics and Gender

Cultural Wars, Censorship and the Arts

All in the Family: Race in Cyberspace - (Mixed) Race Memoir

Knowledge and Power, Truth and Politics

Women's Experiences of Religions

Teaching and School Reform

- **Masculinities in Literature**   What is it to "be a man"? What is it to be a "real man"? Following the insights of feminist criticism, explore writing by and about men assuming that the scripts for behavior are shaped by society rather than biology. Readings in classic American writers such as Whitman and Melville. History of manliness in America. In modern and contemporary writers such as Kipling, Kafka, Richard Wright, Hemingway, examine how representations of manliness differ from nation to nation, from culture to culture, from subculture to subculture, and among racial, ethnic and religious groups.

- **Cosmopolitanism: Philosophy, Globalization and Emancipation**   Historical development of the concept of cosmopolitanism from the time of St. Paul through it's most famous articulation in Kant and up to recent thinkers. Recent developments in global political life under the heading of "Globalization" e.g. the development and function of the UN, the passing of GATT, NAFTA, and other international trends.

- **Faculty Bio**: Ann Snitow   A cultural critic, literary scholar, and feminist theorist and activist, Ann Snitow teaches a wide variety of courses in literature, gender, and cultural studies. Well known nationally and internationally, Ann Snitow is a leading example of the "public intellectual," whose work regularly appears in such places as The Village Voice and Dissent. She has most recently established The Network of East-West Women which has brought scholars and activists in the women's movements in Eastern Europe and the USA together for the first time.

URBAN STUDIES

Concentration includes a number of field-based courses and provides interdisciplinary exploration of urban issues and cultures such as street culture, public health, transportation policy, education, drugs, and AIDS. Students may take courses at the Graduate Faculty and the Milano Graduate School of Management & Urban Policy.

Black Revolt and Urban Crisis
Dynamics of Healthcare
Housing Policy
Mobilizing (in) the City
Politics and the People of New York
Urban Poverty and Public Policy

Community Development
Urban History: Racial Formation in American
Immigration and Public Policy
Political Economy of the City
The American City from WWII to 9/11
Urban Development in International Perspective

RELIGIOUS STUDIES

Approaches to the Study of Religion
Encountering Religious Pluralism
Hebrew Bible in Context
Reading Job
Spiritual Autobiography

Cultures of Islam
Exploring Religious Ethics
New Testament in its Milieu
Women's Spirituality & Contemporary Religion
The Story of the Devil

Pilgrimage in Buddhist Practice   This course looks at the motif of the spiritual journey as a central part of religious practice in Asia by looking at a variety of Buddhist traditions in India and Tibet. Explore how sacred space and religious landscape come to be delineated and canonized and how movement in such spaces is involved in the formation of notions of identity, community, the self and liberation.

EDUCATION STUDIES

In framing schools as cultural sites where race, class, gender, sexuality, language, and ability are intensely contested, the Education Studies concentration is rooted in
strategic critiques that are anti-racist, feminist, and concerned with social justice.

Education and Autobiography
Education Policy
History of Education
Teachers and Writers Collaborative
Teaching to Transgress

Education and Social Change
Global Ideologies of Schooling
Practicum in Urban Education
Race, Class & Ethnicity in American High Schools
Theory & Research in Urban School Reform

PSYCHOLOGY

Abnormal Psychology
Neuropsychology
Dream Interpretation
Emotion
Language and Thought
Psychology, Creativity & the Arts
Psychological Theories on the African-American Experience

Altered Brains: An Introduction to
Autobiographical Memory
Drugs, Culture, Deviance
Evolution and Human Sexuality
Psycholanalyzing Jewish, Christian & Islamic
Stereotypes, etc.

Apply by 2/1, 5/15 for Transfers   Early Admit: 11/15
Average Size First Year Class: 15   Admits Students After 11th Grade
• Interdisciplinary Classes   • Self-Designed Majors • All Seminar Format • Team Teaching • internship
• Distance Learning   • Third World Service-Learning • Recycling & Energy Conservation

Director of Admissions
Eugene Lang College
65 West 11th Street
NY, NY 10011

212. 229.5665
lang@newschool.edu
www.lang.edu

Evergreen State College

4,200 Undergraduates   Olympia, WA

Evergreen is a challenging, high energy, continually evolving community founded on the values of cooperative learning, open inquiry and diversity.

Evergreen earned a national reputation as a pioneer in developing high quality innovative educational programs that bridge the gaps between academic disciplines. Students engage in the study of ideas, concepts and problems that are based on real-world issues and questions.

Evergreen approaches its mission through traditional academic areas: the humanities, arts, natural sciences and social sciences. However, the college's educational programs are transformed by a set of core beliefs that flow through everything the college does both inside and outside of the classroom. Evergreen believes:

- The main purpose of a college is to teach, and good teaching involves close interaction between faculty and students.
- Collaborative or shared learning is better than learning in isolation and in competition with others.
- Teaching across differences is critical to learning.
- Connected learning -- pulling together different ideas and concepts -- is better than learning fragmented bits of information.
- Active learning -- applying what's learned to projects and activities -- is better than passively receiving knowledge.
- The only way to thoroughly understand abstract theories is to apply them to real-world situations.

These beliefs are reflected in the way students learn at all levels of the curriculum. Instead of taking a series of courses on separate topics, Evergreen students typically enroll in a single program that draws together different academic subjects while exploring a central theme, idea or question. Program participants might, for example, study the theme of health-care problems by exploring real-world issues from the viewpoints of biology, history, philosophy, sociology, drama, economics and literature.

Evergreen faculty love to teach. Their enthusiasm, their passion for teaching is infectious. The college's emphasis on students and educational innovation attracts some of the best teachers anywhere. They are hired and evaluated primarily on the quality of their teaching. Most faculty work with 23 to 25 students. Their goal is to be accessible, receptive and open to students; teaching is never delegated to teaching assistants.

At Evergreen, faculty and students are all on a first-name basis. Freshmen typically enroll in a single, full-time interdisciplinary program with 75 to 100 students and three to four faculty members, each representing a different academic discipline. Within this community of learners, students participate in lectures, discuss books they've read in seminars with 25 students, pursue projects with four or five students, work in labs or studios, and learn to navigate the library and other college resources.

Students may stay together as a community for two quarters or an entire academic year. More advanced students typically participate in smaller, more narrowly focused programs that strengthen skills in traditional areas of study – but always drawing on other disciplines and exploring real-world themes. Or students may choose internships, enter into group contracts to work closely with one faculty member and a small number of students, or design independent study contracts.

Rather than signing up for a prefabricated major, Evergreen students have the flexibility to design academic pathways concentrating on subject areas they are passionate about (within the range of expertise provided by faculty). These academic areas include biology, business, communications, computer science, environmental studies, health services, humanities, language studies, marine studies, mathematics, Native American studies, performing arts, physical science, politics and economics, pre-law, pre-medicine and visual arts.

A majority of Evergreen students complete one or more internships by the time they graduate. One student worked as a river ranger with the U.S. Forest Service in the Grand Canyon guiding researchers working on an environmental impact statement. Another worked as a marine mammal researcher documenting the travels of gray whales. Others have served as English tutors for refugees, as researchers in genetic laboratories, as support staff in shelters for abused women, and the list goes on.

Evergreen's Organic Farm has received national recognition. Twenty-four acres of bustling agricultural and academic activity are located on the west edge of campus. Even the farming equipment has been refitted for biodiesel fuel – processed on campus using recycled cooking oil from the cafeteria kitchen.

Student representation is encouraged in all college task forces exploring college issues or new policies. Students also participate in a wide variety of organizations that provide cultural, informational, social, recreational, spiritual and educational services and activities. Current organizations include the Asian Students in Alliance, the Bike Shop, Environmental Resource Center, Native American Student Alliance, Jewish Cultural Center, Women of Color Coalition, MEChA/Chicano Student Movement, and the Math and Science Network. Evergreen competes in the NAIA Cascade Conference in basketball, cross-country, soccer, swimming and women's volleyball.

Evergreen offers two undergraduate degrees, the Bachelor of Arts and Bachelor of Science, and three advanced degrees, Master of Environmental Studies, Master of Public Administration and Master in Teaching.

Evergreen graduates tend to carry their sense of involvement and social responsibility with them in their careers as educators, social workers, counselors, microbiologists, entertainers, lawyers, journalists, health care professionals, administrators, artists, entrepreneurs and a diversity of other occupations.

Evergreen's Tacoma Campus is located in an urban setting, and the college offers programs in six Native American communities

MAKING A DIFFERENCE STUDIES

Evergreen offers over 125 interdisciplinary academic programs every year. The curriculum is never static and the faculty teams re-form and develop new themes annually. Studies listed below are typical.

PROGRAMS FOR FRESHMEN   32 credits (maximum)

Waste and Want: The Science, Psychology and Business of Consumption   Boy was that good! Need a refill? Ever wonder what went into that 15 minutes of morning satisfaction? "I drink two cups a day. At that rate, I'll down 34 gallons of java this year, made from 18 pounds of beans." Farmers will apply 11 pounds of fertilizers and a few ounces of pesticides to the trees this year. Then there is labor, transportation, water, electricity, the cup, sugar, cream and all the resources involved in producing each of these items. Social and environmental impacts of engaging in this daily ritual. How do cultural and historical contexts shape consumption habits.

ENVIRONMENTAL STUDIES   32 credits (maximum)

- Sustainable Design: Green Means   What means do we use to shape the Earth and its living systems, and to live, work and move about? Are these means ethical, sustainable and beautiful? Ecological design proposes means that are responsive and responsible to place and community, that reuse and renew materials and energy, and that draw lessons from natural systems and longstanding human responses to them. Study and research in landscape ecology, energy systems and environmental design history. Projects may range from a comic strip promoting safe disposal of hazardous wastes to portable, self-sustaining shelters for disaster victims. Address how individuals and communities can design spiritually and physically sustaining means of coexisting with the our home planet.

EXPRESSIVE ARTS   48 credits (maximum)

- Local Knowledge: Community, Media Activism, Public Health & the Environment   Community-based work using video, oral history, participatory research and other forms of activist learning. Develop strategies for collaborating with local communities as they respond to change and crisis. Learn to research and analyze locally held knowledge and resources, support community initiatives and implement projects for sustainable community development. Explore case studies, popular education, community-based research and environmental, public health and social justice issues. Examine community projects creating economic, cultural and ecological sustainability. Projects include education, social justice, media, environment, public health, food systems or public policy.

SOCIETY, POLITICS, BEHAVIOR AND CHANGE   32 credits (maximum)

- Political Ecology of Land   An interdisciplinary, in-depth focus on how land has been viewed and treated by humans historically and in contemporary times. Special attention to the political, economic, social/cultural and environmental contexts of land use. Look at land ethics, concepts of land ownership and efforts to regulate land uses and protect land.

NATIVE AMERICAN & WORLD INDIGENOUS PEOPLES STUDIES   48 credits (maximum)

- Patience   What does it means to live in a pluralistic society at the beginning of the 21st century. Look at a variety of cultural and historical perspectives, paying special attention to the value of relationships to the land, to work, to others and the unknown. Explore Native American perspectives and issues that are particularly relevant to Native Americans. Research topics relate to how to live in a pluralistic society and a globalized world under humanistic standards for social justice, freedom and peace

Apply by 3/1   Early Admit: 12/1
- Team Teaching • Interdisciplinary • Life Experience Credit • Self-Designed Majors
- Service-Learning   • Organic Vegetarian & Vegan Meals • Organic Gardens • Green Campus

Office of Admissions
The Evergreen State College
Olympia, WA 98505

360. 867 6170
admissions@evergreen.edu
www.evergreen.edu

FRIENDS WORLD PROGRAM
LONG ISLAND UNIVERSITY
120 in FWP   Southampton, New York

Very few colleges offer a program like Friends World – experiential education by total immersion into other cultures. The Program stands alone in two important ways. The first is its faith in students. Friends World (FW) believes that intelligent young men and women have the ability and the right to be deeply involved in determining their own educational plans. The second is the FW belief that all nations of the world need citizens who are educated to see beyond their own borders and who recognize that as individuals they share the responsibility for the future of the planet.

Friends World Program's (FWP) offers experiential and service-based education through total immersion into other cultures for 3 1/2 years. The Senior Capstone Semester takes place in New York City where you synthesize and integrate your learning that has taken place in Costa Rica, China, India, Japan, Australia, Thailand, Taiwan and/or Turkey. You study in two or more countries outside of your home culture as you earn a Bachelor of Arts degree from Long Island University.

FWP provides a balanced liberal arts education that includes fluency in at least one foreign language through classroom learning, complemented with field experiences, directed independent studies, and internships. In consultation with faculty advisors, you design individualized programs of study in the humanities and social sciences according to your personal interests and goals. Examples of former concentrations include: Peace Studies; Conflict Resolution; Global Youth Culture; Arabic Culture; Music and Media; Dance and Social Change; Environmental Anthropology; Sustainable Agriculture; Community Development; Traditional Healing; Globalization and Society; Indigenous Peoples and Women's Studies. Individualized study is carried throughout the program and at overseas centers.

The Foundation Year prepares freshmen with the fundamentals of experiential education and study abroad. Teaching and learning take place in seminars, lectures, group discussions, workshops, role plays, projects, and directed independent study. The Second and Third Years provide an opportunity to build upon first-year learning, to apply more sophisticated knowledge and skills, to create and execute independent study projects at FWP Centers in China, India, Japan and Australia, and to participate in the traveling semester-length Comparative Religion & Culture program. In the Fourth Year, you spend the fall semester conducting an independent study in a country previously visited, before culminating your FWP education with the Senior Capstone Semester in New York City.

FWP students' education is enriched through work with highly-respected organizations and many leading international professionals and global specialists. Many students eventually enroll in graduate programs or work in a field first explored as a FWP student.

Founded in 1965 by the Quakers, Friends World became a program of Long Island University in 1991. Although non-sectarian, FWP is still respectful of its Quaker roots and encourages students to become involved in service both to the institutional and local communities.

Friends World Program admits freshmen and transfer students. You may attend FWP as Study Abroad students from other educational institutions, enrolling for a semester or a year, with credits transferring back to your home schools.

MAKING A DIFFERENCE STUDIES

Experiential projects, field studies, seminars, workshops, individualized majors, service learning

SOUTH ASIAN CENTER (BANGALORE, INDIA) enables students to explore the country's religious and cultural diversity, the caste system, environmental issues, the situation of Tibetan refugees, the status of women, India's art forms, dance and music.

By Women - About Women   Philosophy and Practice of Yoga
Basic Sanskrit   Indian Cuisine
Holistic Living and Sustainability

LATIN AMERICAN CENTER (HEREDIA, COSTA RICA) offers homestays, service-learning, internships throughout South America, with field trips to Ecuador and Nicaragua.

Spanish Language,   Latin American Issues
Global Health & Traditional Healing   Peace Studies & Conflict Resolution
Global Environmental Issues,   Cross-cultural Research Methods

EAST ASIA CENTER (KYOTO, JAPAN)

Exposes students to the ancient capital of Japan with workshops in haiku, papermaking, tea ceremony, calligraphy, sumie, and Taiko drumming, as well as modern-day subjects such as cinema, photography, literature, creative writing, web-publishing and Teaching English as a Second Language.

Behind the Mask: Alternative Japan   Japanese Language

CHINA CENTER (HANGZHOU)

Study of a wide range of topics including history, religion, traditional Chinese medicine, women's issues, calligraphy, poetry, taiji, Mandarin Chinese language, and modernization and economic development.

AUSTRALIA PROGRAM (BYRON BAY)

Provides a unique opportunity to study the environment and culture of Australia during the spring semester. Students enroll in five three-credit courses organized around classroom lectures, site visits, hands-on projects, workshops, nature experiences, independent research and travel within Australia.

COMPARATIVE RELIGION & CULTURE

Program teaches global citizenship through the lens of world religions as you travel during the semester. Fall 2006 has the theme of Islam & Culture with study in Turkey, India and New York City. Spring 2007 has the theme of Buddhism & Culture with study in India, Thailand and Taiwan

Religions of China -   Chinese Culture and Society
India term: Hinduism, Sufi, Jain, Sikh   Indian Culture and Society
Turkish Identity in the Middle Eastern Context   Peace and Human Rights
Middle East Term: Ankara and Istanbul - Themes in Christianity, Islam and Judaism

NORTH AMERICA CENTER (NEW YORK CITY)

Hosts the Capstone Semester in Brooklyn where you synthesize and integrate overseas experiences from the previous 3? years through courses such as cross-cultural understanding in a globalizing world, internship, senior skills seminar, writing workshop and senior capstone preparation workshop.

Rolling Admissions

• Self-Designed Majors • Interdisciplinary Classes • Service Learning • Team Teaching
• Required Community Service • Optional SAT's • All Seminar Format • Vegetarian Meals

Office of Admissions   718.780.4320
Friends World Program, LIU fw@liu.edu
9 Hanover Place, 4th Floor www.brooklyn.liu.edu/fw
Brooklyn, NY 11201-5882

GOSHEN COLLEGE

925 Students   Goshen, Indiana

Developing "informed, articulate, sensitive, responsible Christians" seeking to become "servant leaders for the church and the world" is the mission of Goshen College. Making a difference permeates everything about Goshen. What's more, Goshen was the first college in the nation to require international education. Operated by the Mennonite Church, one of three historic "peace churches," the college has attracted attention as a place where values are "lived as well as taught."

Goshen College is committed to encouraging students in intellectual, social, moral and spiritual growth. Students are invited to engage in a dynamic and life-giving community here and to mature as individuals through respectful relationships in the classroom, the local community, in the broader Christian church and among other cultures. All are expected to demonstrate sensitivity and concern for others' convictions, perspectives and struggles

Central to that living out of values is Goshen's international education requirement. Since 1968, about 85 percent of GC students have fulfilled the requirement by taking part in Study-Service Term. In the program, students spend a term in a culture significantly different from that of the United States — usually at the same cost as a term on campus. Students typically spend the first seven weeks of the term living and learning in a major city, studying the language and culture of the country. The second half of the term is spent in a service-learning assignment, usually in a rural setting and often related to the student's major. Education majors teach in schools, while nursing and pre-medicine students often work in clinics and other health-related settings.

International education at Goshen isn't limited to a 13-week term in another country. Most GC faculty leaders have lived and worked outside of the country and many bring their international experiences to the classroom. International education at Goshen also plays a significant role in the school's Multicultural Affairs Program.

Students majoring in environmental or related studies such as biology or environmental education can study at the college's nearby Merry Lea Environmental Learning Center, a 1,150-acre plot of bogs and meadow. Outdoor enthusiasts also find the center within easy riding distance by bicycle, and can spend the day hiking the trails, enjoying the hundreds of species of plant and animal life. Adjoining the campus is Witmer Woods, another source of environmental study.

The college also offers a program in Peace, Justice & Conflict studies. Activities around peace include the annual Peace Oratorical contest, the Peace Play, Students for Shalom, public lectures and conferences. Some courses are taught in "real-world" settings, including Guatemala, Ireland, Chicago and Washington, DC.

Goshen's educational goals include:
- Faith that is active and reflective.
- Intercultural openness with the ability to function effectively with people of other world views.
- An understanding of the transcendent reality of aesthetic and spiritual experience.
- Personal integrity that fosters ability to resolve conflict and to promote justice.
- Leadership ability that empowers self and others.
- An understanding of responsible stewardship for human systems & the environment.
- A healthy understanding of self and of others that is reflected in social relation ships of interdependence and mutual accountability

Making a Difference Studies

Social Work

Accredited by the Council on Social Work Education and has, as its primary objective, the preparation of students for professional social work practice.

Social Service Field Experience

Human Services: Services to Families

Human Services: Women's Concerns

Sociology of the Family

Social Work Practice Theory

Social Welfare Policy and Program

Human Services: Child Welfare

Community Development: Local & International

Race, Class and Ethnic Relations

 Social Service Field Experience

Peace, Justice and Conflict

Prosocial Behavior

Conflict Mediation

Violence and Nonviolence

Contemporary Women's Issues

War and Peace Systems

Justice/Restorative Justice

Third World Theologies

War, Peace and Nonresistance

History of Ethnic Conflict

Healing the Wounds of Violence

Poverty and the Church

History of Global Poverty

- **The Spiritual Path of the Peacemaker**   Uses biographical and autobiographical narratives alongside formal and/or theoretical writings of peacemakers. Investigates the question, "How does a peacemaker's inner spiritual journey relate to her/his peace activism work in the world?" Students will make presentations on such individuals as Mother Teresa, Thomas Merton, Thich Nhat Hanh, Dorothy Day, the Dalai Lama, Thoreau, Simone Weil, Elise Boulding etc.

Women's Studies

Marriage and Family

Liberation Theologies

Spiritual Writings of Women

Women's Growth and Development

Womanhood and the Cultures of the U.S.

The Bible and Sexuality

International Women's History

Contemporary Women's Issues

Women in Text and Image

Sexual Violation & Violence

International Studies (Minor) and Study Service Term Abroad

 Service is the true heart of the SST experience, as you meet and engage people from a different culture. You will gain profound insights into the host culture—and the different meanings of service. Service can be as simple and profound as listening to the life experiences of others.

Communication Across Cultures

Comparative Economic Systems

African Societies and Cultures

International Politics

Introduction to Linguistics

Intercultural communication

Asian Religions

Race and Ethnic Relations

First/Third World History

International Literature

Community Development

Family and Kinship Across Cultures

Social Work   Sociology/Anthropology

Apply by 8/15

• Service Learning   • Team Teaching   • Drug, Alcohol, Smoke-Free Campus

• Life Experience Credit • Individualized Majors • Vegetarian Meals   • Energy Conservation

Admissions Office

Goshen College

Goshen, IN 46526

800. 348.7422

admissions@goshen.edu

www.goshen.edu

Green Mountain College

700 Students   Poultney, Vermont

Green Mountain College seeks to prepare students for productive, caring, and fulfilling lives in a rapidly changing world. Established in a setting of natural beauty, the College takes the environment as the unifying theme underlying the academic and social experience of the campus. Through a broad range of liberal arts and career-focused majors and a vigorous, service-oriented student affairs program, the College aims to foster the ideals of environmental responsibility, public service, international understanding, and lifelong intellectual, physical, and spiritual development.

In recent years GMC has refocused its mission with the aim of educating the next generation of thinkers, teachers, and leaders who will help improve and protect the world's diverse environments. GMC is as an environmental liberal arts college with an international focus. All students take a three-course sequence entitled "Perspectives on the Environment": Images of Nature, Dimensions of Nature and A Delicate Balance. This curriculum links disparate disciplines to a set of common environmental concerns facing our global community.

Students select additional courses from four categories: Scientific Endeavor, Social Perspectives, Humanities, and Health and Well-Being. All students explore environmental issues together in these interdisciplinary courses. Each major also contains courses that touch upon environmental themes, an approach GMC calls ecology across the curriculum. For example, an English course examines the influence of nature on writers like Wordsworth and Thoreau. You can also select the option of a self-designed major.

GMC also offers adventure across the co-curriculum beginning with new-student orientation featuring activities such as mountain biking, adventure camping, hiking, white-water canoeing, rappelling or sea kayaking. Weekend outdoor activities for the entire campus community are scheduled throughout the academic year.

The "Greening Green Mountain" program encourages recycling, waste management activities, and water or energy conservation measures. Students work in the college's organic garden and with a stream bank erosion project, design greenhouses, build cold frames, and plan special Earth Day celebrations. Students have renovated one residence hall into an experiment in sustainable living.

Internships and field experiences are vital components of most academic majors. This hands-on experience enables students to serve while they enhance skills, develop role models for success, and achieve a better understanding of career options.

GMC challenges students to think about other people and larger causes, and offers financial aid programs that reward reward volunteer community or environmental service. Service-learning projects include working for community recycling, centers for aging, animal shelters, environmental education, and health care agencies.GMC also offers a wide range of action and service organizations. Clubs on campus include the Environmental Club, Mountain Bike Club, Outing Club, Rugby, Scuba and GMC Cares.

Recent GMC alumni have gone on to earn graduate degrees at such institutions as Columbia, the New School for Social Research, UNC-Chapel Hill and the University of Vermont. They can also be found navigating the waters of Alaska's Inside Passage, teaching English in Korea, running marketing agencies, painting watercolor portraits, coaching cross-country skiing, and making lives – their own and others' – more productive.

MAKING A DIFFERENCE STUDIES

ENVIRONMENTAL STUDIES

Introduces students to increasingly sophisticated studies in biology and ecology with an emphasis on how these fields pertain to regional issues, and on the global implications of such issues as diminished biodiversity, ecosystem loss, and global warming. This interdisciplinary program is committed to developing not only scientific understanding, but also ethical, philosophical, and aesthetic approaches to the natural world.

The Evolution Revolution

Simplicity and Sustainability

Nature in Music

Environmental Ethics

Contemporary Social Issues

Native American Perspectives

Utopias: Envisioning the Good Society

American Views of the Environment

- **The Northern Forest** A team-taught course with extensive field work, draws on the talents and expertise of five GMC professors to address issues from the perspectives of economics, ecology, education, and environmental philosophy. Students who enroll in The Northern Forest take only that 15-hour block course during the semester.

- Faculty Bio: William M. Throop   Environmental ethicist, chair of the Environmental Studies Committee, recently edited the anthology *Renewing Nature* and published articles in *Environmental Ethics* among other places. When not teaching, Dr. Throop enjoys hiking (he's hiked all 46 of the 4,000-foot peaks in the Adirondacks,) canoeing, and working on his family's farm.

ADVENTURE RECREATION

One of four majors, including Therapeutic Recreation, offered by the Department of Recreation and Leisure Studies. Through optional certification tracks, Adventure Recreation students can become certified whitewater canoe or kayak instructors, adventure program facilitators, open water dive instructors, mountain guides, or skiing and snowboarding instructors.

Fundamentals of Outdoor Living

Essentials of Mountaineering (or Paddling)

Essentials of Challenge Course Technology

Leadership and Group Dynamics

Outdoor Emergency Care

Therapeutic Rec. & Developmental Disability

CERTIFICATE IN SUSTAINABLE COMMUNITY DEVELOPMENT

Provides training, requisite skills, a knowledge base and a philosophy that embodies the values of sustainable community and entrepreneurial enterprise. Students will be drawn from GMC and other nearby liberal arts institutions, as well as from professionals working as technical assistance providers, community planners and those in other professions wishing to assist small communities and businesses in implementing locally based sustainable

Economics of the Environment

Sustainable Development: Theory and Policy

Public Policy and the Environment

Building Sustainable Communities

Non-Profits and Policy Making

Land Use Planning

Environmental Advocacy, Public Policy and Corporate Responsibility

EDUCATION   LIBERAL STUDIES   CONSERVATION   BIOLOGY

Rolling Admissions

• Field Studies • Team Teaching • Individualized Majors • Interdisciplinary Majors • Service-Learning
• Interdisciplinary Classes • Enviro Housing • Organic Gardens • Vegetarian/Vegan Meals

Dean of Admissions

Green Mountain College

One College Circle

Poultney, VT 05764-1199

802. 776.6675

admiss@greenmtn.edu

www.greenmtn.edu

GRINNELL COLLEGE

1,450 Students   Grinnell, Iowa

Ask students, faculty, and staff what distinguishes Grinnell and you will hear their agreement that Grinnell fosters a strong sense of community. At Grinnell, individuals are respected for who they are and what they believe, and differences can be expressed and appreciated. Grinnell is a place where great ideas and global issues are considered and debated. Faculty encourages debate over significant issues in the classroom and beyond. Students leave Grinnell believing that they can and should make a difference in their careers and communities.

Grinnell is informed by a pioneering spirit, a willingness to experiment, and a commitment to community. Grinnell seeks and produces good students who take an active part in the campus community and later in the world. The college has traditionally been a community with a conscience. Grinnell's pioneering past began in 1846, when New Englanders with strong social-reformer backgrounds established the college. Influenced by Grinnell's educational and social idealism, the College blends academic accomplishments with service to the world. In 1959, Grinnell established the Travel Service Scholarship, which provided funds to send graduating seniors to developing countries for a year to assist with language instruction, village work projects, or other special needs.

Grinnell continues to link educational goals with society's realities. The College believes that the most valued workers will analyze problems quantitatively and articulate solutions effectively within the context of the broader world. Grinnell graduates not only join business and the professions, but they also can be found in large numbers in the Peace Corps, political campaigns, public official staffs, environmental coalitions and education. The social consciousness developed at Grinnell becomes a life-long commitment.

To introduce students to differing voices and ideas, Grinnell brings to campus many prominent thinkers. Lecturers have included: Ambassador George E. Moose '66, former Assistant Secretary of State for African Affairs; former President of Costa Rica Oscar Arias and former Secretary of State Madeleine Albright. Symposia have focused on such topics as "Culture, Politics and Change in Contemporary Cuba," "The Palestinian-Israeli Conflict in Perspective," "Women, Politics and Leadership for the 21st Century," and "Water: Conflicts and Trade-offs."

Student activities and organizations include the Environmental Action Group, Students in Defense of Animals, and Amnesty International. Also on campus are Stonewall Coalition; Concerned Black Students; International Student Organization; Habitat for Humanity; Native American Alliance; Asian Students Alliance; Student Organization of Latino/as; Chalutzim; Social Justice Action Group; Society for Creative Anachronism and many more.

Many students keep one foot in the surrounding cities and towns work with Head Start, Habitat for Humanity, local school systems and church groups. Student-initiated projects are welcomed, and you are encouraged to link service activities with academic interests and career exploration.

Outdoor activities are organized by the Grinnell Outdoor Recreation Program. Students decide on the group's activities: cross country skiing, backpacking, sailing, caving, whitewater canoeing and others. GORP provides free training workshops and equipment.

MAKING A DIFFERENCE STUDIES

ENVIRONMENTAL STUDIES CONCENTRATION
Off-campus programs in Tropical Field Research in Costa Rica or the ACM Wilderness Field Station.

Organisms, Evolution and Ecology

Human Evolution

Resource and Environmental Economics

Nations and the Global Environment

* **International Politics of Land and Sea Resources** -- Analysis of the international politics of the conflict between the developed nations of the north and the developing nations of the south for control of the world's resources and over a new economic order. Impact of national decision-making processes, international organizations, cartels, and multinational corporations. Case studies on fuel, mineral, and food crises.

FIRST YEAR TUTORIALS
The Anthropology of American Culture

Human: What is and What is Not?

Evolution and Society

Stirring the Pot: Race, Class & Gender in Higher Ed

Color, Culture and Class

Religion and Politics Across the World

Globalization

The Cold Politics of Global Warming

Grinnell thru Pop Culture, Quick Studies & Irreverent Social Commentary

POLITICAL SCIENCE
American Public Policy and Democracy

Consumption and Citizenship in Wider Europe

Disease, Death and International Politics

U.S. Foreign-Policy-Making

Political Economy of Developing Countries

African Politics

The Politics of International Relations

Gender and the American Welfare State

Politics of Middle East

South Africa and the Politics of Transformation

LATIN AMERICAN STUDIES
Latin American Cultures

Political Economy of Developing Countries

State and Society in Latin America

Aztecs, Incas and Mayas

International Economics

Modernization & Innovation: Contemp. Spanish Amer.

Economic Development

Traditions of Independent Spanish America

The Spanish American Colonial World

Radical Movements in 20th-Century Latin America

GLOBAL DEVELOPMENT STUDIES
African Cultures

Resource and Environmental Economics

Ecology

Nations and the Global Environment

The Traditions of Islam

Radical Movements in 20th-Century Latin America

Chinese Women Past & Present

International Politics: of Land & Sea Resources

Grassroots Rural Development

Sustainable Development in Modern World System

SOCIOLOGY
Sociology of Global Development

Social Movements in the 20th Century

Self and Society

Social Inequality

Sociology of Health and Illness

Race and Ethnicity in America

Gender and Society

The Family

Human Sexuality in the United States

Contemporary Sociological Theory

GENDER AND WOMEN'S STUDIES   ANTHROPOLOGY

Early Decision 11/20, 1/1   Regular Decision 1/20

• Individually-Advised Majors • Field Studies • Interdisciplinary Majors • Vegetarian/Vegan Meals

• Local and Organic Foods   • Green Buildings

Office of Admission

800. 247.0113

Grinnell College

641. 269.3600

Grinnell, IA 50112-1690

askgrin@grinnell.edu

www.grinnell.edu

HAMPSHIRE COLLEGE

1,200 Students   Amherst, Mass.

Hampshire's roots are in dissatisfaction with the status quo. In the late 1950's, the presidents of four prestigious New England colleges – Amherst, Mount Holyoke, Smith and the University of Massachusetts – sought ways to practice innovative ideas about education that seemed impossible within their traditional institutions. They wanted students to have the academic freedom to study what they loved in interdisciplinary and in-depth ways that would force connections between the academic and the "real" world. The result of their quest, Hampshire College, opened in 1970. Today, Hampshire remains in a partnership with the four colleges that created it, providing the Pioneer Valley with a Five College Consortium. Each semester the five colleges offer over 5,000 courses collectively – just one of the ways the consortium benefits each of the 30,000 students in the area.

Hampshire's curriculum is organized into five schools of thought, each with its own particular mode of inquiry. These are the schools of: Cognitive Science; Humanities, Arts, and Cultural Studies; Interdisciplinary Arts; Natural Science; and Social Science. This organization blurs the lines between traditional departments so that an anthropology professor daily rubs elbows with historians, psychologists, and political scientists. Faculty trained in different disciplines often team up to teach interdisciplinary courses. For example, a class that explores representations of cultural identities in music, literature, and film is co-taught by a World Music professor and a professor of Cultural Studies.

Hampshire's founders believed that students would be better prepared for a rapidly changing society if they were engaged in substantial independent research projects, internships and field work. Students collaborate with faculty mentors to design individualized programs of study which reflect the students' most passionate interests and concerns. Concentrations typically embrace several subjects; a student concentrating in educational psychology might take courses in education, race, gender, media criticism, writing, psychology, neuroscience, and history. She might also start a program in a local community center exploring racial identity development through poetry. Or, she may spend time in a nearby school testing a curriculum she designed. Throughout her time at Hampshire, faculty advisory committees will guide her with challenging questions, extensive feedback, and narrative evaluations regarding her progress.

A strong commitment to service and diversity is reflected in Hampshire's curriculum. Students are expected, in designing their concentration, to incorporate both community service and a multiple cultural perspectives requirement. Hampshire's motto 'Non Satis Scire' (To Know is Not Enough), challenges students to ask themselves how they will effect change. To this end, Hampshire has several programs designed to prepare students to make a difference through human service, social action, and environmental protection. The Civil Liberties and Public Policy Program promotes the leadership and interests of young women, presents a broad vision of reproductive freedom, and works to develop strategies that are national in scope and impact and yet grassroots in implementation. The Lemelson Assistive Technology Development Center allows students to create innovative products to assist patients, athletes, and people with disabilities. The US Southwest and Mexico Program examines the transnational implications and consequences of living within national and political borders. Students in the program engage in community-based active research in the southwest.

Since 1987, the Community Partnerships for Social Change Program has been a campus resource for students and faculty who wish to integrate their academic interests with their social action and community-based experiences in order to forge a link between the classroom and the community. CPSC offers community-based internship and research opportunities, training seminars, and a variety of resources to strengthen students' social justice organizing skills. The Peace and World Securities Studies Program, a Five-College Program housed at Hampshire, strives to enhance the contribution of the academic community to the search for global peace, justice, and security through course offerings, public lectures, conferences and publications. The Third World Studies Program explores local and global forces that require the majority of the world's population to inhabit the Third World, as well as links between the configurations of power that operate internationally and domestically to the detriment of people of color.

The Hampshire College Farm Center is a working farm, as well as a research, education, and outreach facility, dedicated to sustainable agriculture. The farm staff offers workshops, and involves students in all aspects of small-scale farming, including running a School-To-Farm Program, which offers farm-based educational opportunities for elementary aged students, adolescents with special needs, and urban youth.

The Environmental Studies Program encourages students to probe the workings of ecological systems and the relationship between nature and human culture. Faculty and student research leads to work in such areas as natural resource conservation, biodiversity, population dynamics, the humanly built environment, first and third world development impacts, appropriate technology, sustainable agriculture, political activism, and land use policy. (Hampshire also has a "green" graduation ceremony.)

Hampshire helps students develop confidence in their intellect, creativity, and values. It encourages their desire to be lifelong learners and their capacity to advance the cause of social justice and the well-being of others. The college fosters these attitudes through: a multidisciplinary, multicultural curriculum; self-initiated, individual programs of study negotiated with faculty mentors; students' active participation in original research; and the diverse communities, on campus and off, in which learning takes place.

Approximately 85% of Hampshire graduates are admitted to one of their top two choices of graduate programs. More than 20% start their own businesses, many of which are committed to socially responsible business practices. 47% of graduates have found their places in social service or environmental protection related jobs. Having learned at Hampshire to take charge of their education, and to use that education to make meaningful contributions to society, Hampshire's alumni are engaged in doing exactly that.

Through commitment to testing and evaluating new ideas and new approaches to learning, national efforts to promote inquiry-based learning and teaching, and constructive civic and social engagement, Hampshire's actions serve as models for those of its students.

MAKING A DIFFERENCE STUDIES

SCHOOL OF NATURAL SCIENCE:

Social Determinants of Health
Ecology
Elements of Sustainability
Environmental Education
Organic Farming and Sustainable Agriculture
Research in Nutrition and Pollution

Ecological Footprint: A Tool For A Sustainable Future
Anthropology of Violence
Environmental Impacts: Archeological Perspective
Inventing Reality: the Human Search For Truth
Race, Science and Politics
Research On Women's Health and Diet

SCHOOL OF SOCIAL SCIENCE

Religious Movements and Social Change
The Culture(s) of United States' Foreign Policy
Youth and Justice
Conflict Resolution and Historical Analysis
Making Social Change

Youth, Popular Culture, and Education
Third World Developm't: Grassroots Perspectives
Human Rights: the Legal Framework
Population, Environment and Security
Social Change: Civil Rights & Black Power Struggles

Social Identities & Legal Rights: Race, Feminist & Queer Legal Theories
Fair Division & Fair Representation: Measuring & Modeling Social Phenomena

SCHOOL OF HUMANITIES, ARTS & CULTURAL STUDIES

Citizenship, Freedom and the Good Life
Introductory Topics in Moral Philosophy
Feminist Philosophy
The History of Photography by Women
Asian-American Literature & Life
Politics of Multiculturalism
Parking Lots into Paradise: Next Urban Paradigm

Woman is a Nation: Gender in Music, Lit. & Film
Art Education and the Postmodern Classroom
Music and the Culture of the Caribbean
Music Ethnography
Visual Responses to Cultural and Political Crisis
Authority, Power, Reason and Choice

SCHOOL OF COGNITIVE SCIENCE

Learning Revolutions
Environmental Ethics
Theories and Practices of Literacy Instruction
Ever Since Darwin
Digital Humanities

Introduction To Experimental Psychology
Cognitive Ethology
Language and Society
Diversity, Equity, Opportunity
Bridging the Divide: Service Learning & Practicum

Cognitive Approaches to Learning & Individual Differences in Reading& Mathematics

SCHOOL OF INTERDISCIPLINARY ARTS

American Voices, American Lives
History as Fiction, Fiction as History
Writing the Body: Language and Health
The Architecture of Memory
Public Eye: The Surveillance Society

Prison Literature
African American Poetry
Feminist Fictions
Architectural Design For Diversity & Social Change
Women Playwrights in the 18th & 19th Century

Designing For People in the 21St Century: Universal Design & Adaptive Equipment
Living for Tomorrow: Cultural Contestations, Gender Politics & the Aids Epidemic

Apply by 1/15

• Team Teaching   • Self-Designed Majors   • Interdisciplinary Classes   • Field Studies
• Strong Activism   •Service Learning   • Optional SAT's   • Organic Gardens
• Theme Housing   • Vegetarian & Vegan Meals   • Socially Responsible Investments

Director of Admissions
Hampshire College
Amherst, MA 01002

877. 937.4267
www.hampshire.edu
admissions@hampshire.edu

HENDRIX COLLEGE

1,000 Students   Conway, Arkansas

Hendrix College is a selective liberal arts college in the foothills of the Ozark Mountains. In The Statement of Purpose, Hendrix declares its "dedication to the cultivation of whole persons" and its intention to "prepare its graduates for lives of service and fulfillment in their communities and the world." Hendrix encourages its students to develop "powers of ethical deliberation and empathy for others; discernment of the social, spiritual, and ecological needs of our time; and a sense of responsibility for leadership and service in response to those needs".

For Hendrix, "cultivation of whole persons" includes preparation for meaningful work, satisfying personal relationships, and opportunities for leisure. It also involves global awareness, respect for life and environment, sensitivity to suffering of others, and a desire to help build communities that are compassionate, participatory, peaceful, and free.

This commitment to engaged learning is part of the history and fabric of Hendrix College and is the cornerstone of a new curricular initiative called Your Hendrix Odyssey: Engaging in Active Learning. Tthe Odyssey program guarantees that every Hendrix student will have at least three specific active learning experiences, drawn from six categories. In addition to the personal benefit students receive by linking critical thought with action, Hendrix will also provide an experiential learning transcript to each graduate.

The Global Awareness component of the Odyssey experience helps students understand and appreciate cultures or environments other than their own. Toward that end, students are encouraged to engage in learning outside the classroom that broadens intellectual horizons and deepens understandings of the political, social, cultural, environmental, spiritual and economic issues affecting the world today. Global Awareness opportunities are also designed to promote personal growth and self-reliance as well as to provide new perspectives about the student's own culture or environment.

Another Odyssey component is Service to the World. To meet this requirement, students must arrange to do a minimum of 30 hour service projects for social agencies, service organizations, or faith communities directly involved in providing resources, goods, political access, or other services in response to serious human and environmental problems.

Hendrix students volunteer each year, working at homes for abused women, planting organic gardens, tutoring underprivileged children, finding homes for abused animals, and assisting at a local sanctuary for abandoned elephants.

Numerous student organizations offer opportunities for advocacy for human rights, the environment, and animal welfare. They include Amnesty International, Habitat for Humanity, Regional AIDS Interfaith Network, Student Activities that Value the Earth, and the Volunteer Action Center. Others pursue opportunities for service through the Peace Corps, Teach for America, Heifer Project International and other related organizations. Hendrix recently received an award from the Peace Corps for the high number of graduates who have completed service in the Peace Corps.

The Odyssey Distinction Award is a scholarship, ranging from $1,000 to $5,000 per year, given to students whose high school experiences demonstrate the ability to Think Outside the Book.

MAKING A DIFFERENCE STUDIES

SOCIOLOGY & ANTHROPOLOGY

General Anthropology
Cultures of India
Ethnographic Methods
Medical Sociology
Gender and Family
The Urban Community
Social Inequality

Cultural Anthropology
Cultures through Film
Psychological Anthropology
Medical Sociology
Racial and Ethnic Minorities
Environmental Sociology
Social Change

PHILOSOPHY & RELIGION

Ethics and Medicine
Feminist Thought
Religion in a Global Context
Mysticism, Meditation and Prayer
Environmental Philosophy

Ethics and Society
The Philosophy of Whitehead
African-American Religion
Buddhism
Religion, Animals & the Earth

POLITICS

Current Affairs in Global Politics
Current Issues, Problems, and Events
Public Policy
Political Economy
Communism, Fascism, and Democracy

Global Politics I: History and Theory
Latin American Politics
Public Policy Process
Public Administration
Southern Politics

INTERNATIONAL RELATIONS & GLOBAL STUDIES

Globalization and Transnationalism
English as a Global Language
Religion in a Global Context
Women and Religion

Masterpieces of World Literature
Survey of Global Musics
State of the World
World Religions: Contemporary Perspectives

GENDER STUDIES

Gender and Environment
Gender in Medieval Literature
Introduction to Gender Studies
Gender, Sexuality and American Politics
Feminist Political Thought

Women and African Literature
Gender in African History
Social Inequality
Gender and Family
Anthropology of Gender

INTERDISCIPLINARY STUDIES

Students may design their own major, combining courses from several departments or areas to explore an area of particular interest. Examples of some Interdisciplinary Majors students have intiated include: African Studies & Anthropology; Ecology & Society; Ecology, Society, & Politics; Environmental Education; Environmental Studies; Gender Studies; Holistic Health; International Relations & Global Studies; Non-Profit Leadership; and Sustainability & Global Awareness.

Apply by 8/1
Avg. # of students in 1st year classroom: 15
• Field Studies   • Student Environmental Audits   • Service-Learning
• Interdisciplinary Classes   • Team Teaching   • Self-Designed Majors   • Vegetarian Meals

Director of Admissions   501. 450. 1362
Hendrix College   www.hendrix.edu
1600 Washington Avenue   adm@hendrix.edu

HUMBOLDT STATE UNIVERSITY

6,500 Undergraduates   Arcata, California

Set between redwood groves and the Pacific Ocean, 275 miles north of San Francisco, Humboldt State University is a campus of choice, not convenience. The northernmost institution in the California State University system, the campus tends to attract from afar students who are more adventurous and self-reliant. The intimate, natural setting and small class sizes foster friendliness and close faculty/student relationships. Undergraduates enjoy uncommon privileges: broad access to computers, equipment, and laboratories including the University forest, greenhouse, marine laboratory, and electron microscope. HSU is traditionally known for its sciences and natural resources programs such as forestry and wildlife

The University welcomes the challenges and opportunities of a diverse and rapidly changing society. To this end, it is a community striving to value diversity, to be inclusive, and to respect alternative paradigms of behavior and value systems. Humboldt's mission includes the development of a fundamental understanding of the interdependent web of life; and cultivating capacity for self-initiative, self-fulfillment, and autonomous and responsible action.

Humboldt State has a remarkable array of resources. Students from fisheries, oceanography, geology, biology, and other majors get a chance to test experiments and work on research projects at the University's Marine Laboratory in the coastal town of Trinidad, not far from the main campus. The nearby bay and Pacific Ocean provide rocky and sandy intertidal and subtidal habitats for further study. HSU also has a seagoing vessel available for the primary purpose of providing instructional experiences on the ocean.

Students also find instructional and research opportunities at a 300-acre Dunes Preserve managed by HSU on behalf of the Nature Conservancy. The dunes, bounded by the Pacific and the River Slough, contain rare natural coastal habitats where research can be conducted in a protected ecosystem. A 4,500 acre ranch is being used by students in a wide variety of disciplines. HSU's Waterfowl Ecology Research Group monitors the wetlands and coastal bays crucial to birds and wildlife.

At the edge of Humboldt Bay is a 150 acre sanctuary which benefits students in botany, fisheries, environmental resources, engineering, biology, wildlife, and natural resources interpretation. Among the projects are: a national model natural wastewater treatment process designed by a HSU professor; a co-generation system using methane digesters; and an aquaculture program devoted to rearing salmon, trout, and oysters in treated wastewater.

Students interested in appropriate technology have a unique opportunity at the Campus Center for Appropriate Technology. Students combine theory and practice at the center - a live-in, working demonstration home — including photovoltaic and wind electric systems, a solar hot water system, a greenhouse passive heating system, a composting privy, a graywater system and organic gardens.

The intimacy of the campus mirrors the sense of community along California's North Coast. In the small-town atmosphere, students learn they can make a direct, positive difference in the lives of others. And they do, through programs for senior citizens, recycling, science outreach, legal counseling, health education, and others. Many students acquire a long-lasting sense of social commitment, as evidenced by Humboldt's historically high proportion of graduates entering the Peace Corps.

MAKING A DIFFERENCE STUDIES

ENVIRONMENTAL RESOURCES ENGINEERING/ ENERGY; WATER; WATER QUALITY; GEO ENVIRO.

Water Resources Planning and Management
Environmental Health Engineering
Environmental Impact Assessment
Solid Waste Management

Water Quality Analysis
Renewable Energy Power Systems
Solar Thermal Engineering
Air Quality Management

OCEANOGRAPHY

General Oceanography
Sampling Techniques and Field Studies
Estuarine Ecology
Beach & Nearshore Processes
Solid Earth Geophysics

Biological Oceanography
Physical Oceanography
Marine Primary Production
Zooplankton Ecology
Field Cruise

ENVIRONMENTAL SCIENCE: ENVIRONMENTAL ETHICS

Environmental Ethics
Environmental Politics
Dispute Resolution
Case Studies in Environmental Ethics
Sustainable Campus

Water Pollution Biology
Technology and the Environment
Sociology of Wilderness
The Conservation Ethic
Ecotopia

APPROPRIATE TECHNOLOGY MINOR Very useful for Peace Corps or overseas development work.

Whole Earth Engineering
Technology and the Environment
Social Ecology

Appropriate Technology
Politics of Sustainable Society
Politics of Appropriate Technology in Third World

NATURAL RESOURCES PLANNING AND INTERPRETATION

Environmental & Nat. Resources Economics
Public Land Use Policies and Management
Rural Community Planning
Environmental Communication
Natural Resource Interpretation

Natural Resource Management in Parks
Natural Resource Conflict Resolution
Environmental Impact Assessment
One Earth: Common Ground in Resource Mgm't.
Natural Resource Regulatory Processes

FORESTRY: FOREST RESOURCE CONSERVATION, FOREST HYDROLOGY

Wilderness Area Management
Forest Resources Protection
Natural Resource Management in Parks
Forest Ecosystems and People
Ethics in Forestry

Remote Sensing & Geographic Info. Systems
Advanced Forest Ecology
Forest Administration
The Forest Environment
Wildland Fire Use

RANGELAND RESOURCES   PEACE & CONFLICT   FISHERIES   SOCIAL WORK   WILDLIFE

ENVIRO. TOXICOLOGY   NATIVE AMERICAN STUDIES   INTERNATIONAL STUDIES

GLOBALIZATION   CONSERVATION BIOLOGY   MARINE BIOLOGY   BIODIVERSITY

Apply by 11/30
• Prior Learning Credit   • Self-Designed Majors   • Service-Learning
• Theme Housing   • Organic Gardens   • Community Service & Enviro. Theme Housing

Admissions and School Relations   707. 826.4402
Humboldt State University   www.humboldt.edu
Arcata, CA 95521-8299   hsuinfo@humboldt.edu

Field studies are a frequent component of education at Evergreen State College in the lush Pacific Northwest. Evergreen is nationally recognized for it's innovative teaching and interdisciplinary classes.

Bemidji State University students learn as much about themselves as they do about the environment when they participate in Outdoor Program Center activities and trips. The center is recognized as one of the nation's most active outdoor programs.

Work and community service are integral parts of student life at Warren Wilson College. Environmental studies majors often chose the organic garden work crew while pre-vet students work with animals on the college farm.

Each semester, EcoDwelling students at New College of California balance their classroom learning with an weekend hands-on building campout. Building systems include cob, clay-straw, earthen plasters, carpentry, bamboo and more.

JUNIATA COLLEGE

1,400 Students   Huntingdon, PA

The world is changing at a breathtaking pace. To be successful, students need a different kind of education. At Pennsylvania's Juniata College students are encouraged to break the mold of conformity, to seek their own truth and to think for themselves. Juniata students expect the uncommon in their educational experience, realizing early on that what really matters is the preparation they receive to meet the challenges of the 21st century.

From the time the college was founded in 1876 by members of the Church of the Brethren, one of the traditional peace churches, being uncommon has always been considered a good thing. That's because at this liberal arts college students find their education as personal as it is challenging. Juniata offers a flexible curriculum that empowers students to be in charge of their education. Most Juniata students design their own majors through a tailored Program of Emphasis. That means students pursue their own talents, while gaining the in-depth knowledge that employers and graduate schools value.

A rigorous academic program that involves students in the issues and trends shaping our society distinguishes Juniata's education program. Students study the impact of our actions on the environment through coursework in environmental science. They can put their coursework into action at the 365-acre field station on nearby Raystown Lake. The College's new "Sense of Place" semester provides an opportunity for students to live at the lake for an entire semester.

As a student, you explore new approaches to resolving differences at home and abroad through the college's program in Peace and Conflict Studies - a program that has brought the United Nations to the campus; led to the creation of the college's Peace Chapel designed by Maya Lin, who also designed The Wall (The Vietnam Veterans' Memorial in Washington) and serves as a national model for other institutions.

Juniata students ponder and probe cultural issues through the academic program's cultural analysis component - a course sequence designed to teach you how to think, not what to think. You take two cultural analysis courses, chosen from a selection of approved courses, designed to develop the necessary skills to identify, understand and analyze culture.

Juniata backs up its commitment to students who make a difference through the unique Nomination Scholarship Program. Through this program, the college awards eight students who make a difference as a result of involvement in school, community and beyond. Four of the awards are full tuition, room and board, the other four are full tuition scholarships. Scholarships are offered in The Arts to students who have participated in and who have shown commitment to the arts; in Environmental Responsibility to students who demonstrate personal interest and involvement in environmental issues; in Leadership to students who have demonstrated leadership in school, community or church activities; and in Service and Peace Making to students who have proven involvement in organizations that promote community service, conflict resolution, or mediation.

Juniata College is a community dedicated to providing the highest quality liberal arts education. The aim of that education is to awaken students to the empowering richness of the mind and to enable them to lead fulfilling and useful lives.

Making a Difference Studies

Communication & Conflict Resolution

Introduction to Human Communication
Mediation
Interpersonal Communication
Communicating Diversity
Nonviolence: Theory and Practice
Media Analysis

Introduction to Conflict Resolution
Conflict Intervention
Gender & Conflict
Studies in Communication
News & Feature Writing
Conflict Intervention

Environmental Studies: Public Policy, Conflict Resolution, Human Adaptation

North American Environmental History
Public Policy and Administration
International Economic Issues
Public Interest Groups & Political Participation
Politics of Developing Nations
Environmental Politics
Intro to Environmental Science & Studies

International Political Economy
Economics of the Environment
Conservation Biology
Environmental Monitoring
Economics of the Environment
Topics in Policy: Global Environment
Environmental Problem Solving

International Politics

Intro to American Government
Western Political Thought
United States Foreign Policy
Ideas & Power in the Modern World
International Economic Issues

Intro to International Politics
Politics of Developing Nations
International Law & Human Rights
The Politics & Culture of Modernization
International Political Economy

Criminal Justice

Research in Comparative Justice
Introduction to Criminal Justice
Issues in Law Enforcement
Social Problems & Social Welfare
Drugs & Society
Minorities

Criminalistics: Forensic Science
Social Deviance & Criminology
Corrections
Criminal Law
Child & Family Services
Juvenile Justice

Geology

Remote Field Course
Oceanography
Historical Geology
Mineralogy
Geochemistry of Natural Waters
Petrology of Igneous and Metamorphic Rocks

Introduction to Geology
Weather and Climate
Structural Geology
Mineral Economics , Politics and Law
Petrography
Hydrogeology

Peace & Conflict   Geology   Teaching Credential   Environmental Science   History

Apply by: 3/1   Early Decision 11/1   Early Action 12/1

• Field Studies   • Service Learning   • Team Teaching   • Self-Designed Majors   • Optional SAT's
• Interdisciplinary Classes   • Vegetarian/Vegan Meals   • Theme Housing   • Green Campus

Director of Admissions
Juniata College
1700 Moore St.
Huntingdon, PA 16652

877. JUNIATA
814. 641.3420
www.juniata.edu
info@juniata.edu

LEWIS AND CLARK COLLEGE

2,000 Students   Portland, Oregon

On 137 deeply wooded acres in Portland's southwest hills, the next generation of global thinkers and leaders gathers to discard conventional thinking, civic complacency, and outmoded preconceptions. They gather to explore new ways of knowing through classic liberal learning and innovative collaboration.

Lewis & Clark College welcomes all who are alive to inquiry, open to diversity, and eager to shape life in an interdependent world. The College pursues original research, interdisciplinary studies, and community service, and pushes beyond what is known in order to discover something new every day. L&C does all of this and more to change the world in ways yet unknown.

Lewis & Clark College is a private institution with a public conscience, a residential campus with global reach. The unmatched setting, proximity to a progressive urban center, and Pacific Northwest heritage combine to offer all who teach, study, or work here a deep sense of place and broad opportunities for reflection, renewal, and recreation. The College vigorously pursues the aims of all liberal learning: to seek knowledge for its own sake and to strengthen civic leadership. The highly interactive communities of learning challenge students to connect ideas, reasoning, and thoughtful expression with lives of service as citizens of the world.

This is a college that walks its talk. It was first campus in nation to comply with greenhouse gas emissions targets called for in Kyoto. In 2004 it received a Green Power Leadership Award. In 2005 two new residence halls were awarded LEED Silver and Gold certification by the U.S. Green Building Council for environmentally sustainable design and construction. In was the first private institution in Oregon to sign the International Talloires Declaration of Sustainability. L&C also received a Truman Foundation Institution Award for encouraging outstanding students to pursue public service careers.

The interdisciplinary field of International Affairs rarely exists as a separate department on the undergraduate level. In fact, Lewis & Clark is one of only about 25 institutions in the nation that have an IA department. It is a discipline with broad dimensions, that integrates the information, strategies, and techniques of political science, sociology, economics, history, communication, and psychology to study and understand complex relations among nations. International affairs looks not only at cultural interplay, but at political, military, and economic transactions among nations.

College Outdoors provides students with access to the spectacular outdoor environments of the Pacific Northwest and beyond in a variety of activities including cross-country skiing, backpacking, whitewater sports, sea kayaking, and hiking. Trips go all over the Pacific Northwest – and to the mountains, river, desert, the coast, and on extended adventures into areas of Utah, Arizona, California, Mexico, the Virgin Islands and beyond.

All who gather here –students, teachers, mentors, staff – know that education transforms lives and reforms societies. That is the promise Lewis and Clark makes. To fulfill that promise through lives of knowledge and purpose, to continue always to explore, to learn, and to serve: Students with agile minds come to Lewis & Clark to learn and to lead.

MAKING A DIFFERENCE STUDIES

INTERNATIONAL AFFAIRS

Multinational Corporations
United States Foreign Policy
African Politics
Latin American Politics
Global Resource Dilemmas

Global Inequality
Middle East Politics
International and Internal Conflict
Development: Problems and Prospects
International Relations of Northeast Asia

SOCIOLOGY AND ANTHROPOLOGY

Anthropology of Violence
Crime and Punishment
Radical Social Movements
The Family in Cross-Cultural Perspective
Medicine Healing and Culture
Peoples and Culture of Islam

Women in Developing Countries
Race & Ethnicity in Global Perspective
Class, Power and Society
Myth, Ritual and Symbol
Latin America in Cultural Perspective
Environmental Sociology

RELIGIOUS STUDIES

Early Mahayana Buddhism
Sufism: Islamic Mysticism
Buddhism: Theory, Culture and Practice
Jesus,: History, Myth and Mystery
Religion and Culture of Hindu India

Women in American Religious History
Women in the Islamic World
Witches, Prophets & Preachers: Religion in US History
Religious Fundamentalism: Islamic, Hindu & Christian
Intro to Judaism

ENVIRONMENTAL STUDIES

Seeks to fuse knowledge and analytical ability with leadership and communication skills to successfully devise and implement creative, academically grounded solutions to environmental problems.

Environmental Law and Policy
Philosophy and Environment
Marine Biology
Communication and Conflict
Ecology

European Agrarian Development
Social Change
Economic Development
Energy and Environment, Quantitative Approach
History of the Pacific Northwest

PHILOSOPHY

The critical examination of our most fundamental ideas about ourselves and the world. What is the nature and purpose of human life? What kind of society is best? What is our relation to nature? Philosophy tries to make these beliefs evident and open to reconsideration, hoping thereby to improve human life and the chances for survival of all life on this planet.

Ethics
Philosophy of Science
Philosophy of Law
Metaphysics
Philosophy of Mind

Philosophy of Religion
Philosophy of Art and Beauty
Philosophy and the Environment
Philosophy of Language
Ethics, Society and Politics

Apply by 2/1

• Field studies • Interdisciplinary Classes • Team Teaching • Optional SAT's
• Student Enviro. Audits • Service Learning • Theme Housing • Self Designed Majors
• Vegetarian/Vegan Meals • Green Campus • Organic Gardens

Admissions Office
Lewis & Clark College
0615 SW Palatine Hill Road
Portland, OR 97219-7899

503. 768.7040
800. 444.4111
www.lclark.edu

LIVING ROUTES

Study Abroad for a Sustainable Future

UMass Amherst-accredited January, Summer, Semester
and Year Abroad programs in Ecovillages worldwide

Bring your education to life - in and outside the classroom- in Ecovillages, where issues of ecological sustainability and social justice meet. In Ecovillages around the world, people are creating and modeling sustainable lifestyles in harmony with their local environments - restoring ecosystems and habitat, developing participatory models of governance, growing healthful organic food, building "green" homes, working for justice and social change, and utilizing renewable resources such as wind and solar energy.

These communities provide ideal "campuses" to immerse yourself in academic, experiential and service learning about sustainability, and prepare for lives and careers that make a difference.

Earn transferable academic credit as you:

- Learn about the indigenous use of medicinal plants and intern in teaching in southern India
- Study Human Ecology, help regenerate forests, and live on a self-sufficient island in Scotland
- Get hands-on experience in sustainable development and build fluency in French in Senegal
- Build a super adobe house, learn organic farming and dance Capoiera in tropical Brazil
- Become a skilled consensus facilitator & leader for social change in the volcano belt of Mexico
- Design ecological homesteads/landscapes with expert faculty in beautiful western Mass.
- Learn how High Amazon Fair Trade Coffee coops protect biodiversity & a living wage in Peru

Living Routes offers accredited study programs (January, Summer, Semester and Year Abroad) in Ecovillages in India, Scotland, Senegal, Brazil, Mexico and the U.S. All Living Routes programs contain an intergrated Service Learning component. Students receive an academic transcript from UMass Amherst, and academic credit is widely transferable to colleges and universities throughout the U.S. Additionally, participants who do not need academic credit often participate on Living Routes programs for the skills and experience they provide.

On each program students from diverse backgrounds, ages, and academic pursuits join with faculty to create their own "learning community" within a variety of "living communities". Dialogues with experienced community members, together with service work, internships, and participation in daily rhythms and activities, all facilitate a deep understanding of community life.

In addition, students develop individual and group goals, discuss readings, lead seminars, practice yoga and meditation, pursue independent studies, write essays and papers, visit areas of natural beauty, and create learning portfolios of their work in order to ground and deepen their understanding. In the process, students immerse themselves in the fields of ecological design, sustainable community development, globalization, and international relations.

To learn what students learn and experience day-to-day on one of the programs, check out the student Weblogs at www.LivingRoutes.org. Alumni return to take leadership roles in sustainability initiatives on campus, pursue graduate studies and work in international and grassroots organizations, socially responsible businesses, the arts, justice and environmental advocacy organizations worldwide.

Making a Difference Studies

Semester Programs

Scotland: Human Challenge of Sustainability at Findhorn: 16 credits

Examine the skills, creativity and understanding that are vital to community living. Findhorn is renowned for its environmental consciousness, personal growth, and artistry. Do service learning in organic gardens. Study Worldviews and Consciousness, Applied Sustainability, and Group Dynamics . Visit self-sustaining Erraid Island and build outdoor leadership and habitat regeneration skills.

Field Study: Explore Celtic culture, spend a week on extraordinary Erraid Island with a small farming community, and build outdoor leadership and habitat regeneration skills in a coastal ecosystem

Senegal: Sustainable Community Development: 16 credits

Engage with ecovillagers and indigenous peoples on topics of sustainable development and ecotourism. Partner with Senegalese university students to pursue service learning projects protecting natural resources, creating livelihoods, and improving education. Study French & Introductory Wolof & Senegalese Culture. Internships in envt'l. protection, organic agriculture, health and nutrition.

India: Sustainability in Practice at Auroville: 16 credits

Build ecological skills and learn about Indian and community culture at Auroville - "the city the earth needs" and one of the world's largest ecovillages. Study on an island preserve, site of 4 billion year-old exposed earth, caves and lakes. Discover the jungle ruins of Hindu empires and do a 40-hour sacred solo. Internships in organic agriculture, renewable energy systems, habitat protection, women's empowerment.

Summer and January Programs

Peru: Fair Trade & Bio-cultural Regeneration in the Amazon: 4 credits

Journey to Peru's Andean-Amazon to learn firsthand about empowerment efforts to restore the environment and create right livelihoods for indigenous farmers. Students contribute through service learning and study Shamanism, Fair Trade Organic Coffee Production, Quechua language (optional).

Mexico Leadership for Social Change: 4 credits

Learn the skills needed to bring a group together around a common vision and effect positive change. Huehuecoyotl was founded by an international group of artists and musicians, activists and ecologists. Study Consensus, Basic Facilitation Skills, Participatory Democracy, and Spanish (optional)

Brazil: Permaculture at Ecoversidade: 4 credits

Investigate new ways of creating sustainable habitats at Ecoversidade - a grassroots ecological institute in tropical Brazil. Learn Capoeira, a native mix of acrobatics, sacred dance, and self-defense. Study Sustainable Shelter, Aquaculture, Green building, and Portuguese language (optional)

USA: Permaculture at Sirius: 4 credits

Learn how to integrate plants, animals, buildings and communities in a design for ecological living in western MA. Visit old-growth forests, community-supported agricultural projects, eco-homesteads. Study Reading the Land, Building a Healthy Soil, and Cultivated Ecosystems.

Senegal: Sustainable Development at EcoYoff: 4 credits

Explore the impact of global trends and policies on the grassroots level. Build French language skills as you study the relationship between humans, development needs, and the environment. Partner with Senegalese university students to do community service learning.

Rolling Admissions   Programs can fill up to a year in advance.

Living Routes   888. 515.7333
Ecovillage Education   413. 259.0025
79 S. Pleasant St., #A5   info@LivingRoutes.org
Amherst, MA 01002   www.LivingRoutes.org

Manchester College

1,100 Students   Manchester, Indiana

Manchester College has a long tradition of combining learning and values. Its goal, as presented in the mission statement, is "to graduate people who possess ability and conviction." Manchester recognizes that change cannot come from conviction alone, that those who ardently desire to build a better world need real world skills to accomplish those goals. At Manchester College, skills and abilities are developed through rigorous preparation in a student's academic major(s) and broad coursework in the liberal arts. Graduates leave well trained for graduate school or their first job.

Manchester's mission statement also speaks best to its core values: "Within a long tradition of concern for peace and justice, Manchester College intends to develop an international consciousness, a respect for ethnic and cultural pluralism, and an appreciation for the infinite worth of every person. A central goal of the College community is to create an environment which nurtures a sense of self-identity, a strong personal faith, a dedication to the service of others, and an acceptance of the demands of responsible citizenship." Manchester College is an independent, co-educational college in the liberal arts tradition, and is committed to continue in the tradition of social concern which is a mark of the Church of the Brethren, its supporting denomination.

The learning environment at Manchester College emphasizes an open exchange of thoughts and ideas. Students are taught to ask tough questions and search for satisfying answers. The curriculum allows varied combinations of majors and minors, both in allied fields (e.g. history and political science) and across disciplines (e.g. physics and peace studies, music and gender studies).

Students can take advantage of travel opportunities through international studies programs (a semester or year at campuses in Brazil, China, France, Ecuador, England, Germany, Greece, Indonesia, Japan, Spain and Mexico), and during the three and a half week January Session. Recent January Session classes have gone to Spain, Morocco, Costa Rica, Mexico, Vietnam, Egypt, England, Florida, India and Nicaragua. January Sessions have included NASA research; health, fitness and wellness internships; field experiences in peace studies, social work and psychology, and many other off campus opportunities.

Manchester's emphasis on developing abilities and convictions shapes the academic and extra curricular experiences of students in every major. Action-oriented student groups are open to all students. They include Amnesty International, the Environmental Group, Habitat for Humanity, prison visitation teams, Death Penalty Awareness, Women's Advocacy Group, and many others. Students also participate in the Peace Choir, retreats, coffee houses, concerts, lectures and discussion forums, and in local and national conferences.

The Peace Studies Institute offers college-wide conferences featuring speakers, debates on issues of public policy, and workshops. Manchester also offers an unusually large number of scholarships to students majoring in Peace Studies.

Other special resources include the 100 acre Koinonia Environmental Center, including a 5 acre natural lake and woods, just 11 miles from campus. Koinonia has become a retreat and learning center for church and college groups

MAKING A DIFFERENCE STUDIES

ENVIRONMENTAL STUDIES: INTERPRETATION, EDUCATION & TECHNICAL STUDIES

Over 20 years old, this program was founded before "environmentalism" became popular.

Environmental Philosophy
Plant Taxonomy
Science and the Environment
Field Biology
Environmental Economics

Environmental Studies Practicum
Ecology
State and Local Politics
Environmental Science
Historical Geology

PEACE STUDIES: INTERPERSONAL & INTERGROUP CONFLICT, INT'L. & GLOBAL, RELIGIOUS & PHILOSOPHICAL

The Peace Studies program, founded in 1951, was the first in the nation. Nearly all majors participate in a Peace Studies practicum, an internship, or a year of study abroad.

Current Issues in Peace and Justice
Religions and War
Philosophy of Civilization
International Politics
Confucian and Buddhist Worlds
Microeconomics

Literature of Nonviolence
Analysis of War and Peace
Environmental Philosophy
Conflict Resolution
The Brethren Heritage
Peace and Justice

SOCIAL WORK

The Social Work program has an excellent reputation among professionals in the region, resulting in a strong placement rate for interns and graduates.

Introduction to Human Services
Social Service Policy
Social Welfare as an Institution
Juvenile Delinquency

Human Behavior and the Social Environment
Race and Minority Group Relations
Gerontology
Social Work Practice

PSYCHOLOGY

Students interested in psychology and conflict resolution find an exceptional opportunity in Manchester's mediation program--the Reconciliation Service — one of only a few in the country where students are active participants in mediating disputes for students and outside groups.

Cross-Cultural Psychology
Psychology of Mediation and Conciliation
Psychology of Learning

Psychology of the Young Adult
Counseling Theory and Practice
Psychology of Childhood

GENDER STUDIES

Based on the theory that gender is a cultural construct, not a naturally given aspect of personality, Gender Studies calls on us to reflect on the role gender plays in our lives and in society.

Introduction to Gender Studies
Feminist and Womanist Theology
Self and Society
Women in European History

Women in Literature
Women in the Arts
Women in American History
Feminist Theory

Rolling Admissions
• Average # of Students in a First Year Classroom: 20
• Service-Learning   • Self-Designed Majors   • Interdisciplinary Classes & Majors
• Team Teaching   • Field Studies   • Theme Housing   • Vegetarian & Vegan Meals

Admissions Office
Manchester College
604 E. College Ave
N. Manchester, IN 46962

800. 852. 3648
260. 982. 5055
admitinfo@manchester.edu
www.manchester.edu

MENNO SIMONS COLLEGE

Winnepeg, Canada

Menno Simons College is located in the inner city of Winnipeg on the University of Winnipeg's campus. The U of W is a liberal arts & science university that places its primary emphasis on undergraduate education. Menno Simons College, an affiliated college of The University of Winnipeg, offers solely two degrees: Bachelor of Arts Degrees in International Development Studies (IDS) and Conflict Resolution Studies (CRS).

The College prepares students from diverse backgrounds for participation in local and global communities through an education that addresses conflict, inequality, and poverty. The College combines the values of peace, justice, and service with high standards of academic excellence in the fields of Conflict Resolution and International Development. Rooted in the tradition of the Mennonite Anabaptist faith, the College's interdisciplinary programs are provided in affiliation with other disciplines at the University of Winnipeg and with other institutions in the community. Menno Simons College values interactive learning and facilitates this by limiting class size. MSC students register as, and receive degrees, from the U of Winnipeg.

International Development Studies is an interdisciplinary liberal arts major that challenges students to explore the causes and consequences of processes that promote some individuals, communities, and nations while excluding others. IDS students are prepared for citizenship in an increasingly interdependent global community, and are encouraged to envision paths towards a transformed, just world.

The IDS Program offers students the opportunity to gain practical experience in the development field through local and international practicum experiences. Partnerships have been developed with local community development agencies, and international opportunities are available through a variety of Canadian international development agencies. Past practicum opportunities have included: community development in Winnipeg's inner-city; research on development issues in Bangladesh, Brazil and Haiti; and teaching English as a Second Language in Lebanon and Jamaica.

Conflict Resolution Studies seeks to understand the nature and dynamics of human conflict, and to look at appropriate alternatives for dealing with conflict in ways which develop healthy relationships and prevent violence. Conflicts are analyzed from an interdisciplinary perspective together with topics such as violence, power, justice, peace, culture, communication, war, conflict transformation and dispute resolution. CRS prepares students to understand and interact constructively in response to personal, local, and global conflict situations.

Many international agencies, like the International Institute for Sustainable Development, Mennonite Central Committee, and the Canadian Foodgrains Bank which are headquartered in Winnipeg, facilitate study of the international aspects of these topics.

Winnipeg, situated on the historic banks of the Red and Assiniboine rivers, has a vibrant multicultural flavor. Its urban, multicultural and agricultural character ideally situate it for the study of development and conflict at the community level.

MAKING A DIFFERENCE STUDIES

INTERNATIONAL DEVELOPMENT STUDIES

Rural Development

An Analysis of Development Aid Policies

Voluntary Simplicity

Mennonite Community and Development

Global Processes and Local Consequences

Human Impact on the Environment

Gender and Global Politics

Urbanization in the Developing World

Introduction to International Development

Crisis, Vulnerability and Development

Environmental Sustainability: A Global Dilemma

Do No Harm: Conflict & Humanitarian Aid

Population Geography

Ethnography of South America

Indigenous Peoples and the Industrial State

Energy, Resources and Economic Development

- **Poverty-Focused Development**   The failure of modern development efforts to eradicate poverty in the South (Asia, Africa, and Latin America) has led to a widespread belief that alternative participatory, grassroots development projects are the solution. Course examines historic efforts at participatory development, including community development and cooperative formation, then considers the growing attention given nongovernmental organizations and grassroots movements today. Reviews contemporary strategies to enhance productivity through economic interventions such as credit programs and agricultural extension, or human interventions such as education and health provision. Sustainability issues are considered with reference to the enhancement of social capital.

CONFLICT RESOLUTION STUDIES

MSC encourages students to consider a double major, i.e. an interdisciplinary major plus a major from one of the traditional disciplines or a double major in CRS and Int'l. Development Studies.

Introduction to Conflict Resolution Studies

Conflict as Creative Catalyst

Models For Conflict Transformation

Human Rights and Civil Liberties in Canada

Race and Ethnic Relations

Conflict Within Faith Communities

Restorative Justice

Aboriginal Spirituality

Social Change

Mediation Skills: Dealing with Anger

Cross-Cultural Issues In Conflict Resolution

Conflict and Communication

Environmental Perception and Human Behavior

Conflict and Culture

Conflict and the Construction of the Other

Issues in Sustainable Cities

Environmental Economics

Peace Theory and Practice

Faith and Justice

Program Planning, Monitoring & Evaluation

Conciliation Skills

Issues in Sustainable Cities

- **Conflict & Development Issues In Indigenous Communities**   Explores dynamics of indigenous peoples globally, with special reference to the Canadian context, within the broad frameworks of development and conflict resolution. Key elements of indigenous culture and worldview.From the perspective of conflict resolution studies, inter- and intra-group conflict and conflict resolution processes involving indigenous communities will be explored. From the perspective of int'l. development studies, processes of marginalization and underdevelopment will be presented to understand the indigenous communities' social, economic and political situation. Strategies for community development and conflict resolution highlighted as means to achieve transformation.

Menno Simons College
520 Portage Ave. Suite 210
Winnipeg, Manitoba
Canada R3C 0G2

204. 953. 3855
http://io.uwinnipeg.ca/%7Emsc/
adm@uwinnepeg.ca

MIDDLEBURY COLLEGE

2,350 Students   Middlebury, VT

A small, academically rigorous liberal arts college tucked away in Vermont, Middlebury College surpasses all expectations. Its students are among the most engaged activists, volunteers, and civic-minded citizens in the nation, cultivating a sense of community wherever they go to study or work— literally around the world.

The Alliance for Civic Engagement is the nexus of campus activism. The office works with faculty to develop new and creative ways of using coursework to create visible change in the community. Students can go there to find ways to foster mutual understanding of diverse cultures in rural schools, organize a voter registration drive, or serve as volunteer firefighters and EMTs. ACE staffers are actively involved in reducing local poverty and routinely help students secure local and national internships in nonprofit service organizations. The office assures that all areas of the College make their community a better place.

Students who want to make a difference at the global level immerse themselves in the College's renowned language and interdisciplinary international studies programs, which are rooted in the philosophy that to effect change one must be able to see the world from different points of view, embodied by language and unconstrained by rigid disciplinary boundaries. The College administers more overseas direct-enrollment programs in language than any school its size, in 11 countries and 28 cities. Sixty percent of students prepare themselves for lives as global citizens by studying abroad. Activist opportunities abroad are available to interested students. After graduation, many Middlebury alumni live and work abroad, and the College consistently ranks among the top small schools sending graduates to the Peace Corps.

Middlebury is second to none in its commitment to the environment. The College was the first to offer an undergraduate major in environmental studies, which compels students to look at the environment from scientific, political, and humanistic perspectives. The College supplies "Green Grants," one of which funded six students' transcontinental tour in a biodiesel bus that made national headlines. Students can staff the recycling center, which diverts about twice the percentage of waste of its peer institutions, serve on the College's Environmental Council, or live in a dorm that requires sustainable living. Middlebury sets award-winning standards for buildings and renovations that mandate the use of lumber from sustainable forests and locally produced building products and that promote low carbon emissions. Twenty-five percent of the food in the dining halls is grown or produced in Vermont, yet Dining Services also supports "buy local" initiatives elsewhere, such as the small free-range salmon industry in Alaska.

In all areas of life, Middlebury College teaches skills and strategies for leadership and activism. Its academic calendar provides a month of intensive study in one subject that might culminate in a trip to rebuild New Orleans, or give students the extra time they need to plan fundraisers for children in developing countries the following spring. Students put on events to raise awareness of AIDS, racism, homophobia, dilapidated prisons, and the rights of indigenous people, problems that could be forgotten in the idyllic setting if not for the activity of the student body. From all corners of the globe, students come to Middlebury to engage the world.

Making a Difference Studies

Environmental Studies

Conservation Biology; Chemistry; Geology; Economics; Policy; Geography; Human Ecology; Architecture & Enviro; Creative Arts; History; Writing; Literature; Religion, Philosophy & the Enviro

Nature's Meanings	Sound Artists and the Environment
Architecture and the Environment	Place & the Environment in Spanish American Lit.
Environmental Economics	Global Climate Change
Faith, Freedom, and Ecology	Human Impact on the Global Environment
Africa: Environment and Society	Conservation and Environmental Policy

International Studies

African; East Asian; European; Latin American; Middle East; Russian & Eastern European; South Asian

Terrorism	Imperialism and Culture
Film and Anthropological Representation	Diaspora and Exile
Jihad vs. McWorld	Development and Democracy
Religion and Conflict	Ethnicity, Nationalism, and the State
New Social Movements	Rethinking E-W Divide: Connections Across Feminisms

Sociology/Anthropology

Human Origins, Culture, and Biodiversity	Sociology of Education
Anthropology of Human Rights	Sociology of Heterosexuality
Continuity and Change in Africa	Anthropology of China
Poverty and Public Policy	Sociology of Mental Illness
Medical Sociology	Contemporary Israel: State and Society

Political Science

Politics, Philosophy, and Education	Power and Powerlessness
Ethics and War	International Politics
Politics of the Middle East and North Africa	The Media as a Political Institution
Conservation and Environmental Policy	Religion, Nation & State in the Contemporary World
Science, Politics and Public Policy	City Politics

- **Local Green Politics** How do local communities manage their local natural resources? How do they avoid a "tragedy of the commons" of natural resource degradation or ecological imperialism? Through case studies in wildlife conservation, ecotourism, protected area management, and environmental and conservation planning, we study community-based natural resource management efforts. Case studies - from ancient times to the present - from Africa, Asia, Europe, Latin America & the U.S.

Economics

Economic Development: Theory and Practice	Urban Economics
Poverty, Inequality and Distributive Justice	Population Growth and the Global Future
Trade and Foreign Aid in Latin America	The Post-Communist Economic Transition
Development and Democracy	Theories of Economic Development in Latin America
Health Economics and Policy	Labor Economics

Apply by 1/1   Early Admit: 11/15
- Average # of Students in a First Year Classroom: 15
- Field Studies • Service-Learning • Self-Designed Majors • Interdisciplinary
- Team Teaching • Theme Housing • Student Environmental Audits
- Optional SAT's • Vegetarian & Vegan Meals • Green Campus • Organic Gardens

Admissions Office
The Emma Willard House
Middlebury College
Middlebury, VT 05753

802. 443. 3000
admissions@middlebury.edu
www.middlebury.edu

University of Minnesota

32,000 Undergraduates   Minneapolis, Minnesota

At the University of Minnesota, students in the College of Liberal Arts integrate fields of knowledge through interdisciplinary and thematic courses. They have the opportunity to examine values, ethics, and social responsibility and to learn about the cultural diversity of the world and U.S. society. Students also have opportunities for active learning, such as internships and study abroad. Carlson School of Management is known for its particular emphasis on socially responsible business practices.

The College provides a variety of programs to enhance or personalize chosen degree programs. Programs such as the Honors Program, the Martin Luther King Program – and those offered through the Office of Special Learning Opportunities, the Foreign Studies Office, and the Career Development Office – help students get the most from their undergraduate experience. Students earning a Bachelor of Individualized Studies (BIS) design their own program with three areas of concentration. The program must have a coherence based on stated academic objectives. Also available is an individually designed interdepartmental major; a program with an interdisciplinary theme that meets the students individual academic interests. Established interdepartmental majors include African, American, East Asian, Jewish, Latin American, Middle Eastern, urban and women's studies, and international relations.

In order for students to transcend the boundaries set by major European and North American educational traditions, B.A. and B.I.S. degree students are asked to examine cultures substantially different from their own. At least two courses are required dealing with the cultures of Asia, Africa, Latin America or with traditional Native American cultures. Students are also required to take a course in U.S. Cultural Pluralism, with aprimary focus on social and cultural diversity and with special attention to race and ethnicity.

Field-experience learning at UM is a form of study in which community resources are used to explore the questions and issues raised in the classroom. Students work in a paid or volunteer position, usually in locations such as a museum, social service agency, government office, or community program. Fieldwork (sometimes called an internship or practicum) takes the place of the campus, but is carried out under the direction of a faculty member.

The College of Natural Resources seeks to increase the economic, social and environmental benefits of our most important renewable resources. The CNR offers six majors: Fisheries and Wildlife; Forest products; Forest Resources; Natural Resources and Environ-mental Studies; Recreation Resource Management; and Urban Forestry. Most majors require to completion of a 31/2 week summer term at Lake Itasca Forestry and Biological Station, at the source of the Mississippi River. The College's Cloquet Forestry Center includes more than 3,700 acres of virgin and second-growth timber.

In support of local agriculture, dining services have developed an on-going partnership with an organization that provides certification of products grown using environmentally friendly and socially responsible agricultural practices in the Midwest. UDS uses Minnesota grown produce including apples, strawberries, eggplant, green peppers, cabbage, radishes, cucumbers, green beans, potatoes, and sweet corn when in season. Fair Trade coffee is served in all college restaurants, and organic produce is available on campus. Dining services are also beginning to recycle frying oil to be converted into diesel fuel

MAKING A DIFFERENCE STUDIES

JOURNALISM AND MASS COMMUNICATION

Media in American History and Law
Public Affairs Reporting
Supervision of School Publications
Mass Media and Popular Culture
Communication & Public Opinion

Visual Communication
Community Newspaper
Racial Minorities & the Mass Media
Mass Media and Politics
Mass Communication & Public Health

URBAN AND COMMUNITY FORESTRY

Urban Forest Management
Insect Pest Management
Identifying Forest Plants
Northern Forests Field Ecology
Agroforestry in Watershed Management
Ecological Anthropology

Forest Economics and Planning
Farm and Small Woodlands Forestry
Managing Green Spaces for People
Landscape Management
Group Process, Team Building, and Leadership
Conservation of Plant Biodiversity

ENVIRONMENTAL EDUCATION

Emphasis is on environmental issues at local, regional, and global levels; human dimensions of environmental education; and best practices for diverse audiences, teaching and learning in informal settings.

Principles of Environmental Education
Environmental Interpretation
Restoration and Reclamation Ecology
Visitor Behavior Analysis
Ecological Vegetation Management

Economics and Natural Resources Management
Natural Resources Consumption & Sustainability
Ethics and Values in Resource Management
Problem Solving & Planning in Natural Resources
Enviro. Conflict Mgm't, Leadership & Planning

ENVIRONMENTAL ISSUES AND PLANNING

Economic Dev. of American Agriculture
Energy Research Use
Recreation Land Policy
Politics, Planning and Decision Making
Politics of the Regulatory Process

Resource Dev. & Environmental Economics
Assessing the Ecological Effects of Pollution
Environmental Policy
Management of Recreational Lands
Impact Assessment and Enviro Mediation

GLOBAL STUDIES: ENVIRONMENT & SUSTAINABLE DEVELOPMENT; GOVERNANCE, PEACE & JUSTICE IN A GLOBAL CONTEXT; INT'L. POLITICAL ECONOMY; POPULATION, MIGRATION, & IDENTITY; CULTURE, POWER, PLACE

Theoretical Approaches to Global Studies
Colonialism and Modernity
Debating "Development": Contested Visions
Change in the Contemporary Global Order
The Age of Global Contact

Knowledge and Power in Global Studies
Environment and Empire
International Human Rights Law
Grassroots Development Internship
Knowledge, Power, & Politics of Representation

FOREST BIOLOGY/HARVESTING/RESOURCES FISHERIES & WILDLIFE WASTE MGM'T.
WATER/SOIL RESOURCES INT L. RELATIONS WOMEN'S STUDIES PHILOSOPHY SOCIOLOGY
AFRICAN-AMER. STUDIES HISTORY OF SCIENCE & TECHNOLOGY LANDSCAPE ARCHITECTURE

Apply by 12/15

University of Minnesota
Office of Admissions
100 Church Street, SE
Minneapolis, MN 55455

612. 625. 2000
800. 752. 1000
www.umn.edu/tc
admissions@tc.umn.edu

Monterey Bay/ California State

California State University, Monterey Bay is the California State University system's 21st campus for the 21st Century. Founded in 1994, CSUMB is located on the beautiful and historic Monterey Peninsula area on California's central coast. With its truly innovative curriculum, CSUMB is preparing students to become socially and professionally capable and well-rounded. CSUMB's academic programs are designed for people of diverse backgrounds who want to work hard at learning, have fun while learning, and consciously add value to their lives through the learning they do.

The vision for CSUMB includes a model pluralistic-academic community where all learn and teach one another in an atmosphere of mutual respect and pursuit of excellence. Graduates will have an understanding of interdependence and global competence, distinctive technical and educational skills, the experience and abilities to contribute to a high-quality workforce, the critical thinking abilities to be productive citizens, and the social responsibility and skills to be community builders. The curricula is student and society-centered and of sufficient breadth and depth to meet statewide and regional needs, specifically those involving both inner-city and isolated rural populations (Monterey, Santa Cruz, and San Benito counties).

CSUMB's innovative curriculum is outcome based rather than "seat time" based; that is, students will be assessed in terms of what they actually know and what they can do rather than how many classes they have completed or how many tests they have passed. Graduates will have mastered seven learning outcomes which are:

- Effective and ethical communication in at least two diverse languages;
- Cross-culturally competent citizenship in a pluralistic and global society;
- Technological, aural, and visual literacy;
- Creative expression in the service of transforming culture;
- Ethics, social justice, and care for one another;
- Scientific sophistication and value for the earth and earth systems; and
- Holistic and creative sense of self.

The seven goals are achieved by demonstrating competencies including technology, language, cross-cultural competence and service to the community. Service learning is an important and integral component of CSUMB's vision, philosophy, and educational programs. All students must complete two service learning courses. Service learning involves active learning - drawing lessons from the experience of performing service work that meets community needs, as defined and determined by the communities. Typical courses include: Monterey Bay - A Case Study in Environmental Policy; Marine and Coastal Management-Integration of Science and Policy; and Fieldwork in Multicultural Child Care.

At CSUMB, the class size is kept small and students work side by side with faculty to develop their unique learning paths. CSUMB has state-of-the-art technology and works with several high-tech industries right on campus.

It takes a special kind of pioneering student to succeed at CSUMB. Students must be adaptable, able to appreciate rigorous academic programs, and want to play an active part in a dynamic and diverse educational evolution.

MAKING A DIFFERENCE STUDIES

HUMAN COMMUNICATION: MULTICULTURAL STUDIES, ETHICS, WOMEN'S STUDIES...

Emphasizes community building, peaceful co-existence, the development of individual and group potential, effective and ethical decision making. Covers fields such as Chicano/Latino Studies, Communication, History, Humanities, Journalism & Media Studies, Liberal Arts, Oral History.

Creativity and Social Action
Media Ethics
Interpersonal Communication & Conflict
The Social Impact of the Mass Media
Gender and Communication
Communication Ethics

Chicana/Latina Experiences
Leadership in Multicultural Communities
Ways of Knowing
Social Movements and Communities
Restorative Justice
Free Speech and Responsibility

GLOBAL STUDIES

A concrete expression of CSUMB's commitment to contribute directly to the development of cross-cultural, competent citizenship in a pluralistic global society.

Global Political Economy
Intercultural Communications
Introduction to Global Studies
Gender and Violence in Global Life

Changing Politics of Global Life
Earth and Social Systems
Global Organizations & the United Nations
Genealogy of Globalization

EARTH SYSTEMS SCIENCE AND POLICY: MARINE & COASTAL ECOLOGY, SCIENCE EDUCATION, WATERSHED SYSTEMS

Understand the earth's systems and their interactions through applied learning and research. Most of the environmental issues we are facing today are interdisciplinary in nature. Problems such as land degradation, climate change, pollution, deforestation and loss of biodiversity cross the boundaries of classical disciplines. We combine disciplines to form an integrated science, economics and policy program.

Environmental Geology
Science and Policy of Global Change
Marine Robotics
Intro to GIS and GPS
Physical Marine Ecology
Interpreting Monterey Bay Natural History
Community-Based Watershed Restoration Service Learning

Aquaculture and Fisheries Systems
Enviro. Justice & Enviro. Policy Service Learning
Electronic Projects for Enviro, Measurements
California Ecosystems
Marine Science
Environmental Ethics and Environmental Policy

COLLABORATIVE HEALTH & HUMAN SERVICES

Innovative and interactive classroom exercises include team-based assignments, student-policy debates, case-study discussions, and guest lectures by health and human service professionals and policy experts.

Community Health
Health and Social Policy Analysis
Public Policy Analysis
Collaborative Community Leadership
Conflict Resolution and Collaborative Negotiation

Social Work
Cross Cultural Competency
Personal and Professional Ethics
Public and Nonprofit Systems Management

Apply by: 11/30
Student Body: 38% Minority

• Service Learning   • Interdisciplinary Classes   • All Seminar Format   • Self-Designed Majors
• Team Teaching   • Field Studies   • Life Experience Credit   • Vegetarian Meals

Admissions & Financial Aid
CSU Monterey Bay
100 Campus Center
Seaside, CA 93955-8001

831. 582. 3544
moreinfo-prospective@csumb.edu
http://csumb.edu/

NAROPA UNIVERSITY

450 Undergraduates   Boulder, Colorado

Naropa University provides the unique educational environment that balances personal meaning and creative expression with academic excellence. The degree programs cultivate a spirit of openness, critical intellect and the development of effective action, while transmitting the principles of awareness and wisdom.

Naropa's faculty is remarkable in its diversity and achievements. They are distinguished by a wealth of experience in the professional, artistic, and scholastic applications of their disciplines. They are committed to a heart-felt philosophy that brings out the individual insight and intelligence of each student. The faculty and student body at Naropa form a close-knit community, and this relationship between the students and faculty is a unique part of the educational experience. From the small class size, to the low teacher to student ratio, to the vibrant atmosphere of creative risk-taking, an integration of intellect and intuition is modeled and encouraged. Drawn from over 35 states and nearly 20 countries, Naropa students represent a wide range of life experiences, ages, cultures and backgrounds. Activism, altruism and community involvement are among the many notable characteristics of Naropa's unique student environment.

The unique Contemplative Psychology program is designed to support students in self-discovery, inner wisdom, and the development of interpersonal skills. Founded on the mindfulness/awareness teachings of Buddhist and Shambhala lineages, world wisdom traditions and Western psychology, the program guides students in the understanding of who they are. Students develop compassion and a knowledge of the functions of the mind. Becoming more expansive, they are able to act with skill toward themselves and others

Naropa University was founded in 1974 by Tibetan mediation master and scholar Chogyam Trungpa and is patterned after Nalanda University, an 11th century Indian university renowned for joining intellect and intuition and for its appreciation of various contemplative traditions. Naropa offers a full four-year undergraduate program in a wide range of majors, a BFA in Performance as well as several degrees at the graduate level. An active study abroad program in Bali, Sikkim North India, South India, Prague and Costa Rica mixes academic study and experiential learning with the philosophy, music, painting, environmental and peace studies, dance and traditional awareness practices of each country.

Naropa University seeks students who have a strong appetite for learning, enjoy experiential education in an academic setting and who have demonstrated an ability to live independently. Nontraditional students and those with a high school degree or GED are welcome to apply.

Naropa University is nestled in the foothills of the majestic Rocky Mountains on 10 acres in the center of Boulder, Colorado. The main campus and surrounding grounds include the Performing Arts Center, a mediation hall, the Allen Ginsberg Library, the Naropa gallery, and the Naropa Café. The north campus is home to the three graduate psychology programs and the west campus, Nalanda, is home to the performing and visual arts. All three campuses are within a few miles of each other and are connected by an excellent public transportation system. The city of Boulder, 25 miles northwest of Denver, is a town of 100,000 and was rated by Outside Magazine as one of the top ten places to live for health and outdoor recretion.

MAKING A DIFFERENCE STUDIES

"When human beings lose their connection to nature, to heaven and earth, then they do not know how to nurture their environment. Healing our society goes hand in hand with healing our personal, elemental connection with the phenomenal world."

- Chogyam Trungpa Rinpoche

ENVIRONMENTAL STUDIES
Integrates science, spirit, and personal engagement in a broad multidisciplinary environmental curriculum with specialization in American Indian Studies, Anthropology, Ecology and Horticulture.

Global Ecological Issues
Science and Medicine
Environmental Justice
History of the Environmental Movement
Sustainability

Pilgrimage and Sacred Landscape
Garden World
Global Corporatism
Beholding the Body of the Earth
Green Building

CONTEMPLATIVE PSYCHOLOGY: CONTEMPLATIVE RELIGION & WESTERN PSYCH; PSYCHOLOGY OF HEALTH & HEALING; TRANSPERSONAL & HUMANISTIC PSYCHOLOGY; BODY PSYCHOLOGY AND EXPRESSIVE ARTS AND WELL BEING
This major trains students to work with their own personal process in such a way that they deepen their understanding of themselves and discover the courage and wisdom to genuinely help others.

Embodying Process & the Individual
Cultural Diversity
Expressive Arts & Healing
Buddhist Psychology I: Meditation

Herbal Medicine
Family Systems
Abnormal Psychology
Contemplative Psych: Compassionate Outreach

EARLY CHILDHOOD EDUCATION
Personalized teacher education with teaching skills drawn from the holistic and spiritual traditions of Montessori, Waldorf, and Shambhala.

Teaching Methods
Kindergarten Magic
Education, Culture and Critical Theory

Observing Early Development
Holistic & Contemplative Teaching Traditions
Body Mind Development and Expression

- Foundations of Contemplative Education   Lays the ground for discovering the full blown richness and dignity of ourselves and children. Through an exploration of the traditional Shambhala and Buddhist approaches, we study contemplative dynamics of teaching young children. These practices enable students to perceive and bring forth children's true natures without prejudice and aggression.

INTERDISCIPLINARY STUDIES
Students explore an individualized course of studies in two or more departments in a focused manner. The result is the creation of new or unusual pints of view, questions, knowledge, perception and experience regarding a personally defined central object or matrix of study. Examples include:

"Documentary Poetics"
"The Embodied Teacher"

"Social Ecology"
"The Responsibility of Freedom"

MUSIC
The practice of music encompasses the whole musician: the ear and its sensitivity to pitch and rhythm, the intellect and the intricacies of music theory, the body and the technical demands of playing an instrument, and the contemplative and expressive world of the heart.

Ear Training
Sabar Drumming
Jazz Ensemble

Afro-Pop Ensemble
Music Appreciation
Recording Studio

RELIGIOUS STUDIES

Offers courses of study that examine the phenomenon of religion as it affects individuals, as it operates in culture, and as it addresses questions of life's ultimate values.

Zen Meditation Practicum
Contemplative Islam
Sacred Earth

Queer Theory, Feminism & Religion
Contemplative Judaism
Contemplative Christianity

TRADITIONAL EASTERN ARTS

The only degree program in the country offering training in the Traditional Eastern Arts of Aikido, T'ai-chi Ch'uan, and Yoga. Focus is integration of body, mind, and spirit through practices grounded in meditative awareness and physical acumen.

T'ai Chi Chu'an
Ikebana: Japanese Flower Arranging
Shambala Meditation Practicum
Indian Devotional and Raga Singing
Daoist Healing Qi Gong

Aikido
Yoga
Kyudo: Zen Archery
Mudra Space Awareness
Yoga: Integral Practice and Teacher Training

VISUAL ARTS

Provides a context for exploring mind and phenomena where disciplines are studied, not just as artistic techniques, but also as expressions of innate wakefulness. Artistic creation, as a statement of one's true nature, further develops an understanding of one's place within the world, and thus illuminates the ordinary practicalities of how we live.

Pottery from the Earth
Figure Drawing
Sculpture

Photography
Chinese Brushstroke
Thanka Painting

WRITING AND LITERATURE

Naropa University's department of writing and poetics aspires to the classical Greek academia, a "grove" of learning where elders and students met to explore traditional and innovative technique and lore, in this case, the literary arts. A disciplined practice of writing and cultivating a historical and cultural awareness of literary studies is encouraged.

Eco Literature
Letterpress Printing
Contemplative Poetics

Poetry Workshop: It happens almost everywhere
Reading & Writing: What a Character
Trends in Contemporary Literature

PERFORMANCE

An innovative four-year program designed for the student who wants to pursue conservatory style ensemble training in theater, dance and voice in an environment that cultivates individual creativity, and the development of mindfulness and awareness practices. Dance and theater courses for non-majors are also offered. Bachelor of Fine Arts degree.

Contemporary Dance Technique
Discovering the Artist: Improvisation
Community Process/Diversity Training
Contact Improvisation

Voice
Acting
Dance of African Movement
Acting Foundations

Rolling Admissions
• All Seminar Format • Service-Learning • Self-Designed Majors • Life Experience Credit
• Interdisciplinary Classes & Majors • Graduate Programs • Vegetarian & Vegan Meals

Director of Admissions
Naropa University
2130 Arapahoe Ave.

303. 546. 3572
800. 772. 6951
admissions@naropa.edu

NATIONAL LABOR COLLEGE

700 Undergraduates   Silver Spring, MD

"You cannot uneducate the person who has learned to read. You cannot humiliate the person who feels pride. You cannot oppress the people who are not afraid anymore."

Cesar Chavez

The George Meany Center for Labor Studies - the National Labor College (GMC-NLC) is located on a beautiful 47-acre campus in Silver Spring, Maryland. It began with the vision of George Meany, former President of the AFL-CIO, that labor have its own college that would provide continuous labor education for all union activists.

GMC-NLC offers campus labor programs as well as undergraduate and graduate degree programs. The fundamental mission of the George Meany Center for Labor Studies- the National Labor College is to serve the higher education needs and desires of working men and women and their union representatives. As GMC-NLC grows and develops to accommodate changing circumstances and provide greater opportunities, these two central goals remain consistent: bringing higher education to workers and preparing union representatives for the challenge of leadership in a global economy.

The Bachelor's Degree program is a flexible, largely external program that enables students to pursue a Bachelor of Arts degree while continuing their trade union work. It recognizes the educational value of the union experience that active officers and staff gain over the years, and credit is awarded for the learning which this experience has generated. NLC is proud to announce a 100% nonresidential college degree, the Bachelor of Technical/Professional Studies that provides union members who have participated in challenging apprenticeships and training programs with online access to the courses need to earn a college degree.

The curriculum revolves around seven fields of labor study which enable you to relate day-to-day activities in the trade union movement to general developments in the American economic, social, and political arenas. The areas of concentration are:Labor Studies; Labor Education; Labor Safety and Health; Labor History; Labor Organizational Dynamics and Growth; Political Economics of Labor and Union Leadership and Administration.

The program also requires a large component of liberal arts courses, providing students with a broader perspective that reaches beyond the areas of labor concentration into the social sciences, humanities, and sciences. Demonstrated competency in some essential skill areas is also required for graduation. This combination of core curriculum, general education, and basic skills enables graduates to function as educated members of an increasingly complex society, as well as to serve more effectively as leaders in the American labor movement.

The program is structured to provide contact with faculty and fellow students through a week-long "in-residence" session held at the College every four months – January, April, July, and October. At these sessions, students begin courses with intensive classroom experience. After the conclusion of the in-residence session, students work independently on their courses -- completing assignments, conferring by mail and phone with instructors. Students are encouraged to take non-major courses at home-based institutions when possible.

Since becoming an upper division, degree-granting institution in 1997, nearly 500 working men and women have earned a Bachelor of Arts Degree from GMC-NLC. Advanced degree programs are offered in partnership with the University of Baltimore. The college received it's accreditation as of 2004.

Making a Difference studies

Labor Education

Designed for students who are interested in teaching activities associated with the labor movement, such as training programs. The course of study includes teaching practicum, curriculum design, distance education, and exposure to theories of adult learning.

Introduction to Labor Studies

Comparative Research Methods

Grant and Proposal Writing

Instructional Systems Design

Distance Learning in Education

Educational Planning

Survey Research for Unionists

Social Psychology of Organizing

Designing Collective Actions

Theories of Adult Learning

Labor Studies

Overview of issues and theories of interest and concern to working women and men. Historical, political, legal, social, and theoretical aspects of the labor movement. Good for students who want to pursue a graduate degree in labor studies, or who are seeking a broad range of knowledge.

Labor and the American Political System

Labor and Participation in Work

Culture of the Workplace

Images of Labor in Film

Organizing & Representing the New Work Force

Employee Rights

Comparative Labor Movements

Union Organizing and Governance

Ethics in Decision Making

Negotiations and Mediation

Political Economy of Labor

Provides a thorough understanding of the economic theories and practices that affect the organization and operation of the workforce. Includes a review of economic research techniques, strategic planning, and changing legislative mandates as they impact upon bargaining and negotiation.

Economic Policy

Bargaining in a Changing World

Labor Law

Political Economy of Labor

Grant and Proposal Writing

Current Economic Problems

Investment Strategies

Strategic Planning in Labor

Futuristics

Introduction to Labor Studies

Labor Safety and Health

Focuses on those issues relating to workplace injuries and their prevention. Includes occupational safety legislation, industrial hygiene, hazardous materials, and economic issues which impact upon safety considerations. Ideal for students who work in occupations strongly affected by safety issues.

Social Psychology of Organizations

Hazardous Materials Training

Industrial Hygiene

Hazardous Recognition and Abatement

Theories of Adult Learning

OSHA Law

Ergonomics

Industrial Sociology

Labor History   Organizational Dynamics   Union Leadership

Distance Programs in Occupational Safety & Health, Leadership, communications & Tech.

Special tuition rates for union members and union employees.

This college is tailored for union members already in the labor market.

Rolling Admissions

GMC-NLC Admissions
The National Labor College
10000 New Hampshire Ave.
Silver Spring, MD 20903

301. 431. 6400
www.georgemeany.org

New College of California

500 Undergraduates   San Francisco, CA

New College of California is committed to education in support of a just, sacred, and sustainable world. New Colleges cherishes intellectual freedom, the search for social justice, respect for differences, and a belief in collective responsibility for the welfare of all people and the Earth. NC offers a Bachelor of Arts degree in Humanities with two options, a full undergraduate Weekday/Evening Program and an accelerated Weekend B.A. Completion Program. Both programs have emphasis areas to help focus your studies, small classes, the opportunity to design your own curriculum, and one-on-one advising.

New College's Weekday and Evening Humanities B.A. Program is dedicated to education that encourages critical thinking, interdisciplinary learning, diversity, activism, and community-building. This program offers an array of stimulating seminar and workshop courses in literature and writing, the visual and performing arts, psychology, education, culture, politics, and ecology. Students may enter the Weekday/Evening B.A. Program with as few as zero units, and classes are held in the fall and spring semesters. Each student works with a core faculty advisor to design a semester-by-semester educational program customized to the student's interests and abilities. This individualized program builds on a core curriculum that grounds the student in essential skills and bodies of knowledge. Using flexible learning options, students enroll in of a mix of coursework, independent study, and a practicum (an internship or volunteer experience). Each student's explorations inside and outside the classroom converge in an area of emphasis in the Interdisciplinary Humanities that the student can either design from scratch or choose from the following: Arts and Social Change; Media Studies; Irish Studies;, Poetics; Psychology; Social Theory/Social Change; Writing and Literature; or Youth in Society/Education.

The Weekend B.A. Completion Program enables working adults to finish their degree in 2-3 semesters and provides an environment in which they can develop critical skills and understanding to further their personal and career development. It offers a community of support for students serious about questioning dominant cultural values and strengthening their commitments to a more just society and sustains a conversation in which the voices of non-Western cultures and of marginalized communities including LGBTs; youth; people defined as disabled; and people of color, can re-energize human discourse. By attending classes on weekends and studying in between, students can integrate their work and other aspects of their lives with their academic and career goals.

Weekend B.A. Completion emphasis areas include:
- Activism & Social Change
- Culture, Ecology & Sustainable Community (Santa Rosa campus)
- Experimental Performance
- Interdisciplinary Studies

The Weekend B.A. Completion Program offers a cohort-style learning environment and has classes during the fall, spring, and summer semesters. Students may transfer to New College with a maximum of 90 transferable units, of which only 78 can be lower division. Students who enter with the minimum required 54 units or more can receive a fully-accredited

B.A. degree in the field of their choice in three consecutive semesters through a combination of weekend seminars, independent study with a faculty member, and, if needed, credit for prior learning experience and standardized testing. Students who enter with 88 units may be able to complete the program in less time.

Students in the B.A. Completion Program at the North Bay Campus do an emphasis in Culture, Ecology and Sustainable Community. Its Core Seminar Series is a sequenced critical examination of the ways that modern industrial society has dysfunctionally organized its life-ways from agriculture to technology to economics, combined with a visionary exploration of alternative ways of organizing society that are more ecologically sustainable and socially just. Students also conduct a project and, as part of their concentration, take classes in one of the following areas: Ecological Agriculture, Holistic Nutrition, Eco-dwelling, Consciousness Healing & Ecology, Activism & Social Change, or Self-designed.

The Activism and Social Change emphasis is designed to address the educational needs and social concerns of both aspiring and engaged activists. The program links the study of Critical Social Theory, Social Movements of the Past and Present and Activist Strategies and Skills with opportunities to work and learn with skilled local, national and international activists. Working closely with their academic and community advisors, students develop concentrations such as environmental justice, health care, affordable housing, union organizing, human rights, peace activism, etc. Students complete a Senior Thesis/Project that enables them to pursue their individualized research/activist interests through written or multimedia projects.

The B.A. Completion Program with an emphasis in Experimental Performance is designed to fuse personal vision, artistic discipline and cultural transformation in and across the mediums of dance, theater, voice and writing for performance. The program's structure emphasizes community building as well as an understanding of the historical and cultural context and impact of the emerging work. Students learn and train in both community and independent study environments and ultimately, through the creation of artistically innovative and socially provocative works of experimental theater and performance.

In the Humanities BA Completion Program, students explore an Interdisciplinary emphasis as an alternative to the traditional humanities. Students who enter with sixty or more units can receive a fully-accredited BA degree in the field of their choice in three semesters through a combination of one-weekend-per-month seminar series, independent study with a faculty member, and, if needed, credit given for prior learning experience and standardized testing. On a case-by-case basis, students with less than sixty units, but more than forty-four, will be considered for admission. Students who enter with eighty-eight units may be able to complete the program in two semesters.

Many traditional colleges now have majors, departments, or civic engagement centers as a small commitment to social or environmental justice. At New College, the entire school is dedicated to creating a just, sacred, and sustainable world. You won't have to search through catalogs to find classes that are socially relevant. All classes are socially relevant. You won't have to look for that one professor who cares about social or environmental justice. New College is filled with teacher and student activists who are passionate about changing the world in ways that are cutting-edge, creative, and address the root causes of the problems we face today. New College can teach you how to be a better activist or the activist you've always wanted to become - it's what New College does best.

MAKING A DIFFERENCE STUDIES

ECOLOGICAL STUDIES

Environment, Civilization & Development
Environmental Justice
Appropriate Technology
Natural Building
Ecological Agriculture
Environmental Activist Skills

Eco-Psychology
Alternative Economics
Intentional Community
Permaculture
Consciousness, Healing and Ecology
Eco/Global Literacy

POLITICS & SOCIETY

Contemporary critical thinking challenges established versions of history and politics. Emerging movements demand accountability to women, queers, ethnic "minorities," to working-class and poor people, and to the biosphere.

Social Theory for Social Change
Social Movements
Histories of Resistance
Political History of San Francisco
Alternative Press and Social Change
Race, Class, and Gender Oppression

The Anarchist Tradition
Post-Modernism & Commodification of Urban Space
War and Peace
Schooling, Inequality, & Social Change
Globalization and its Discontents
Youth in Society/Education

CULTURE AND SPIRITUALITY

Spiritual Activism
Queer Culture
Social Foundations of the Self
Irish Studies
Women's Spirituality
Cuba and Globalization

Tibetan Buddhism
Latin American Women's Literature
Wisdom Traditions/Journeys of Mind
Focus on the Middle East
Ethics, Spirituality, and Social Change
Indian Subcontinent and Southeast Asia

THE ARTS & SOCIAL CHANGE

Experimental, Activist & Queer Performance
Writing and Literature
Creating Community Theater
Community Theater Making
Screenwriting and Propaganda
Theater Arts-Reflections on the World

Arts and Social Change
Arts and Learning
Performance/Urban Ritual
Art vs. Trash: Intro to Cultural Studies
Charting the Americas thru Literature, Art & Music

ECODWELLING (GREEN BUILDING) Santa Rosa campus

Design with Site and Climate
Small-Space Design
Water and Waste Systems
Human Environmental Health
Intentional Community

Intro to Permaculture
Natural Heating and Cooling
Renewable Energy Systems
Green Building Materials
Natural Remodeling

Rolling Admissions   No Housing

• Service Learning   • Weekend & Evening Classes   • Accelerated Degree Completion
• Team Teaching   • Self-Designed Majors   • All Seminar Format   • Life Experience Credit
• Interdisciplinary Classes & Majors   • Required Practicum

Weekend BA Completion Admissions   415.437. 3420
Weekday/Evening BA Humanities Admissions 415. 437. 3462
New College of California   888. 437. 3460
777 Valencia St.   www.newcollege.edu
San Francisco, CA 94110

UNIVERSITY OF NEW ENGLAND

1,600 Undergraduates   Biddeford and Portland, Maine

The University of New England offers a unique educational environment that blends the traditional liberal arts and sciences with professional focused programs to prepare students to make a difference in the world through meaningful and rewarding careers, lifelong learning, and enlightened lives. The University fosters critical inquiry through a student-centered, academic environment rich in research, scholarship, creative activity, and service while providing opportunities for acquiring and applying knowledge in selected clinical, professional, and community settings.

Central to the undergraduate educational experience at the University of New England is the Core Curriculum. It provides an innovative common learning experience for all UNE undergraduates. Students are invited to explore four college-wide themes from multiple disciplinary perspectives and to develop important intellectual skills. Students focus on a theme each year - (1) Environmental Awareness, (2) Social and Global Awareness, (3) Critical Thinking: Human Responses to Problems and Challenges, and (4) Citizenship. Designed to provide a foundation in the liberal arts, the core reflects the values of the college and is designed to prepare students for living informed, thoughtful, and active lives in a complex and changing society.

The core curriculum emphasizes active, collaborative, and experiential learning. It challenges students to transfer knowledge from one arena to another, appreciate different disciplinary perspectives on the same topic, and integrate what they have learned to construct their own knowledge. College of Arts and Science Dean Paul Burlin explains, "we expect UNE graduates to have been exposed to certain major issues, have learned about them, analyzed their own views and developed more informed perspectives."

UNE offers over 40 programs at the undergraduate level and various graduate programs that provide unique opportunities for graduates to serve their communities. Students have the opportunity to major in programs leading to careers in aquaculture and marine science, education, environmental and political science, health and medical science, and social and behavioral science fields. Unique learning experiences are offered through hands-on programs such as the Applied Sociological Experience which expands the understanding of culture, social issues, and political life on a global scale and study abroad programs with focus topics such as Social and Environmental Justice in Latin America, Sustainable Development and Social Change in Central America, and Nation Building, Globalization, and Decolonizing the Mind: Southern African Perspectives.

All entering first-year environmental students participate in a year-long learning Green Learning Community (GLC) focused on the fundamental themes of environmental studies. The GLC integrates courses in biology, literature, environmental issues and an integrating seminar experience over two semesters. This interdisciplinary approach enables students to understand more clearly the relationships between environmental issues, biology and humanities and at the same time improve skills in critical thinking, writing, oral communication, research, and use of computers. Experiential learning activities are central.

The Salt Institute for Documentary Studies at UNE can be thought of as a domestic "study abroad" program which complements campus-based education by providing the opportunity to actively engage in field research in one of three mediums of documentary expression: photography, radio, and nonfiction writing.

The Marine Science Education and Research Center provides state-of-the-art facilities for marine education and research and includes a Marine Animal Rehabilitation Center licensed by the National Marine Fisheries Service. The Marine Science Education and Research Center provides students, faculty and visiting researchers a window to the sea, and the opportunity to create important new knowledge in marine science, the environment and human health.

In keeping with the University's mission to protect the health of the environment, the Marine Science Education and Research Center incorporated state-of-the-art "green design" principles into its construction and operation. The central principle of "green design" is that a building should have as little negative impact on the environment as possible. In application, this principle extends beyond construction materials to issues from site planning and preparation to energy usage. Even the distance that materials come from can be a factor when you consider fuel (and resulting pollutants) for transportation.

UNE's Center for Sustainable Communities is an internship and service learning program that creates mutually beneficial partnerships between students and environmental organizations in the communities surrounding the Biddeford campus. Through hands-on involvement with local governments, non-profit organizations, and community groups, students are able to field test academic learning in situations that make tangible the challenge to "think globally, act locally."

UNE's Maine Women Writers Collection has a pre-eminent special collection of published and non-published literary, cultural and social history sources, by and about women authors, all either native or residents of Maine.

The New England Institute fosters research and education into the interdisciplinary nexus of cognitive science and evolutionary psychology while the Center for Transcultural Health that helps improve the overall health of an expanding culturally and ethnically diverse population.

UNE's two campuses are located in the beautiful coastal region of southern Maine, and both utilize all that the New England region has to offer. The Westbrook College Campus, home to UNE's College of Health Professions, is located in a residential area of Portland, Maine's largest city. The College of Arts and Sciences and the College of Osteopathic Medicine are on UNE's University Campus in Biddeford, situated on a beautiful 540-acre site where the Saco River flows into the Atlantic Ocean with more than 4,000 feet of water frontage.

You can boat and sail along the Southern Maine coast past scenic lighthouses, or you can swim and relax at nearby beaches. The area offers more than 100 miles of trails for jogging, biking, hiking, cross country skiing and other activities. The White Mountains of Maine and New Hampshire, as close as 1 1/2 hours, are great for skiing and hiking.

Making A Difference Studies

SOCIOLOGY

Pop Culture
Tribal Cultures
Poverty
Social Identification and Globalization
Applied Sociology Experience II: Salt Institute

Environmental Sociology
Displaced Cultures and Society
Race/Class/Gender: Social Perspective
Applied Sociology Experience I: Study Abroad
Society in Latin America

ENVIRONMENTAL STUDIES

Environmental Geology
Wetland Conservation & Ecology
Environmental Movements & Social Change
Women and the Environment

Design with Nature: Site Planning
Wetland Restoration: Science & Policy
Environmental Advocacy
Enviro Racism & Environmental Justice Movement

MARINE BIOLOGY, AQUACULTURE AND AQUARIUM SCIENCE

Deep Sea Biology
Marine Biology
Finfish/Shellfish Culture Tech
Polar Biology
Marine Mammals and Policy
Museum Specimen Preparation

Marine Conservation Biology
Coral Reef Biology
Principles of Aquaculture
Principles of Aquarium Operations and Science
Tropical Biology
Biology of Marine Mammals

PSYCHOLOGY AND SOCIAL RELATIONS

Cultural Anthropology
Classical Sociological Theory
Deviance
Displaced Cultures & Society
The Family

Social Psychology
Contemporary Theory
Abnormal Psychology
Social Identity & Globalization
Cross Cultural Communication

POLITICAL SCIENCE

Focuses on fundamental issues confronting modern society - globalization, war, inequity, poverty, the environment and evaluate the processes, policies and theories devised to deal with them.

Theories and Politics of Nationalism
Exploring Political Ideas and Issues
The Politics of Law
Intro to Politics and Environment
The Politics of the Middle East

Law and American Society
Intro to International Relations
Ancient and Medieval European Political Theory
The Challenge of the United Nations
Pol. Theory/Lit.: Egypt Thru the Eye of Mahfouz

HISTORY

American Identity and History
American Women's History
History Hands On
Slavery and Race in the U.S. and Brazil
Cuba: History, Society & Culture

Growing Up Female
Cultural Imperialism, Latin American & the U.S.
The European Enlightenment
Latin American History Thru Film
Revolution and Social Protest in Mexico

EDUCATION   WOMEN'S STUDIES (MINOR)   HEALTH SERVICES MGM'T.

Rolling Admissions

• Field Studies   • Interdisciplinary   • Service Learning   • Self Designed Majors
• Required Community Service   • Life Experience Credit   • Vegetarian/Vegan Meals

Admissions Office
University of New England
11 Hills Beach Road
Biddeford, Maine 04005

207. 602. 2297
800. 477. 4UNE
admissions@une.edu
www.une.edu

Northland College

750 Students Ashland, Wisconsin

The abundant natural beauty of the northern lakes and forests of Lake Superior country provide the perfect setting for a school like Northland. Over twenty five years ago the faculty committed themselves to a new vision: a liberal arts/environmental college. Since then the idea that our natural and social worlds - and the knowledge they support - are inextricably connected, has flourished and matured at Northland. A premise of Northland's educational mission is that we must strive to free ourselves from the alienating and self-destructive assumption that humans live in isolation from the natural environment. We dwell simultaneously in the human realm of institutions, cultures, and ideas as well as in the life-giving realm of nature. As long as we separate these two realms we can never feel completely at home – at peace with ourselves and our environment.

Northland is unique in that it does not restrict its study of the relationship between humanity and nature to a few courses in ecology or environmental studies. Almost a third of Northland's courses may be said to have some clear relevance to environmental issues. A concern for the natural world around us runs throughout Northland's curriculum.

Northland fosters an atmosphere in which there is a distinctive concern for both the individual human being and the natural world. Northland offers a value-sensitive education focused on the study of our interactions with the environment, ranging from aesthetic and spiritual values to complex social and scientific issues. There is also emphasis on the study of human behaviors and interaction in such areas as environmental studies, outdoor education, cross-cultural and global understanding, education, and business. The faculty includes environmental subject matter or methodologies in their classes whenever appropriate.

In keeping with Northland's commitment to apply in practice what it teaches about environmental issues and ways to develop a sustainable future. The Environmental Living & Learning Center residence was designed with hundreds of environmental considerations in mind. Among the special features are a 20 kilowatt wind tower, three photovoltaic arrays, fourteen solar hot water panels, and composting waterless toilets. The apartments have passive solar design and share two greenhouses to be operated by the residents. Students joined architects and others on the campus committee to select the most environmentally friendly materials. The College has adopted a goal of achieving zero-discharge for eliminating waste materials. The Environmental Council, a college-wide task force, serves as the vanguard of environmental consciousness on campus and an energy audit is done once a year.

Lake Superior, the Apostle Islands, and Chequamegon National Forest offer a natural setting for field studies. Outdoor Education majors may spend a full semester at the Audubon Center of the North Woods. Academic adventures abroad provide in-depth exposure to international culture and environments from the rainforests of Costa Rica and the tropical lowlands of Mexico to the mammals of Kenya and natural history of the Galapagos.

Students participate in many outdoor activities and excursions, from sea kayaking and biking to backpacking and cross-country skiing. The outdoor orientation program for freshmen gives students an opportunity to canoe, kayak or participate in small group activities.

Making a Difference Studies

Teacher Certification: Enviro. Studies & Education (Grs. 1-9, 6-12), Native American

Concepts of Biology
Environmental Public Policy
Sociology of the Environment
Ecology

Environmental Education Curriculum Review
Concepts of Earth Science
Environmental Law
Environmental Citizenship

Environmental Studies

Sustainable Development
Applied Problem Solving
Native Peoples and Rainforests
Cultural Ecology
Environmental Policy Analysis

Environmental Ethics
Land and Water Use Planning
Global Resource Issues
Artic Environments
The Nature of Sound

Government: Environmental Policy

Environmental Public Policy
Land and Water Use Planning
Sociology of the Environment
Environmental Ethics

Seminar in Environmental Law
Environmental Citizenship
Global Resource Issues
Policy Analysis Techniques

Outdoor Education

Whitewater Canoeing
Orienteering
Winter Exploration and Interpretation
Therapeutic Recreation Design
Ecological Ecosystem Interpretation

Rock Climbing
Group Process and Communication
Search and Rescue
Environmental Education Curriculum
Philosophy & Theory of Experiential Education

Conflict and Peacemaking

War, Peace and Global Issues
Exploring Alternative Futures
Theory and Practice of Nonviolence
Sociology of the Third World

Nuclear Age
Group Process and Communication
Conflict Resolution
Social Change and Social Movements

Government: Social Welfare Policy

Economics of Labor
Social Problems
Nature of Inequality
Social Change & Movements
Global Resource Issues

Conflict Resolution
Crime, Deviance and Criminal Justice
Sociology of the Community
Population
Introduction to Public Administration

Native American Studies   Natural Resources   Forestry Dual Degree/Michigan Tech U

Apply by 5/1

• Student Environmental Audits   • Field Studies   • Self-Designed Majors   • Team Teaching
• Service-Learning   • Theme Housing   • Interdisciplinary Classes   • Green Campus
• Vegetarian & Vegan Meals   • Organic Gardens   • Socially Responsible Investing

Director of Admissions
Northland College
1411 Ellis Ave.
Ashland, WI 54806

715. 682. 1224
800. 753. 1840
www.northland.edu
admit@northland.edu

OBERLIN COLLEGE

2,800 Students   Oberlin, Ohio

As long as there has been an Oberlin, Oberlinians have been changing the world. As an institution and as a community, Oberlin is characterized by a heady spirit of idealism. Do Oberlinians arrive with the conviction that a single person's efforts can have far-reaching effects, or does Oberlin instill this idealism in them? Most likely it is a combination of the two, one reinforcing the other. Whatever its source, the results of this idealism are dramatic. It impels Oberlinians to be open to new perspectives, to rethink their positions when necessary, to speak their minds, and to strive to make the world a better place. This spirit of idealism, this sense of conviction, unites the many different individuals in the Oberlin community. Students, faculty members, and alumni believe they can change the world.

What unifies this diverse and often opinionated group of students into a community of scholars? First, they are all extraordinarily committed to academic achievement. Second, their vision and progressive thinking - that Oberlin spirit of idealism - allows them to seize every opportunity as a learning experience. They educate one another on important issues and they work to solve problems on campus, in the community, and in the world. Their ongoing debate is evidence of their willingness to confront issues that society often chooses to ignore. Oberlin students put their idealism to work on a variety of issues. Reflecting Oberlin's traditional concern for the betterment of humanity, about 30% of Oberlin graduates work in the field of education. Alumni also stay close to important social causes.

Oberlin was the first coeducational college in the country. Three women graduated in 1841, becoming the first women in America to receive bachelor's degrees. The admission of women caused Oberlin to be the center of controversy over coeducation for years. Similarly, Oberlin decided to admit blacks in 1835 in exchange for financial backing by two wealthy abolitionists. As a result of this decision, by 1900 nearly half of all the black college graduates in the country - 128 to be exact - had graduated from Oberlin. To put it in even greater historical perspective, in 1835 the state of Ohio was still debating whether to allow blacks to attend elementary and secondary schools, while Southern states were drafting even stricter slave codes.

Once set on this progressive course, Oberlin became a center for abolitionism. The progressive impulse that inspired Oberlin's commitment to minorities and social justice in the 19th and 20th centuries spurred innovations in academic and campus life. Programs focusing on cultural diversity have been part of Oberlin's new-student orientations since the early 1980's. While Oberlin has never been a utopia, neither has it been willing to give up its quest for perfection. In 1991 Oberlin began requiring students to take at least nine credit hours in courses that deal with cultural diversity in order to graduate. Faculty members are also incorporating material on the environment, the experience of minorities and women, and other new areas into current courses, as well as developing new courses in these areas.

Freshman colloquia are interdisciplinary, seminar style courses in which enrollment is limited to 14 first-year students. This small size allows students to become familiar with the give-and-take nature of class discussions at the college level. Recent colloquia included "The Religious Thought of Mahatama Gandhi," "The Personal is Political: Representations of Activist Women in American History," "The Palestinian-Israeli Conflict," and "Explaining Social Power."

Students frequently work as research assistants for their professors. Biology students have assisted in research on the use of rock dust to remineralize soil and increase its fertility. Six students worked on a sociology survey investigating problems encountered by local low-income people. More than 350 Oberlin students participated in a year-long planning process with architects and the wider Oberlin community to ensure that Oberlin's Adam Joseph Lewis Center for Environmental Studies would not only house environmental studies courses, but would itself embody the principles of environmentally sustainable architecture. The building is powered by sunlight and causes no discharge or disposal of toxic materials.

In keeping with Oberlin's tradition of community service and social activism, Oberlin formed a chapter of the Bonner Scholars Program on campus in 1992. The program provides scholarship funds to first generation and low-income students by providing the equivalent of a full work-study award to students who complete ten hours of community service per week during the school year.

One of the highlights of Oberlin's Fall Orientation is the Day of Service program hosted each year by the Center for Service and Learning. More than half of the College's new students will spend a day volunteering with community organizations including Murray Ridge Group Home, Oberlin Early Childhood Center, Boys and Girls Club, and Oberlin City Schools. Students will spend more than 1,500 hours serving the community during the Day of Service Program.

Off-campus study is quite popular and, by graduation, about half of each class has spent at least one semester studying away from Oberlin. Nearly two dozen programs are available in countries such as Ireland, England, France, China, Kenya, Liberia, Nigeria, Sierra Leone, Japan, Costa Rica, Spain, India, and Scotland. The Mystic Seaport program, a wilderness program, and an urban planning and historic preservation program with Columbia university are among other options.

For members of the Oberlin Student Cooperative Association (OSCA), cooperative houses and dining rooms are as much a statement of political conviction as they are place to live and eat. OSCA, a student run business with a $1.6 million operating budget operates four room-and-board co-ops and four board-only co-ops on campus. Members emphasize the democratic nature of decision making in each co-op and in the organization as a whole. Working together also saves students money: the board fee charged by co-ops is about 30% less than that charged in College dining halls, and the fee for a double room was 15% less. Co-ops purchase food from local family farms and send work crews every week to help in harvesting on the farms.

Oberlin has more than 140 extra-curricular organizations. Some of the most popular are the various community service, environmental, human rights, multi-cultural and Lesbian/Gay/Bi-sexual groups.

Oberlin's Experimental College is a student-run organization which sponsors courses (for limited academic credit) taught by members of the community - faculty, students, administrators, and townspeople. Each year a very heterogeneous list of subjects is offered including crafts, special interests, community service, and academic subjects not found in the regular curriculum.

Graced with marshlands, lush woodlands, natural springs and rocky shorelines, Oberlin's home county is part of the Lake Erie Wing Watch Region. Each year it attracts hundreds of migrating species, plus bald eagles, warblers, and great blue herons.

MAKING A DIFFERENCE STUDIES

ENVIRONMENTAL STUDIES

Environment and Society
American Environmental History
Environmental Education Practicum
Environmental Economics
Organic Agriculture
Environment, Current Destitution, Future Generations and Moral Responsibility

American Environmental Policy
Ecology and the Environment
Energy Technology
Colloquium on Sustainable Agriculture
Conservation Biology

- **Oberlin and the Biosphere**   Examines food, energy, water and materials flows, and waste management on the Oberlin campus; what enters and what leaves the campus community. Attention will be given to mines, wells, forest, farms, feedlots, dumps, smokestacks, outfall pipes, and alternative technologies and practices. Students participate in a joint research project.

AFRICAN AMERICAN STUDIES

Practicum in Black Journalism
Education in the Black Community
African-American Drama
Pan-African Political Perspective
African-American Women's History

West African Dance Forms in Diaspora
Modern African Literature
Traditional African Cosmology
Cinema and Society: Racial Stereotyping
Langston Hughes and the Black Aesthetic

WOMEN'S STUDIES

The Challenge of Gender and Race
Experiences of Religious Women
Issues in Language and Sexuality
Gender, Race and Rhetoric of Science
The Emergence of Feminist Thought
Feminist Theory and Challenge of Third World Feminism

Turning Points in Women's History
Nature and Statue of Women
Paid & Unpaid Work: Sexual Division of Labor
Power and Marginality: Women & Develop't
Women in the Transition from Socialism

SOCIOLOGY

Community and Inequality
Urban Sociology
Gender Stratification
Race and Ethnic Relations
The City and Social Policy

Youth Subcultures, Movements & Politics
Revolution and Reform in Latin America
Sociology of the Black Community
State, Society & Social Change: Latin America
Social Change in Contemporary Societies

RELIGION

Issues in Medical Ethics
Themes in Christian Ethics
Christian Social and Political Thought
Zen Buddhism
Mysticism in the West
Christian Utopias & Communitarian Movements

Islamic Spirituality and Mysticism
History of African-American Relig. Experience
Religion and the Experience of Women
Taoism
Selected Topics in Early Judaism

HISTORY

Latinos in the U.S.
Roots of Feminist Analysis
Nourish or Punish? Ideologies of Poverty in 18th and 19th Century England
Caribbean History: Slaves and Slavery in the New World
Peasant Movements and the Agrarian Condition in Latin America

Race, Class and Gender in the Southwest
History of Vietnam

ECONOMICS

Poverty and Affluence

Labor Economics

Economic Development in Latin America

Economics of Discrimination

Public Sector Economics: Health Care Policy

Environmental Economics

Environmental & Resource Economics

Econ. of Land, Location & the Environment

- **Introduction to Political Economy** Economic problems of unemployment, inflation, the distribution of income & wealth, and the allocation of resources. Basic tools of analysis for studying these problems are developed and the role of public policy in securing economic objectives is explored.

POLITICS

Political Change in America

Government and Politics of Africa

Public Policy in America

Emergence of Feminist Thought

Political Economy of Women in Late Industrializing States

Federal Courts and the Environment

Urban Politics

Third World Political Economics

Nuclear Weapons and Arms Control

LAW & SOCIETY

Explore philosophical, political, economic, historical, sociological, ethical, scientific, and religious issues that are central to understanding the role of law and legal institutions in society.

Philosophy and Values

Christian Social & Political Thought

Economics, Ethics and Values

Equal Protection of the Law

Moral Problems in Religious Perspective

Crime, Law and Order in Colonial India

Social & Political Philosophy

Deviance, Discord and Dismay

Reproductive Biology in the 80's

Individual Responsibility

Turning Points: American Women's History

Intro to the Talmud: Argument & Interpretation

LATIN AMERICAN STUDIES

Folklore and Culture of Latin America

Dirty Wars and Democracy

Hispanics in American Politics

Revolution and Reform in Latin Amer.

Latin American History: Conquest and Colonialization

Economic Development in Latin America

State, Society and Social Change

Int'l. Political Economy / North-South Relations

Female and Male in Latin American History

ANTHROPOLOGY

Native American Literature

Immigration and Ethnicity in US

Immigration and Ethnicity in Israel

Ancient Civilizations of New World

Engendering the Past

Ideology, Power and Prehistory

Jewish Society and Culture in Middle East

Anthropology of Sub-Saharan Africa

THIRD WORLD STUDIES   EAST ASIAN STUDIES

Apply by 1/15   Early Decision: 11/15
50%+ Perform Community Service   Avg. Size First Year Classroom: 20
- Internships   • Theme Housing   • Green Campus   • Self-Designed Majors
- Service Learning   • Student Environmental Audits • Vegetarian / Vegan Meals

Admissions Office

Carnegie Building

Oberlin College

101 Professor Street

Oberlin, OH 44074

800. 622. OBIE

440. 775. 8411

college.admissions@oberlin.edu

www.oberlin.edu

Olivet College

1000 Undergraduates   Olivet, Michigan

Among many towering oaks in south central Michigan is Olivet College. A campus of more than 1,000 students, this 160-year-old institution has stayed true to its historic roots of offering a higher education to all, regardless of race, gender or financial ability.

In 1993, the Olivet College community established an academic vision for the college titled Education for Individual and Social Responsibility. This vision helps shape curricula and challenges traditional assumptions about the purposes and assessment strategies you use to earn a college education. The system that arose, known as The Olivet Plan, charges students to focus on individual and social responsibility, character and competence, and service as well as career.

The Olivet Plan provides a system for you to build the skills essential for success in a highly competitive marketplace while instilling lessons in character. Emphasizing goal setting, interpersonal and small group skills, critical thinking, global awareness, diversity sensitivity and ethics, The Olivet Plan serves as a guidepost for all students.

Demonstrating responsibility in action – the college sponsors a bi-annual Service Day where you can work hand-in-hand with faculty and staff volunteering in Olivet and surrounding communities. Some of the projects include spending time with Hospice patients, the "Tell a Friend" event coordinated with the American Cancer Society, writing letters to service men and women, making bird houses to include in local habitat and coordinating food and coin drives for the SIREN/Eaton Shelter, which provides emergency shelter, transitional housing, crisis counseling, and other support services to homeless families and battered women and children in Eaton County.

You could spend your spring break traveling to Arkansas to work on the Heifer Project International heifer ranch. This service learning experience includes completing farm chores, doing light construction, learning about Third World economics and spending part of your experience living in a Third World simulated environment.

Understanding the importance of hands-on service learning, the college's faculty is proactive in coordinating activities that highlight your area of study. Most notably, students in the college's Department of Business Administration and Economics volunteered to assist area low-income residents in preparing their taxes through the Volunteer Income Tax Assistance program. Many students from the Department of Natural and Physical Science spend time at the college's Kirkelldell Biological Preserve participating in spring prescribed burns to reduce aggressive non-indigenous plants. Additional projects these students help coordinate include creating a seed bank area to provide native plants and seeds that can then be transplanted to other sites to speed the spread of native species, and an ongoing research project comparing the efficacy of habitat restoration techniques.

Olivet College also offers a Community Responsibility Scholarship to prospective students who show a history of civic responsibility and volunteerism.

MAKING A DIFFERENCE STUDIES

ENVIRONMENTAL SCIENCE

Environmental Economics

North American Geography

Biocultural Ecology

Entomology

Plant Ecology

Environmental Health and Toxicology

Environmental Science

Biodiversity

Nature, Technology and Humanity

Environmental Law

Ecosystems Ecology

Introductory Zoology

ECONOMICS

During the 1990s, Olivet completed a comprehensive review of its educational philosophy and programs. The is an intentional focus on individual and social responsibility and on character as well as competence. All programs in the Business and Economics Department are committed to this vision.

Labor Economics

Economic Development

Industrial Organization

Studies in Entrepreneurship

International Economics

History of Economic Thought

Public Finance

Self and Community

EDUCATION: ELEMENTARY AND SECONDARY

Elementary Certification in Social Studies, History and Science. As a minor, students may get certification in Political Science, Psychology, Sociology, Biology....

Teaching Reading in the Secondary School

Methods of Teaching Language Arts

Education of the Exceptional Learner

Foundations of American Education

Teaching Reading in the Secondary School

Teaching Hands-On Science in Elementary School

Art Education: Foundation, Theory and Practice

Psychology of Human Development & Learning

Teaching Hands-On Math in Elementary School

Media, Methodology, Technology & Art Advocacy

- **Art Education: Integration and Expansion** Planning, organization and delivery of art content at an advanced level. Complexities of questioning "cultural relativism", teaching "Multiculturalism", exploring the integration of other content areas in the art classroom. Six weeks off-campus teaching.

SOCIOLOGY - ANTHROPOLOGY

Myth, Symbol and Meaning

Conflict and Cooperation

Topics in Inequality

Sport, Culture and Society

Religions and Social (Dis)order

Childhood and Culture

Work, Culture and Society

Power and Social Control

People, Resources and the World

Biocultural Ecology

JOURNALISM

Media Impact, Ethics and Management

Mass Communication Theory

Broadcast Production

Editing

Basic Reporting

Photojournalism

Practicum in Mass Communication

Advocacy and Persuasion

American Government: State and Local

Fundamentals of Communication

Apply by: 2/1

- Self-Designed Majors • Required Service Learning • "Learning Communities"

Olivet College

Admissions Office

320 South Main Street

Olivet, MI 49076

800. 456. 7189

www.olivetcollege.edu

admissions@olivetcollege.edu

UNIVERSITY OF OREGON

16,500 Undergraduates   Eugene, Oregon

Students at the University of Oregon take the university motto, Minds Move Mountains, to heart. For more than a decade, Mother Jones magazine has recognized the UO as one of the most activist campuses in the country, often ranking the university number one. The UO is also consistently among the top ten universities in the nation for the number of graduates who volunteer for the Peace Corps. Whether at home or abroad, UO students are making lasting progressive change in health care, education, environmental protection, social justice, and many other areas.

The UO landed in the top three in a list of environmentally-friendly colleges recently published by the National Wildlife Federation. Green chemistry labs are one example of the UO's environmental consciousness. The UO was the first school in the world to develop cutting edge technology that allows comprehensive scientific experiments without production of toxic chemicals that are harmful to the environment. Biology professor Bill Bradshaw and a team of student researchers are investigating the evolutionary adaptation of species in conditions that simulate global warming.

More than 250 student-run organizations let you venture beyond the classroom, across cultures, and into the world. You can promote conservation and renewable energy with the Solar Information Center. You can help work towards environmental solutions that benefit everyone, regardless of race or class, through the Coalition Against Environmental Racism. Facilities such as The Center for the Study of Women in Society -the best-funded research facility of its kind in the country - and student-run groups such as OSPIRG (Oregon Student Public Interest Research Group), the Multicultural Center, and the award-winning Student Recycling Program bring students together to create a better world.

Student impact extends beyond the borders of the Eugene campus. Students can participate in internships or community service experiences within the Eugene community—a center of political and environmental activism. Students taking a course in non-profit and community economics gain practical experience by providing local organizations with data used in real-world decision-making. The UO also has three off-campus facilities: the Pine Mountain Observatory, the Malheur Bird Refuge Field Station, and the Oregon Institute of Marine Biology (OIMB). OIMB, situated on 107 acres of coastal property along Coos Bay, offers an interdisciplinary course encompassing marine ecology, marine mammals and birds, and biological oceanography, as well as other programs of individualized study.

You could also travel abroad through one of the UO's nearly 80 overseas study and international exchange programs. For example, international studies major Sarah Dobra attended the Universidad San Francisco de Quito. After several months in Ecuador, she designed an independent research project and received a scholarship from the UO Honors College to support her work in two rural hospitals in Ecuador. Sarah is now working for Mercy Corps in Guatemala, implementing nutritional training in rural communities and establishing women's health and micro-finance initiatives.

Students also benefit from UO's status as a center for conferences on positive change. The Holistic Options for Planet Earth Sustainability conference, a sustainable business symposium, and the public interest environmental law gathering are just a few of the annual events at the UO. The panel discussions and keynote lectures, which have included Julia Butterfly Hill, Sister Helen Prejean, David Brower, Ralph Nader, and other well-known activists, are major events for undergraduate students.

At the University of Oregon, exploration, independent thinking, and activism are reflected in the impressive legacies of alumni. Nine Pulitzer Prize winners, two Nobel Prize winners, and 26 national political leaders are among the UO's distinguished alumni. The late Ken Kesey, author of One Flew Over the Cuckoo's Nest and Sometimes a Great Notion was a UO alumnus and faculty member. Kesey was a mentor to Rob Elder, a 2000 UO grad, now a journalist at the Chicago Tribune. Of Kesey, Elder wrote, "What kept Kesey going, kept him writing, was what he described as a single note. 'If you've got love in your heart, whatever you do from that moment out is likely to be right,' Kesey said."

The University of Oregon is located in Eugene (pop. 137,500), a city known for its commitment to individuality, in the heart of the Willamette Valley. Two rivers run through town, bordered by 250 miles of bike paths and running trails. The Pacific Ocean is one hour west; snow-covered Cascades peaks are one hour east. The student-run Outdoor Program organizes activities that include biking, hiking, kayaking, mountaineering, and windsurfing. If you want to challenge your spirit as well as your mind, you'll love it here.

MAKING A DIFFERENCE STUDIES

ARCHITECTURE: LANDSCAPE AND INTERIOR ARCHITECTURE
All are five-year programs subscribing to the concepts of green architecture and sustainability.

Architectural Form and Urban Quality	Housing in Society
Hydrology and Water Resources	Landscape Preservation
Natural Resource Policy	Preservation and Restoration Technology
Solar Heating	Urban Farm
Passive Cooling	

PLANNING, PUBLIC POLICY & MANAGEMENT
Concentrations include sustainable community development, environmental policy and management, health and social policy, policy analysis, and public and nonprofit management.

Communities and Regional Development	Contemporary Housing Issues
Environmental Health	Planning in Developing Countries
Managing Fiscal Austerity	Managing Nonprofit Organizations
Energy Policy and Planning	Neighborhood and Community Revitalization
Planning & the Changing Family	Planning and Social Change

ENVIRONMENTAL STUDIES

American Environmental History	Solar Heating
Conservation Biology	Architectural Form and Urban Quality
Environmental Politics	Community, Environment, and Society
Population Ecology	Gender and International Development
Urban Geography	

ETHNIC STUDIES

Asian Americans and the Law	Chicanos and the Law
Intro to the Asian American Experience	Intro to the Chicano and Latino Experience
Intro to the Native American Experience	Minority Women: Issues and Concerns

PEACE STUDIES

American Radicalism
Political Ideologies
Value Systems in Cross-Cultural Perspective
Social Issues and Movements

Socioeconomic Development Planning
Systems of War and Peace
Sociology of Developing Areas
Environmental Politics

INTERNATIONAL STUDIES

Aid to Developing Countries
International Protection of Human Rights
Population and Global Resources
Global Ecology
International Community Development

Environmental Planning
Introduction to World Value Systems
Rich & Poor Nations: Conflict & Cooperation
Ethnology of Tribal Societies
Anthropological Perspectives on Health & Illness

LATIN AMERICAN STUDIES

Latin American Communism
Latin Amer. Development & Social Change
U.S. Foreign Policy
Cooperative Global Conflict Resolution

British Imperialism in Latin America
Hispanic Culture and Civilization
Cross Cultural Communication
International Political Economy

EDUCATION

Cultural Diversity in Human Services
Family Policy
Innovative Education
Mental Health
Self as Resource

Change in Educational and Social Systems
Community Organization and Social Planning
Interventions with Individuals and Families
Learning Environments for Diverse Students
Professional Communication & Collaboration

ANTHROPOLOGY

Culture, Illness, and Healing
Pacific Island Societies
Women and Culture : Creativity and Symbols
Economic Anthropology
State, Society, Gender in Asia

The Americas: Indigenous Perspectives
Immigration and Farmworkers Political Culture
Scientific Racism: An Anthropological History
Anthropology and Folklore
Feminist Methods in Anthropology

JOURNALISM

The Mass Media and Society
Journalism and Public Opinion
Communications Law
Mass Media Ethics
Cultural Approaches to Communication

Advertising as a Social Institution
Environmental Journalism
Third World Development Communications
International Journalism

OUTDOOR PURSUITS LEADERSHIP   BURMESE, THAI, INDONESIAN LANGUAGES

GEOLOGY   GEOGRAPHY   LANDSCAPE ARCHITECTURE

Apply by 1/15   Early Admit: 11/1

• Interdisciplinary Classes & Majors   • Co-op Work Study   • Team Teaching   • Self-Designed Majors
• Service Learning   • Third World Service Learning   • Student Enviro Audits   • Theme Housing
• Vegetarian & Vegan Meals   • Green Campus   • Organic Gardens   • Socially Responsible Investments

Office of Admissions
240 Oregon Hall
1217 University of Oregon
Eugene, OR 97403-1217

541. 346. 3201
800. BE-A-DUCK
uoadmit@uoregon.edu
www.uoadmit.uoregon.edu

PAUL SMITH'S COLLEGE

850 Students   Paul Smith's, New York

The Paul Smith's College community provides a dynamic educational environment which encourages students to be actively engaged in their own learning experience by fostering creative, ethical and intellectual growth. The College's comprehensive educational approach offers the integration of traditional and experiential learning to encourage discovery, discipline and creativity.

Paul Smith's College is set in the Adirondacks of Northern New York amid awe-inspiring mountains, sparkling lakes and lush forests. The 14,200 acre main campus on the shores of Lower St. Regis Lake, providing a safe, comfortable and invigorating environment. Bachelor's programs include Biology, Fisheries and Wildlife Sciences, Forestry, Hotel, Resort and Tourism Management, Natural Resources, and Recreation, Adventure Travel and Ecotourism. Alternatively, careers also start with Associate degrees in programs such as Fish and Wildlife Technology, Forest Recreation, Outdoor Recreation, Surveying, or Urban Tree Management.

Paul Smith's College is committed to promoting and practicing the principles of sustainable development, encouraging environmental awareness and maintaining an environmentally sound campus. The forest management operations at Paul Smith's College have received FSC Certification from Smartwood through the certifier's partnership with the National Wildlife Federation.

The low student-to-faculty ratio means teachers, mentors, and advisors are always close at hand to listen and encourage individual growth. Although the community is small, it's scope extends far beyond the Adirondacks. Paul Smith's student population is increasingly culturally diverse with young people coming from around the world. Ireland, Bosnia, Italy, Tibet, Japan, and Kenya are countries recently represented within the student body.

Extensive hands-on training, field work, internships, externships and experiential learning sets Paul Smith's apart. Students start gaining valuable, hands-on experience in each chosen career in the first semester. Forestry, surveying and the environmentally-based programs utilize the six-million acre Adirondack Park for their classroom, You can study the works of poets, writers and philosophers in the very surroundings that inspired their ideas and helped shape how our society now thinks of the natural world.

The College's academic and extracurricular programs capitalize on the natural surroundings providing students with unparalleled opportunities for practical study and recreation. Hiking, canoeing, kayaking, skiing, snowshoeing, swimming, and mountain biking are readily available, and down hill skiing opportunities abound. The Adirondack Park provides a dramatic natural setting, as well as an historical perspective on stewardship and hospitality.

Students' participation in a broad range of recreational, cultural, student life and community service activities promotes individual growth, and serves to enhance understanding and awareness of others.

Upon graduation, opportunities are virtually unlimited, and for the past ten years the transfer and job-placement rate has been a near-perfect 99 percent,

MAKING A DIFFERENCE STUDIES

FISHERIES & WILDLIFE

Techniques in Wildlife Management
Conservation Biology
Forest Ecology
Microbial Ecology
Physiological Ecology
Wetlands Ecosystems and Management

Aquatic Plants
Watershed Management
Fish Biology and Management
Wildlife Management
Tropical Ecology
Winter Ecology

RECREATION, ADVENTURE, TRAVEL & ECOTOURISM (RATE)

Students will be actively engaged on- and off-campus in projects which utilize our own 14,200 acres and the surrounding six-million-acre Adirondack Park. They may find themselves rock climbing in the High Peaks region and camping out under the stars, planning Adirondack expeditions and leading orienteering classes all in one semester. Tropical destinations such as Costa Rica will be the setting for an Eco-Adventure Practicum, and students will complete an Externship as well.

Adventure Travel and Ecotourism
Expedition Planning
Entrepreneurship
Natural Habitat Interpretation
Adirondack Expedition

Eco-Adventure Practicum
Introduction to Recreation
Sustainable Development
Issues in RATE

ECOLOGY & FIELD BIOLOGY

Stream Ecology
Plant Ecology & Systematics
Plant Physiology
Landscape Ecology
Understory and Ground Cover Flora

Limnology
Plant Biology
Entomology
Paleoecology
Advanced Conservation Science

ECOLOGICAL FORESTRY MANAGEMENT

Forest Resource Economics
Silviculture
Forest Ecology
Wildlife Conservation
Forest Mensuration
Insects and Diseases of Trees
Forest Soils

Environmental Simulation Modeling
Forest Mapping
Aerial Photo Interpretation
Forest Measurements
New Paradigms in Forestry
Forest Health
Introduction to GIS

ENVIRONMENTAL STUDIES (TWO YEAR A.A. PROGRAM)

Stream Ecology
The Adirondacks
Wilderness In American Literature
Ecology

Environmental Studies
Biology
Natural Habitat Interpretation
Politics of the Environment

Rolling Applications
• Field Studies • Self-Designed Majors

Paul Smith's College
P.O. Box 265
Paul Smiths, NY 12970-0265

518. 327. 6227
800. 421. 2605
www.paulsmiths.edu

PITZER COLLEGE

975 Students   Claremont, California

Founded in 1963, Pitzer is a coeducational liberal arts college with a progressive educational philosophy. Pitzer College is part of a uniquely stimulating higher education environment consisting of five schools known as the Claremont Colleges. These Colleges bring a vast range of courses and facilities to Pitzer students. Students enjoy a level of resources usually associated with mid-sized universities together with the close student-faculty relationships found within small, human-scale colleges.

Pitzer College offers a setting rich in possibilities, and if Pitzer graduates are more creative, more independent of spirit, and more willing to seek new answers, then it could be that the opportunities unique to Pitzer helped to make them this way. Pitzer tends to attract students that concern themselves with the critical social and political issues facing our world. Most students arrive at Pitzer already committed to various social or political issues. Once at the College, they're encouraged to develop these interests to a greater degree; to take them further and test them harder. But mostly, the ideals that bring people to Pitzer continue to guide them after graduation.

Pitzer presents a unique opportunity for exploration of the self, the world and our involvement in that world. The College believes that students should take an active part in formulating their individualized plans of study, bringing a spirit of inquiry and adventure to the process of academic planning. Through innovative offerings, team taught and interdisciplinary courses, independent studies and highly participatory experiences both on and off campus , students have the opportunity to participate fully in the creation of their educational path. Pitzer stresses social and ethical responsibility, critical thinking, research and service learning. By bringing together the perspectives of several disciplines, students gain an understanding of the powers and limits of each discipline and of the kind of contribution each can make to an exploration of the significant issues.

By learning about their own culture and placing it in comparative perspective, students come both to appreciate other cultures and to recognize the ways that their own thinking and actions are influenced by the culture in which they live. By examining the social consequences and ethical implications of the issues they explore, students learn to evaluate the effects of individual actions and social policies and to take responsibility for making the world a better place. Independent study allows students to create a curriculum that meets their individual needs and goals by working individually with faculty.

Since its founding in 1963, Pitzer College has committed itself to educating students to be effective and responsible citizens at a local or global level. Such citizenship is fostered through the effective engagement of our students in local communities, in conjunction with a strong theoretical and applied curriculum. Internships affirm Pitzer's commitment to connecting knowledge and action, and provide opportunities to link students to social issues in Los Angeles communities thus developing feelings of social responsibility.

Pitzer won the Idealism in Action award given to a college that has demonstrated depth and breadth in their commitment to civic engagement. This award, which requires additional application elements, recognizes a campus that has demonstrated commitment to community service, activism, service learning, and socially responsible careers or that has made vast strives in doing so over the past two years

MAKING A DIFFERENCE STUDIES

ENVIRONMENTAL STUDIES

Environmental Arts and Action
Enviro. Awareness & Responsible Action
Environmental Policy
Community, Ecology and Design
Reading and Painting the Landscapes
Progress & Oppression: Ecology, Human Rights & Development
Building Sustainability: Environmental Assessment at Pitzer College

A Sense of Place
Population and Society
Theory & Practice of Environmental Education
Ethnoecology
Social Justice and Natural Resources

SCIENCE, TECHNOLOGY AND SOCIETY

Mathematics in Many Cultures
Media and Society
Science & Technology in the Modern World
Politics of Environmental Action

Mathematics, Philosophy & the Real World
Philosophy of Science
Science, Technology and Politics
Science, Politics and Alternative Medicine

MEDIA STUDIES

Anarchy and the Internet
Documentary Media
Imagined Communities
Language of Film

China & Japan Through Film and Ethnography
Feminist Documentary and Production
Intro to Latin American Literature and Film
Mexican Film History

ORGANIZATIONAL STUDIES

China and Japan: Economy and Society
Labor Internships
Political Psychology
Sociology of Work and Occupations

Economic Development
Manufacturing Tales
Social Responsibility and the Corporation
Human Resource Mgm't. & Organizational Analysis

POLITICAL ECONOMY

International Political Economy
Public Choice
Third World and the Global Economy
State and Development in the Third World

Agricultural Development in the Third World
Politics of Water
Issues of International Trade Development Policy
Environmental Economics

INTERNATIONAL AND INTERCULTURAL STUDIES

Nature, Movement & Meditation in Qigong
Culture and Power
The Third World & the Global Economy
Mexican Visual Culture
Ethnoecology

Ecology, Human Rights & Development
Economic Change & the Environment in Asia
Ecology and Culture Change
Chinese Philosophy, Culture & Traditional Medicine
Resistance to Monoculture: Gender, Spirituality & Power

CHICANO STUDIES   BLACK STUDIES   GENDER & FEMINIST STUDIES   ASIAN STUDIES

Apply By 1/1

• All Seminar Format   • Team Teaching   • Interdisciplinary Classes
• Self-Designed Majors   • Full Recycling & Energy Conservation Since 1963
• Field Studies   • Organic Gardens   • Vegetarian/Vegan Meals

Office of Admission
Pitzer College
1050 North Mills Ave.
Claremont, CA 91711

909. 621. 8129
800. 748. 9371
admission@pitzer.edu
www.pitzer.edu/

Audubon Expedition Institute's unique field studies program takes students on extended bus tours to different regions of the country. Here students overlook Manning Provincial Park in British Columbia.

The California University campus chapter of Habitat for Humanity creates a cardboard village to remind the campus community of the importance of affordable, decent housing. They collect money for HFH as part of the activity.

The scenic St. Olaf campus includes 150 acres of native tall-grass prairie, 15 wetlands, a bluebird trail, 350 acres of farmland, 10 miles of trails and 80 acres of woods.

The aha moment of education . . . in College of the Atlantic class on intertidal biology, faculty member Dr. Helen Hess and student Henry Steinberg work on methods of ecological censusing.

Photo by Toby Hollis

PORTLAND STATE UNIVERSITY

18,000 Undergraduates   Portland, Oregon

Portland State University is Oregon's only urban public university and is defined by its relationship with the community. PSU is committed to the delivery of quality academic programs for undergraduates and graduates. These programs are integrated with a campus-wide commitment to community service, and to collaborative strategies linking faculty and students in learning and research experiences that bear directly on the problems and opportunities of the community and state.

Portland State has won praise from scholars nationwide by replacing its traditional general education requirements with an inquiry-based interdisciplinary undergraduate program that meets the needs of today's students. The undergraduate experience at PSU offers many of the advantages found at small selective private schools, but at the price of a public university. The general education program, called University Studies, is designed to facilitate the acquisition of the knowledge, abilities, and attitudes which will form a foundation for lifelong learning among its students. This foundation includes the capacity and the propensity to engage in critical thinking, to use various forms of communication for learning and expression, to gain an awareness of the broader human experience and its environment, and to appreciate the responsibilities of persons to themselves, each other, and to their communities.

Freshmen and Sophomores enroll as small groups in interdisciplinary inquiry courses each taught by teams of five faculty, facilitated by peer mentors, and supported by dedicated high tech classrooms and labs. Upper division students enroll in clusters of theme-related courses that offer in-depth learning as well as advanced skill development in communication, information technologies, group work, and research. Many of the inquiry and cluster courses contain elements of service learning. The general education program culminates in a two-term six-credit Senior Capstone course. These students are organized in small interdisciplinary teams to apply and interpret their undergraduate learning experience in a community-setting focused on a real-life issue. The capstone also offers an opportunity to connect with potential employers and gain work experience, while addressing a priority need of the community.

Service learning is also integrated into many courses in the majors; more than 200 courses at PSU involve some aspect of community-based learning. One example is the Center for Columbia River History, which engages undergrads in history and related research disciplines educational programs to enhance understanding of River Basin history. Using folklore, geology, literature, history, economics etc, the project asks small Oregon communities to focus on changes since the big dams were built.

Located around a tree-lined city park in downtown Portland, PSU offers access to jobs, shopping, sporting and cultural events, and relatively low-cost housing. The campus has strong connections with its immediate neighborhood and the University district is becoming a model urban community with a blend of retail, business, housing, education, recreation and transportation services.

Making a Difference Studies

COMMUNITY DEVELOPMENT: COMMUNITY ORGANIZATION & CHANGE, HOUSING & ECONOMIC DEVELOPMENT, COMMUNICATIONS & COMMUNITY DEVELOPMENT

One of only a few undergrad programs nationwide in the growing field of community development. Trains citizen activists and professionals empowered to take leadership roles in public affairs. Interdisciplinary approach includes anthropology, communications, cultural studies, ecology, environmental studies, history, political economy, social psychology and urban design.

Methods of Community Development
Minority Business Perspective
Urban Economics
Housing Development
Green Economics & Sustainable Development
Urban Transportation

Theory & Philosophy of Community Development
Social Change
Downtown Revitalization
Neighborhood Conservation & Change
Afro-American Community Development
Urban Planning: Environmental Issues

ENVIRONMENTAL STUDIES: ENVIRONMENTAL SCIENCE & ENVIRONMENTAL POLICY

Understanding Environmental Sustainability
Institutions and Public Change
Environmental Ethics
Culture and Ecology
Applied Enviro Studies: Policy Considerations

Environmental Risk Assessment
Environmental Economics
Urbanism and Urbanization
Groundwater Geology
Epidemiology of Cancer

CHILD AND FAMILY STUDIES

Collaboratively designed by faculty and professionals in cooperation with community agencies

Child in Society
Anthropology of the Family
Preparation for Early Intervention Settings
Child Psychology
Communication and Gender

Family in Society
Admin. of Programs for Children & Families
Health Promotion Programs: Children & Youth
Community Resources & Family Support
Interdisciplinary Perspectives on Children & Families

GEOGRAPHY

The Developing World
Urban Geography
Resource Management
Environment & Society: Global Perspectives
Himalaya and Tibet

Climate and Water Resources
Problem of World Population & Food Supply
Sustainable Cities
Metropolitan Economic Geography
Cultural Geography

HEALTH EDUCATION: COMMUNITY HEALTH/HEALTH & FITNESS PROMOTION

Drug Education
Emotional Health
Stress Management
Principles of Environmental Health
Mindbody Health: Human Potential

Foundations of Health Education
Epidemiology
Nutrition and Health
Planning & Evaluation: Health Educ. Programs
Communicable Diseases & Chronic Health Problems

ENVIRONMENTAL ENGINEERING (MINOR)   WOMEN'S STUDIES   INTERNATIONAL STUDIES
MIDDLE EASTERN STUDIES   ANTHROPOLOGY   PSYCHOLOGY   SOCIOLOGY   ECONOMICS
URBAN STUDIES   SUSTAINABLE URBAN DEVELOPMENT (MINOR)

Rolling Admissions
• Interdisciplinary Classes   • Team Teaching   • Over 200 Classes with Service Learning (all majors)

Portland State Universitys
Office of Admission
POB 751
Portland, OR 97207-0751

503. 725. 3511
800. 547. 8887
www.pdx.edu
admissions@pdx.edu

PRESCOTT COLLEGE

425 Students   Prescott, Arizona

Prescott College is a small, private, liberal arts college nestled in the pine-covered mountains of central Arizona. Founded in 1966 with a grant from the Ford Foundation, the College is committed to engaging students in a rigorous, well rounded liberal arts education centered on scholarship, innovative teaching methods, and close relationships between students and faculty. In keeping with the College's mission, students are encouraged to think critically and act ethically with sensitivity to both the human community and the biosphere and to live productive lives of self-fulfillment and service to others.

Small class size, a field-based curriculum, and real-life experiences distinguish Prescott College as a leader in undergraduate education. The faculty-student interaction at Prescott is very different from more extensively classroom-based programs and allows ample opportunities for participating, debating, and interacting one-on-one with faculty who serve as role models and mentors and often become life-long friends and colleagues. At Prescott College faculty and students travel and study and research and write and work more closely together than at any other college.

At Prescott College a wide variety of majors/emphases are supported through six multi-disciplinary programs that collectively explore what are traditionally considered separate fields of inquiry. Students design the direction and the methodology of their overall degree program in close collaboration with advisors, frequently combining coursework from one or more areas to create unique courses of study.

Prescott College is an "experiential education" school. Students learn by doing, going, seeing, hearing, tasting, experimenting, working, thinking, reflecting, and touching as much as they learn from reading and lectures. Many courses have strong field components, and some are conducted entirely in the field, going on-site throughout the Southwest, Mexico, Africa, Europe, Central and South America, the Caribbean, and throughout the world. With this approach every class moves along at warp speed, and students are expected to keep up with the academic side of their assignments as they travel, camp, relocate, mesh with local communities, conduct field studies, and otherwise pursue the "experiential" side of their education. Internships, apprenticeships, independent studies, community service, and study abroad are encouraged so that students may study and live in cultural contexts outside their normal experience. Because of this Prescott College students are much more prepared for careers in their fields, as well as for life in general, than mainstream college students.

Prescott grads have advanced to graduate study at Cornell, Stanford, Tulane University Law School, Tufts University School of Medicine, Union College, University of Oregon, University of Arizona, Loyola University, and Antioch College, among many others. They have also gone on to thrive as educators, ecologists, conservationists, field biologists, botanists, public policy consultants, social workers, authors, outdoor guides, kayak instructors, emergency medical technicians, financial consultants, recording engineers, journalists, poets, psychologists, and activists, to name just a few examples.

Prescott College Adult Degree Bachelor of Arts Completion and Graduate Programs

For the most part, students in Prescott College's community-based programs are focused on making a positive difference in the world. The programs' hands-on, self-directed approach works for motivated learners with a desire to engage in social change and environmental action. The College was an early pioneer in experientially-based education. As a result, students co-design their own programs of study with the assistance of faculty and complete projects that demonstrate competence and mastery. It's a form of education that works; year after year Prescott College has been awarded the highest academic rating in the state of Arizona by the Princeton Review.

It's often said that "the sky is the limit" when it comes to degree options for Prescott College's adult learners. These programs are community based as opposed to online programs, meaning that students continue living and working in their home communities while in school. Students work one-on-one with mentors, professionals in their community, or graduate advisors to complete their coursework. While students live all over the country and in a growing number of international locales, many are served locally by the College's satellite center in Tucson, Arizona.

As well as studying with mentors and graduate advisors, students develop close working relationships with Core Faculty members who guide them throughout their programs of study. Graduate students also attend quarterly seminars or colloquia at the College's sustainably-designed Crossroads Center on the main campus in Prescott, Arizona, where they present work, network, and attend classes and presentations.

Prescott College was also an early pioneer in interdisciplinary learning and environmental education, and as a result all programs require students to examine both cultural and environmental aspects and impacts of the subject matter. Many students create programs specifically tailored to a job or field they'd like to work in. This often includes incorporating their current profession into their schoolwork.

As part of its 40th Anniversary initiative this year, the college has expanded the availability of scholarship funds. The College partners with several organizations to provide creative, full-ride fellowships for employees who gain valuable workplace experience while earning graduate degrees. These include the Arizona Wilderness Coalition and Prescott Alternative Transportation Master's Fellowship programs. Other scholarships include the William Randolph Hearst Endowed Scholarship for Native American students studying teacher education; the Haide Koskinen Memorial Scholarship for environmental research, carried out at the College's marine research field station in Kino Bay; the James Stuckey Commemorative Scholarship for students whose academic work demonstrates excellence and commitment; and the Adult Degree Programs New Student Scholarships.

> *I shall pass through this world but once. Any good therefore that I can do, or any kindness that I can show to any human being, let me do it now. Let me not defer or neglect it, for I shall not pass this way again.*
> Mahatma Gandhi

Making a Difference Studies

Environmental Studies

Students often major in Agroecology, Conservation, Earth Science, Ecological Design, Environmental Policy, Human Ecology, Marine Studies, Natural History and Ecology.

Environmental Education	Park and Wilderness Management,
Conservation Biology	Weather and Climate
Ecosystem Biology	Botany
Wildlife Management	Marine Studies/Conservation
Ecological Design	Environmental Ethics
Agroecology	Environmental Policy,

Adventure Education

Self-designed majors in Adventure Education, Outdoor Experiential Ed & Wilderness Leadership.

Aboriginal Living Skills	Kayaking (Whitewater, Sea)
Expeditionary Skills	Wilderness Leadership
Alpine Mountaineering	River Guiding,
Rock Climbing	Outdoor Education and Recreation
Maps and Wilderness Navigation	Ropes Facilitation
Search and Rescue	Outdoor Program Administration

Cultural and Regional Studies

Students often majors in Peace Studies, Religion & Philosophy, Cultural & Regional Studies.

Anthropology	Economics
Political Economy	Political Science
Government	Public Policy, Law, Philosophy, Human Rights,
Sociology	Native American Studies
Gender Studies	Latin American Studies
Peace Studies	Spanish Language and Literature

Education

Self designed majors in Elementary & Secondary Teacher Certification and Environmental Education.

Special Education	Environmental Education
Experiential Education	Elementary Education
Curriculum Design	Learning Theories
Language Arts	Science Education
Social Sciences	Secondary Education

Human Development

Students often major in Ecopsych; Human Developm't; Counseling Psych; Therapeutic Adventure Ed.

Holistic Health and Wellness Anatomy	Transpersonal Psychology
Counseling Psychology	Bodywork
Equine Assisted Therapy	Lifespan Development
Yoga	Sexuality
Therapeutic Use of Adventure Education	Nutrition

Apply by 8/15

55% Transfer Students   No housing; a housing specialist assists students in finding housing

• Self-Designed Majors   • Field Studies   • Interdisciplinary Classes   • Optional SAT's   • Team Teaching
• All Seminar   • Green Campus   • Distance B.A. Programs   • Organic Café with Vegetarian /Vegan Options

Admissions Office   800. 350. 2100
Prescott College   928. 350. 2100
220 Grove Ave.   admissions@prescott.edu
Prescott, AZ 86301   www.prescott.edu

RUDOLF STEINER COLLEGE

250 Students   Fair Oaks, California

Rudolf Steiner College strives to provide a creative educational environment for men and women of diverse ages and backgrounds who seek a deeper understanding of the challenges of modern life and wish to develop new capacities as a basis for their life's work, for social service, and cultural renewal. Founded on the spiritual scientific work of Rudolf Steiner, the College has as its mission to provide programs that:

- Awaken independent thinking and healthy judgment about the deepest issues of human life;
- School powers of perception;
- Cultivate and enrich artistic faculties;
- Strengthen capacities for practical life.

The view of the human being as an individual, encompassing body, soul, and spirit is central to the programs of the College, along with an emphasis on the cultivation of the inner life as a source of strength, creativity, and initiative. Programs strive to address the students' quest for the knowledge, insight, and moral imagination needed to bring balance and healing to human beings, communities, and the earth itself.

Rudolf Steiner College offers upper division and graduate level courses. Most students are between the ages of 22 and 45 with a range of 20 to 70. Most have already earned at least one academic degree. The cosmopolitan community is comprised of students and faculty from many different countries. They have explored some of the world through travel, study, work; many are also raising families. They come seeking to make a difference.

Students seek to make a difference for the world through Self-Development Through the Arts by cultivating the imagination, insight, and initiative required to address modern problems. The arts are an integral part of the curriculum and are studied as a basis for sensitivity, to deepen perception, social awareness, and balance of soul.

Using Goethean phenomenological approaches to science in Self-Development Through the Sciences, in a context of small group dialogue, students are encouraged to explore their own soul processes looking for potent images that can be used as analogs for their own path in life. This is a year of self exploration and community development.

Waldorf Education: Making a difference for the next generations. Waldorf education (K-12 curriculum) seeks to cultivate balanced human beings by educating head, heart, and hand in harmonious interplay. People preparing to teach in Waldorf schools study: human development, based on the assumption that a human being is a spiritual being; curriculum appropriate to different age levels; and multiple visual and performing art forms. Waldorf education is the fastest growing independent education movement worldwide. Upon graduation, teacher placement is 100% with most graduates getting multiple job offers.

Bio-Dynamic Gardening recognizes the basic principles at work in nature and how the health of the soil, plants and animals depends on reconnecting nature with the creative forces of the cosmos. Students seek to make a difference through the study and applications of the knowledge gained from the practical methods outlined by Rudolf Steiner.

MAKING A DIFFERENCE STUDIES

FOUNDATION PROGRAM

One-year full-time and two-year weekend options. This speaks directly to the quest for deeper understanding of the human being, to a yearning for self-knowledge and higher wisdom of the world. It is designed to introduce and explore the insights and endeavors of Rudolf Steiner, as well as focusing on artistic development and personal growth. Taken in preparation for the second year of Waldorf teacher education.

Introduction to Waldorf Education
Spiritual Streams in American Literature
Painting, Drawing, Sculpture
Movement and Spatial Dynamics
Karma and Reincarnation

Eurythmy (Movement)
Choral Singing
Parsifal: The Quest for the Holy Grail
World Evolution and Spiritual Development
Philosophy of Freedom

WALDORF TEACHER EDUCATION PROGRAMS

Full-time, part-time, weekend/summer options including two part-time programs in the Bay Area; certificate; B.A. & M.A. options. Preparation for early childhood, elementary, or high school teaching in a Waldorf school (over 800 schools worldwide). Specialties offered in early childhood education, remedial education, eurythmy, foreign language, music, handwork, and administration.

Storytelling, Gardening
Learning and Development
Inner Work of the Waldorf Teacher
Painting, Drawing, Crafts
Psychology of Adolescence
Teaching Math, Science, Languages, History & Geography

Puppetry and Festivals for the Young Child
Speech, Eurythmy, Music
High School Curriculum Subjects
Teaching Science in the Elementary Grades
Working With Colleagues

ARTS PROGRAM

Watercolor painting: veil and wet-method. Use of these techniques in the Waldorf curriculum and art therapy. Supplemental studies of singing, eurythmy (movement), and clay sculpture.

BIODYNAMIC GARDENING COURSE

Soil preparation, composting, Bio-dynamic preparations and sprays, crop rotation, earthly and cosmic forces in plant growth, pest management, seed saving.

GOETHEAN STUDIES PROGRAM

Goethe's theory of knowledge as a path to deepened perception and higher cognition. Botany, color study, meteorology, comparative morphology, and study of sacred geometry, Gaia/Sophia and the alchemy of the soul. Exploration of science through artistic media.

Numerous courses are offered throughout the year including childcare provider training, caregiving for infants and toddlers, family series for parents and toddlers, nature and arts for Japanese, professional development for teachers of at-risk youth, and Waldorf methods applied in the public school classroom.

Rolling Applications   Student Body: 20% international
Those who have successfully completed at least two years of general education courses, may enroll in
Rudolf Steiner College programs leading to a B.A. in Anthroposophical Studies or Waldorf Education.
• Interdisciplinary • Part-Time, Weekend, and Summer Study   • Vegetarian Lunch
• Organic Gardens • Tranquil setting on 13 acres of beautifully landscaped grounds

Admissions Counselor
Rudolf Steiner College
9200 Fair Oaks Blvd.
Fair Oaks, CA 95628

916. 961. 8727
www.steinercollege.edu
rsc@steinercollege.edu

RUTGERS STATE
SCHOOL OF ENVIRONMENTAL & BIOLOGICAL SCIENCES

3,000 Students   New Brunswick, N.J.

The School of Environmental & Biological Sciences (formerly Cook College) is one of four residential colleges on the New Brunswick campus of Rutgers University. Although the college is a professional school offering B.S. degrees solely in programs in environmental sciences, food, nutrition, marine sciences, and natural resources, the university's vast array of courses and activities are also available. SEBS combines a rural setting on the outskirts of New Brunswick with state-of-the-art laboratory and research facilities in bioremediation, geographic information systems, marine and coastal sciences and sustainable agriculture.

COOK/SEBS has long been recognized as the national leader in land-grant college curriculum innovation. The Department of Environmental Sciences was the first of its kind in the nation. SEBS thus broadened the established land-grant agricultural mission to include its environmental effects and the environmental problems of urban and suburban development. The faculty has a commitment to a multidisciplinary, problem-oriented undergraduate program. This program now includes the social, cultural, aesthetic, and ethical dimensions of problems in food, agriculture, natural resources, and the environment – in addition to the scientific and technical aspects that had been the focus of land-grant colleges.

The College's mission is to integrate teaching, research, and outreach to anticipate and respond to issues and challenges in agriculture, food systems, environment and natural resources, and human and community health and development, in order to empower people to improve their lives, the lives of others, and the environments on which they depend. A growing emphasis in the coming years will be on internationalizing our curricula and providing greater opportunities for study/work abroad.

A required "Perspectives on Agriculture and the Environment" course introduces entering students to the mission of the College and the complexity of environmental problems. A capstone "Junior-Senior Colloquium" requires students to work as a team drawn from a variety of majors, to propose solutions to a well-defined "real world" problem. The College believes that to sustain the integrity of our ecosystem, students should develop the ethical sensitivity and the analytical skills to address questions of social responsibility, environmental ethics, moral choices and social equity.

SEBS offers traditional land-grant college programs in agricultural, animal, atmospheric, food, nutritional and plant sciences. Discipline-based programs in the natural sciences, journalism, communication, and public health are offered in cooperation with other faculties of the university, but SEBS students focus on the application of these disciplines to problems in the environment or human health. Nine multidisciplinary majors are open only to SEBS students.

An organic farm was established on campus in 1993, operated by students who remain in New Brunswick for the summer. The farm is a CSA (community-supported agriculture); the shareholders and student farmers consume approximately 25% of the produce, the balance is donated to local soup kitchens and food banks. Students learn the fundamentals of organic gardening and the complexities of distributing fresh produce

MAKING A DIFFERENCE STUDIES

ENVIRONMENTAL PLANNING & DESIGN

Environmental Design Analysis
Legal Aspects of Conservation
Land Planning and Utilization
Conservation Vegetation

History of Landscape Architecture
Land Economics
Horticulture in the Residential Environment
Weather, Climate & Enviro. Design

PUBLIC HEALTH

Biology, Society, and Biomedical Issues
Human Rights, Health, and Violence
Health and Public Policy
Housing and Health Care
Air Pollution
Elements of Solid Waste Mgm't & Treatment

Public Health Economics
Social & Ecological Aspects of Health & Disease
Urban Policy in Developing Nations
Enviro. & Public Health: Epidemiological Aspects
Elements of Water and Wastewater Treatment
Environmental Toxicology

ENVIRONMENTAL POLICY, INSTITUTIONS AND BEHAVIOR: U.S. OR INT'L. ENVIRO STUDIES

Environment & Development
Population, Resources and Environment
Rural Communities
Environmental Teacher Education
International Environmental Policy

Enviro. Problems: Historical & Cross-Cultural
Economics of World Food Problems
Social & Ecological Aspects of Health & Disease
Environmental Communication
Culture and Environment

ENVIRONMENTAL SCIENCES

Solid Waste Management and Treatment
Soils and Their Management
Air Pollution Control
Environmental Health
Soil Ecology

Topics in Agroecology
Problems of Aquatic Environments
Tropical Agriculture
Water Resources -Water Quality
Perspectives on Agriculture & the Environment

ENVIRONMENTAL AND RESOURCE ECONOMICS

Labor Economics
Food Health and Safety Policy
Natural Resource Economics
Environmental Law
Ecosystems Ecology and Global Change

Ethics in Business
Environmental Economics
Fundamentals of Environmental Geomatics
Watershed Management
The Greenhouse Effect

CONSERVATION & APPLIED ECOLOGY

Fishery Management
Soils and Water
Introductory Biochemistry
Legal Aspects of Conservation
Air Photo Interpretation
Fundamentals of Environmental Planning

Forest Management
Conservation Ecology
Natural Resource Biometrics
Ecosystems Ecology and Global Change
Environmental Toxicology
Wetlands Ecology

MARINE SCIENCES   AGROECOLOGY   ENVIRO. HEALTH SCIENCE   JOURNALISM & MASS MEDIA

Apply by 12/1

• Field Studies   • Team Teaching   • Self-Designed Majors   • Multidisciplinary Classes
• Service-Learning   • Organic Garden   • Vegetarian Meals

RU Undergraduate Admissions
65 Davidson Road, Room 202
Piscataway, NJ 08854-8097

732. 932. 4636
www.cookcollege.rutgers.edu
https://www.ugadmissions.rutgers.edu

St. Olaf College

3,000 Students   Northfield, Minnesota

Founded in 1874 by Norwegian Lutheran immigrants, St. Olaf is an academically rigorous, liberal arts college of the church with nationally ranked music, science and mathematics programs. The student-faculty ratio of 12.5 to 1 encourages individual learning and teaching, while the residential nature of the 300-acre campus helps students become part of an enduring community that takes pride in its traditions and innovations.

A St. Olaf education is about academics first. But it is also about connecting reason and faith, learning and service, the classroom and the community. Topics of conversation on campus range from the ethical impacts of computer science to federal environmental regulations, international health care and the major epochs of Western civilization. Students study the frequency of a particular human behavior in one class and the frequency of a high note played through a pipe organ in the next.

Consistent with the college motto, "Ideals to Action," St. Olaf students strive to use their knowledge to serve others. Whether they are mathematics majors working with Twin Cities corporations to solve real-world business problems or "green" chemistry students using non-toxic chemicals, St. Olaf students develop their critical-thinking skills and a stronger sense of global citizenship. The student congregation always engages in outreach and stewardship. Over the past 10 years, thousands of dollars and books have gone to children and teachers in Tanzania . Offerings and sponsorships have also supported Pine Ridge Indian Reservation, the children of prison inmates, children in Bosnia and a health clinic in Mexico.

A longtime leader in international education, St. Olaf continues to be the No. 1 baccalaureate institution in the United States in both number and percentage of students who study abroad. The Association of International Educators has recognized St. Olaf as one of the top 17 institutions in the country that does exemplary work in internationalizing its campus.

St. Olaf students study theater in London, religion in South Africa, art history in Florence and medicine in Peru. Currently, more than 120 international and U.S. off-campus study programs are offered in 38 countries. Several programs are environmental: Biology in South India, Tropical Field Research in Costa Rica, Environmental Studies in Australia, Island Biology, Equatorial Biology, Superior Studies at Wolf Ridge, Winter Ecology, and the Washington Semester in International Environment and Development.

In the last ten years St. Olaf has been a "groundwater guardian," making a concerted effort to keep its stormwater runoff on its own lands, relieving stress on local storm sewers and helping purify water for recharging the aquifer. Land restorations and the trail system provide opportunities for hiking, running, skiing, and birdwatching. As St. Olaf turns to local and organic sources for food, it supports Minnesota farmers and the regional economy.

St. Olaf ranks among the top contributors of volunteers to the Peace Corps and provides the largest contingent of volunteers to the Lutheran Volunteer Corps each year. Graduates have gone on to pursue advanced degrees at Harvard, Oxford University and M.I.T.

Today's world needs citizens who think deeply, collaborate effectively and lead with dignity in a fast-moving, complex and multicultural environment. St. Olaf graduates will continue to provide imaginative and ethical leadership while confronting tomorrow's challenges.

MAKING A DIFFERENCE STUDIES

ENVIRONMENTAL STUDIES

Introduction to Environmental Studies
Conservation Biology
Biosphere Ecology
Environmental Policy and Regulation
Saving Wild Places

The Culture of Nature
Topics in Global Environmental Politics
Environmental Political Theory
Global Climate Change
Remote Sensing & Geographic Information Systems

- **Campus Ecology**   Explores key concepts of ecology, focusing explicitly on the ideal of ecological sustainability for the St. Olaf College campus. Students attend both to contemporary environmental issues and to the ideas and institutions that shape human resource use. Working groups research topics such as curriculum, clothes, cars, water, waste, food, energy, procurement, and landscape in the context of American religious and environmental values.

AMERICAN RACIAL AND MULTICULTURAL STUDIES

An interdisciplinary program committed to the study and celebration of American racial and cultural diversity. The ARMS faculty represent many different disciplines and help students integrate multiple perspectives on racial issues. Students are introduced to the cultures, histories and experiences of African Americans, Asian Americans, Latinos and Native Americans. Concentrate on the cultural contributions of these groups and on the conflicts that have arisen from cultural differences.

Black Drama
The Civil Rights Revolutio
Native American History
Women and Slavery
Race and Class in American Culture

American Racial and Multicultural Literature
African-American History
Civil War and Reconstruction
Contemporary Native American Issues
Gender in Cross-Cultural Perspective

THE GLOBAL SEMESTER, TERM IN THE MIDDLE EAST, AND TERM IN ASIA

Three study abroad programs examine issues facing developing countries. The itineraries take students and professors around the world with visits to such places as India, Hong Kong, Egypt, Morocco, Turkey, Thailand and China. Participants study at prestigious universities in each of these countries.

Religions of India
Korean Society
The Arts of China
Eastern Christianity
Thai Language

Global Issues: Cultural Identity & Technology
Social Change in the Middle East & North Africa
Egypt in the Ancient and Modern World
Thai Society
Modern Vietnam History

WOMEN'S STUDIES

Women and Literature
Women in America
Biology of Women
Psychology of Women

Human Sexuality
Introduction to Feminist Theology
Philosophy and Feminism
Contemporary Chinese Women Writers

ECONOMICS

Environmental Economics
Economics of Health Care
Economics of Public Policy
Economic Justice

Economic Development in Japan
Urban Economics
International Economics

- **Development Economics**   The study of economic, political, and institutional requirements necessary to bring about relatively rapid and large-scale improvement in the standards of living for Third World populations in Latin America, Asia,and Africa. Major theories of economic development are employed to analyze specific problems such as population growth, poverty and hunger, agricultural stagnation, industrialization, export-led growth and debt.

Hispanic Studies

Spain's Cultural and Linguistic Legacy

The Maya: Colonial Times to Present

Modern Latin America

20th Century Cuba

Forging a Latin American Culture

Cultural Heritage of the Hispanic U.S.

Contemporary Issues in the Spanish-Speaking World

Slavery, Race and Ethnicity in Latin America

U.S.-Latin American Relations

Interim (January) Studies

Water Resource Management

Urban Alternative Education

Family Violence

Politics and Human Rights

Anthropology of War and Peace

Family Social Service in Central Mexico

Cross Culture Media

Biomedical Ethics

Christian and Islamic Ethics

Global Health Biostatistics

- **Multicultural Education in Hawaii** Examine the influence of race, class, and multiculturalism in American schools by participating as teachers' assistants and tutors in two distinctly different K-12 settings. Through guest lectures, readings, field trips, and seminars, students explore the unique geography and culture of the Hawaiian Islands and develop a framework for examining diversity on the mainland.

Sociology & Anthropology

Sociology, in the words of C.Wright Mills, is the search for "public issues" that underlie private trouble". Anthropology is the study of how culture influences every aspect of human life and society.

Anthropology of War and Peace

The Arab World

Indigenous Peoples

Global Interdependence

Religion, Culture, and Society

Native North American Cultures and Religions

Modern Southeast Asia

Sociology of Dying, Death and Bereavement

Social Movements

Health Care, Medicine and Society

Family Studies

Provides academic linkages across disciplines based in the liberal arts and reflects the college's emphasis on cross-cultural and experiential learning.

Family Relationships

Social Welfare in the Global Community

Cross-Cultural Psychology

Family Values

Psychology of Counseling

Human Sexuality

Human Rights in Cross-Cultural Perspective

Family Social Services in Central Mexico

Indigenous Cultures of Australia & New Zealand

Social Policy

Africa and the African Diaspora   Social Work   Philosophy

Apply by 2/1   Early Decision 11/15   Early Action: 12/1

Avg. # of students in first year classroom: 27

• Interdisciplinary Classes • Field Studies   • Service Learning   • Third-World Service-Learning

• Team Teaching • Self-Designed Majors • Evening Classes • Vegetarian & Vegan Meals

• Green Campus   • Some Socially Responsible Investment Policies

Director of Admissions

St. Olaf College

1520 St. Olaf Ave.

Northfield, MN 55057-1098

800. 800. 3025

507. 646. 3025

www.stolaf.edu

admiss@stolaf.edu

SARAH LAWRENCE COLLEGE

1,300 Students   Bronxville, New York

Sarah Lawrence, a coeducational liberal arts college, offers a unique education to students who want to shape their own curriculum with the guidance of a talented faculty. Sarah Lawrence was the first college in the United States to propose that education should be shaped to fit individuals and have a sustained commitment to their needs and talents, and the first to realize that genuine learning engages the imagination as well as the intellect. Other innovations include:

- A seminar/conference system where students learn in small interactive classes (limited to 15 students) and private tutorials. Student/faculty ratio of 6:1 is one of the lowest in the country.
- Faculty advisers, called dons, with whom students work to design individual programs of study. The don also teaches the student's First Year Studies Seminar, meets weekly with first-year students, and provides ongoing guidance throughout the undergraduate years.
- Written evaluations for coursework, with grades kept on file for graduate school applications only.
- No graduate assistants, instructors, or adjunct lecturers. Each professor is fully a teacher, available to first-year through fourth-year students.

Sarah Lawrence endows students with the efficacy and will to make a difference in their own lives and in other's. They are given the resources and support needed to study their areas of interest with intensity and to explore the moral, social, and political implications of the subjects studied. The College believes that an educated human being is one who combines skepticism with reverence, who will question everything but the dignity and worth of others, and who recognizes an obligation to serve the larger community.

The College was a pioneer in incorporating field work into its curriculum. Students can arrange to receive academic credit for interning at numerous social and political organizations if they work with a faculty member to explore and write about an academic aspect of their experience. Past field-work sites include the NAACP Legal Defense Fund, the American Civil Liberties Union, the Landmark Preservation Commission, and the Mount Sinai Center for Occupational and Environmental Medicine. Theater and dance students participate in outreach groups that work with area public schools.

In an expansion of its field-work option, Sarah Lawrence has service/learning courses in which all class participants do field-work in a social service or public policy organization; their combined experiences are formally integrated into the course content. The College's Community Partnerships & Service Learning Program provides students with the opportunity to learn about and engage in social change through course study, community-based learning placements, immersion trips, advising, and service projects. The program serves as a hub for students and faculty interested in working for social changes in Yonkers, Westchester County, and New York City.

Sarah Lawrence prepares students for global citizenship — to meet the challenges of living and learning in a multicultural world. In recognition of this, the College is a member of the International 50, a select group of schools that graduate a disproportionately high number of people entering careers in international affairs, or areas of government or academia with an international focus.

Making a Difference Studies

Public Policy

Economics of the Environment

The Meaning of Work

Global Economic Development

Women, Families & Work

Changing Places: Social/Spatial Dimensions of Urbanization

Survival & Scarcity: Resources for the Future

Econ. Policy & the Environment of the Future

Science, Technology & Human Values

Ecological Principles: Science of Environment

Political Science

African Politics

Politics of American Elections

Politics & Government of Latin America

Perspectives on Politics & Society in 20th Cent.

Drugs, Trade, Immigration: U.S.-Mexico Relations in the Late 20th Century

Nuclear Weapons: Selected Explorations of their Impact on Modern Life

Is America a Democracy? Class, Race, Gender, & Political Participation

Politics & History: Conservative, Radical & Liberal

Area Studies

Images of India

Islam, Flower in the Desert

Literature of Exile

Asian Religion

Middle East History & Politics

Culture & Society: Anthro Perspectives

Chinese & Japanese Literature & History

Tradition & Change in Modern China

Russian History, Literature & Politics

Latin American Literature & Politics

African Identities: Lives in Contemporary Sub-Saharan Africa

Sociology

Crime & Deviance Theory

Contemporary Urban Lives

Social Movements & Social Change

Inequality: Social & Economic Perspectives

Social Theory: Class, Race, Gender & the State

African-Americans & Social Science Research

Colonialism, Imperialism, Liberation: Third World Perspectives

Psychology

Education: Theory & Practice

Moral Development

Social Psychology

Social Development Research Seminar

Ethnicity, Race & Class: Psychosocial Perspectives

Ways of Knowing: Gender & Cultural Contexts

Deception & Self-Deception: The Place of Facts in a World of Propaganda

Women's Studies

Equality & Gender

Mothers & Daughters in Literature

Women in Asian Religions

Psychology of Women

Gender, Sexuality & Kinship

Women & Resistance in the Muslim World

The Female Vision: Women & Social Change in American History

Theories & Methodology of Women's History & Feminism

Environmental Studies   International Studies   Science, Technology & Society

Apply by 1/1   Early Decision 12/15

• Service Learning   • Self-Designed Majors   • Interdisciplinary Courses   • Field Studies

• Seminar/Conference Format   • Continuing Education   • Vegetarian Meals

Office of Admissions
Sarah Lawrence College
Bronxville, New York 10708

800. 888. 2858
www.sarahlawrence.edu
slcadmit@mail.slc.edu

SEATTLE UNIVERSITY

4,200 Undergraduates   Seattle, Washington

Seattle University, founded in 1891, is the largest independent university in the Northwest. A teaching institution, it is one of the 28 Jesuit universities in the United States. The University's mission has four central themes: Teaching and Learning, Education for Values, Preparation for Service, and the Growth of Persons. These provide an intellectual environment promoting the growth of creative, ethically-aware individuals with the skills, values, and motivation to lead and serve their communities and professions.

Seattle University's developmental and unified Core Curriculum embraces the unique tradition of Jesuit liberal education. The three phases of this Core Curriculum are: Foundation of Wisdom, Person in Society, and Responsibility and Service. Together they provide a developmental approach to educating students for a life of service, a foundation for questioning and learning, and a common intellectual experience for all students. Many Seattle University courses incorporate "service learning"–students commit to volunteer service, then reflect on the experience through class assignments.

The purpose of education is not just to expand intellectual capacity to attain a better life for oneself, but also to develop moral competency, leading to the pursuit of a more compassionate and just society for all. In order for students to understand these dualities, they must grapple with the challenging questions that arise when they put their education into action. By mobilizing students to address significant needs of the community and by connecting these service endeavors to learning opportunities, the Center for Service and Community Engagement helps students more fully understand the meaning of their education and their lives.

Seattle University has a solid environmental institutional philosophy and culture, and recycles or composts more than 50% of its waste. Close monitoring of campus lighting, heating/cooling, and transportation makes Seattle U. a community leader in energy conservation. In 1981 Seattle U. was the first university to initiate Integrated Pest Management, relying on alternative strategies to develop a balance of nature by allowing beneficial insects to control non beneficial insects.

Seattle U. was selected as one of five "lead institutions" in a national program - "Theological Education to Meet the Environmental Challenge". In response, Seattle University has been preparing its students, through three undergraduate environmental programs, for careers which maintain a clean natural environment while attaining a sustainable economic environment.

Seattle University's Ecological Studies major explores the complex web of human-nature relationships constituting earth's many ecological systems. The program aims to develop ecological and scientific literacy to understand the function of natural ecological systems and the nature and complexity of human interactions with these systems. The program considers local, national and global issues; students learn about local and regional ecosystems and the attitudes of human cultures towards these ecosystems. Coursework leads students to consider ecological dimensions of natural science, politics, history, philosophy and religion. As part of Seattle University's Jesuit identity, students consider the importance of the spirituality of nature, and the critical role of spirituality and ethics to ecological issues.

International internship opportunities abound, including the International Development Internship Program, which sends students to developing countries in Latin America and Africa to work with established non-governing organizations.

Making a Difference Studies

Ecological Studies
Collaboration with community and environmental leaders through four service-learning courses.

Introduction to Geosystems
Human Ecology and Geography
Environmental Politics
Religion and Ecology
Statistical Methods

Introduction to Global Politics
Environmental History
Environmental Philosophy
Marine Biology
Nature Writing

Social Work
Intro. to Social Work
Race and Ethnicity
Human Behavior in the Social Environment
Social Work Research
Mental Illness: Introduction to Social Work

History of Social Policy
Social Work with Children and Youth
Contemporary Social Policy
Race and Ethnicity
Human Development and Social Work

Civil and Environmental Engineering
Engineering Geology
Soil Mechanics
Water Supply & Waste Water Engineering
Environmental Law and Impact Studies

Environmental Engineering Chemistry
Surface and Ground Water Hydrology
Solid and Hazardous Waste Engineering
Engineering Design Course Series

Public Affairs
Race and Ethnicity
Community Design Workshop
Nonprofit Leadership
Working with Nonprofit Staff
Community Planning and Leadership

Urban Politics/Public Policy
Housing Design & the Sustainable Community
Introduction to the Nonprofit Sector
Nonprofit Fundraising
Local and State Politics

Asian American Experience: Culture, History and Community
Exploring the American City: Urban Design and Community Development

Theology and Religious Studies
Spiritual Traditions: East and West
The Gospel of Jesus Christ
Church as Community
Biomedical Ethics

Women and the Hebrew Bible
Women and Theology
Jesus and Liberation
Religion and Ecology

Political Science
Principles of Public Administration
Local and State Politics
Citizenship
Diversity and Change
Native American Politics and Protest

The Policy Process
Public Sector Analysis
Planning, Budgeting & Information Systems
Leadership in the Public Sector
Urban Politics and Public Policy

Apply by 2/1
• Field Studies • Service-Learning • Third World Service-Learning
• Self-Designed Majors • Interdisciplinary Classes • Green Campus

Office of Undergraduate Admissions
Seattle University
PO Box 222000
Seattle, WA 98122-1090

206. 296. 2000
800. 426. 7123 (out-of-state)
admissions@seattleu.edu
www.seattleu.edu

Sheldon Jackson College

275 Students   Sitka, Alaska

Sheldon Jackson College is for the student choosing a decidedly different and bolder path through life. The campus is located on the western shore of Baranof Island in Southeast Alaska and enjoys a moderate climate year round. Encircled by mountains and settled between ancient forests and the Pacific Ocean, it provides a vast wilderness classroom for education and discovery. Within walking distance of campus students can investigate tidelands and old-growth spruce and hemlock forests, observe freshwater estuaries, high alpine meadows or kayak through Sitka Sound, paddling past sea lions and humpback whales. The campus borders on the 16.8 million acre Tongass National Forest, the largest temperate rain forest in North America.

While many colleges make commitments to ethnic diversity and cultural sensitivity in attempting to create a multicultural learning environment, Sheldon Jackson College provides the reality of such a community. Alaska Natives currently comprise seventeen percent of the student body. Some of these students come from villages in Alaska where subsistence hunting, fishing, and gathering are essential to survival. Others celebrate their native heritage within a westernized society. The Annual Gathering of the People celebrates the heritage, culture and current experiences of Alaska's Native Peoples — complete with dancing and a potluck dinner in which traditional Native foods (seal, whale, herring eggs, moose, and Eskimo ice cream) can be sampled. This is a College of rich cultural and geographical diversity. Overall, students come from 40 states and several foreign countries.

Sheldon Jackson believes that it is important for students to explore and develop the spiritual component of their lives, and to commit themselves in very practical ways to the application of that understanding in the profession of service. SJ is affiliated with the Presbyterian Church, and while providing an education in which the exploration of Christian faith and values is nurtured, it challenges students to develop a sensitivity to other faith traditions. The Community Service Program provides opportunities for students to volunteer while receiving tuition assistance for service.

The Environmental Awareness Team and Outdoor Recreation Program sponsor a very successful city-wide Spring Expo to celebrate Earth Day, complete with Intertribal Native drumming, an Eskimo blanket toss, sea kayaking, a river traverse, climbing wall session, snorkeling, tree planting, and bald eagle release from the Alaska Raptor Rehabilitation Center.

The Wilderness Orientation Program allows new students to participate in a wilderness adventure which could include sea kayaking, a hike to the crater of Mt. Edgecumbe on nearby Kruzof Island, and a sampling of wild edibles. Opportunities abound for students to become involved as explorers and caretakers of the ancient forests and Pacific Ocean which surround Sheldon Jackson College. Sea kayaking, hiking, camping, scuba diving, hunting, and fishing are all popular pastimes.

Sheldon Jackson takes pride in offering top rate academic programs, adventurous experiences outside the classroom, and the comfort and security of a small, close-knit campus community. It is also proud of the fact that annual tuition is about 50 percent less than other private colleges around the country.

MAKING A DIFFERENCE STUDIES

FISHERIES

Sheldon Jackson has the only college-owned private salmon hatchery in the U.S. Hands-on work experience includes culturing shellfish and algae, taking eggs, and collecting samples.

Salmonid Culture
Fish Health Management
Ecosystem Analysis
Marine Invertebrate Zoology

Marine Biology
Oceanography
Fish Ecology
Hatchery Practicum

• **Mariculture**   Methods of growing marine invertebrates and sea vegetables in the North Pacific. Species include oysters, clams, scallops, mussels, abalone, sea urchins, kelps and others. Lab emphasizes biology of organisms that could be cultured and collection of immature specimens to culture.

NATURAL RESOURCE MANAGEMENT & DEVELOPMENT

Surveying and Mapping
Field Studies in Resource Management
Native Perspectives on Resource Mgm't.
Natural Resource Policies and Law
Economic Considerations in Natural Resources

Forest Ecology
Forest/Range Soil
Photogrammetry
Wildlife Ecology and Management

OUTDOOR LEADERSHIP

Foundations of Experiential Education
Hiking
Sea Kayaking
Wilderness First Responder
Outdoor Recreation Planning

Ethics and Leadership
Marine Safety Instruction
Expedition Coastal Kayaking
Rock Climbing and Mountaineering
Intro to Outdoor Education

ECOLOGY

Systematic Botany
Animal Physiology
Limnology
Fish Genetics & Health Management
Environmental Interpretation

Plant Ecology
Global Perspectives in Environmental Sciences
Marine Invertebrate Zoology
Intro. to Geographic Information Systems
Conservation Biology

MARINE BIOLOGY

Introduction to Marine Biology
Ichthyology
Mariculture
Conservation Biology
Advanced Open Water SCUBA Diving

Marine Invertebrate Zoology
Fish Genetics/Health
Oceanography
Basic Open Water SCUBA Diving
Global Perspectives in Environmental Science

EDUCATION   HUMAN SERVICES

Rolling Applications
Student Body: 26% Native American, 10% Other Minority

• Service-Learning   • Self-Designed Majors   • Required Community Service   • Field Studies

Director of Admissions
Sheldon Jackson College
801 Lincoln St.
Sitka, AK 99835

800. 478. 4556
907. 747. 5208
www.sj-alaska.edu
admissions@sj-alaska.edu.

SIERRA INSTITUTE

HUMBOLDT STATE UNIVERSITY

At the end of his sophomore year the young John Muir left the University of Wisconsin for what he called the "university of the wilderness". He traveled to the Sierra Nevada mountains in California and began a lifelong adventure in learning directly from nature. It is that first-hand contact with the natural world that Sierra Institute programs seek to provide.

Sierra Institute offers academic field courses taught entirely in wildlands – students never enter a campus classroom. For up to a full academic quarter, students form small traveling field schools, backpacking through the western U.S., Central and South America.

Program coursework is diverse, interdisciplinary, and always focused on specific places. You can study field ecology and natural history in Utah's canyon lands, California's Sierra Nevada, or the rainforests of Belize. If you study environmental ethics and philosophy in the Sierra, you will read John Muir and Gary Snyder while following in their footsteps. In the Pacific Northwest you experience old growth forests, northern spotted owls, clearcuts, and conservation biology while studying public lands management.

Whether studying natural science or nature philosophy, Sierra Institute students all share a common experience – their classroom is alive. There is an immediacy to coursework that enhances and supplements the educational process. Academic and experiential learning combine to create a richness rarely found on campus. The direct knowledge of the rhythms of the natural world that students get by learning outside also fosters a deep sense of place.

All instructors have advanced degrees and are skilled wilderness leaders with appropriate first aid training. With credit conferred by relevant departments at Humboldt State University, our class curriculums have been designed to include the landscapes and cultures in which they are taught. Group size is limited to 10-12 students. Most programs are 9 weeks in length and grant 12 semester units. In the summer some shorter programs of 3 and 6 weeks are offered, granting a maximum of 4 or 8 semester units. Humboldt State is on the semester system (1 semester unit equals 1.5 quarter units).

The physical pace is slow, allowing participants to sink into the place and come to know it well – no prior backpacking experience is necessary. Because of the small group size, daily lectures and discussions are usually lively and always intimate.

A Sierra Institute experience can serve as a powerful springboard back into the university life that surrounds – and increasingly threatens – the backcountry. Many students, upon returning to campus, are inspired to work on the environmental problems facing society. One recent student remarked that "until Sierra Institute I had thought environmental issues were not worth discussing because they were hopelessly unsolvable. Now I know there exist positive solutions and that change is possible."

Sierra Institute seeks to combine critical perspectives with profound personal experience and to stimulate an overall ecological literacy. It asks students both to understand the ecology of their place and to work toward sustainable living in school and beyond. In an urban culture that continues to separate itself from its wild roots, we need educational opportunities that reconnect culture with nature. It is just these bonds that Sierra Institute programs foster.

MAKING A DIFFERENCE STUDIES

Sierra Institute field programs can vary from year to year. These are a recent example.

THE HIGH SIERRA: NATURAL HISTORY FIELD STUDIES

Spend three weeks exploring one of the most spectacular mountain areas in North America. Focus will be the high country of the central Sierra Nevada. The lofty granite peaks, secluded alpine lakes, and flower-strewn meadows are as inspiring to today's student as they were to John Muir, who called it the "gentle wilderness." You will study principles of ecology and geology and learn techniques to identify the plants, birds, and mammals of the Sierra. Issues concerning human history and attitudes towards wilderness will enrich our ecological studies.

Sierra Nevada Natural History   Wilderness Skills and Nature Awareness

RECLAIMING YOUR PLACE: BIOREGIONALISM, COMMUNITY & SUSTAINABLE LIVING

How you express your personal relationship to place is unique to you and your gifts, skills, and passions. It may be as habitat restoration, community organizing, art, music, dance, gardening, involvement in local politics, ritual, etc. Through the study and practice of a multitude of expressions, spanning hunter-gatherer culture to contemporary bioregional activism, we develop our own understanding of how we want to claim, and be claimed by, the place in which we live.

Wilderness Skills and Nature Awareness   Bioregionalism & Sustainability: Theory & Practice
Perspectives on Nature   Environmental Ed. & the Wilderness Experience

CALIFORNIA WILDERNESS: NATURE PHILOSOPHY, RELIGION & ECOPSYCHOLOGY

All our actions begin with some understanding of who we are and what our place is in nature. This program is an interdisciplinary exploration of worldviews, blending philosophy, psychology, religious studies, literature, and natural sciences. Perhaps grand questions are best pursued in grand locations. Travel to three different wild areas of and make backpacking excursions into each enabling you to see some diversity of the state, and a variety of landforms, textures, and moods.

RAINFOREST FIELD STUDIES: GUATEMALA AND BELIZE

Provides the opportunity to immerse yourself firsthand in the tropical ecosystems of northern Central America, and in the cultural milieu of local peoples. Primary focus will be tropical forest ecology and natural history. Discuss tropical forest conservation and issues of sustainability and cultural survival. The practicum course will examine the process of experiential and wilderness education. One must comprehend rainforests mysterious workings, appreciate their pivotal role in the well being of the planet, and develop effective strategies for their protection.

Natural History of Central American Rainforests   Evolution & Conservation of Neotropical Diversity
Wilderness Skills and Nature Awareness   Environmental Ed. & the Wilderness Experience

HAWAIIAN CULTURAL RENAISSANCE, ETHNOBOTANY AND HISTORY

Study archeological and historical evidence for the foundation and development of pre-European contact Hawaiian culture, the most complex society in Oceania at the time of contact with Europeans in 1778. Consider transformations of Hawaiian society from the arrival of Polynesian voyagers (circa 300 AD) to the present. Learn about Hawaiian life from people of Hawaiian descent who are maintaining and revitalizing key aspects of "traditional" culture—language, ocean voyaging, hula, martial arts, taro farming, medicinal plant cultivation, healing, 'awa (kava) ceremony, and temple ceremony. These efforts constitute the flourishing Hawaiian Cultural Renaissance Movement.

• Field Studies   • Team Teaching   • Multidisciplinary Classes   • Vegetarian & Vegan Meals

Sierra Institute   707. 826. 3731
Office of Extended Education   sierra@humboldt.edu
Humboldt State University   www.sierrainstitute.org
Arcata, CA. 95521-8299

STANFORD UNIVERSITY

6,500 Undergraduates   Palo Alto, California

At Stanford, students are engaging in community service in growing numbers. Service has become part of student life in classrooms, in the residences, and in extracurricular programs. According to recent senior surveys over 70% of undergraduates are involved in public service during their Stanford careers. Numerous student service organizations have taken root in the ethnic community centers, student residences, and religious organizations on campus. The Haas Center for Public Service serves as a focal point for public and community service locally, across the U.S., and overseas. By engaging students in the widest variety of service activities – through hands-on action, policy research, or community problem solving – the Center enriches their education and inspires them to commit their lives to improving society.

The act of service is only the beginning for the Stanford-educated citizen who seeks to make an impact in society. Volunteer work does not end with the completion of a "service action;" rather, it provides an experiential foundation for intellectual work, including academic scholarship, that attempts to answer questions raised by the service experiences.

Interest in study-service connections is growing among students and faculty. More than 50 courses integrate public service activity with study. A few of the courses with a service component include: The Process and Practice of Community Service; Aging: From Biology to Social Policy; Children and Society Program; The State of Public Education in Urban Communities; Women in the African-American Freedom Struggle; The Impact of AIDS; HIV/AIDS Training Education; Policy Making at the Local and Regional Level; and Urban Studies Community Organization.

Among the most intensive courses is "Poverty and Homelessness", in which students gain an understanding of the nature of poverty and homelessness from readings, class discussions and working with homeless families or individuals at shelters. The Community Writing Project has involved thousands of freshmen, matching students with more than 100 community agencies that need newsletter articles, grant proposals, public education materials, and other kinds of writing.

The Goldman Honors Program in Environmental Science & Policy brings students from the schools of Humanities and Sciences, Engineering, and Earth Sciences together into small project-focused seminars to analyze important environmental problems. Stanford is highly interdisciplinary, and the "thin walls" between disciplines cultivate an environment of intense creativity that redefines what it means to be intellectually well rounded. With each seminar you take, faculty member or classmate you meet, you will make connections between classroom conversations and real-life applications. You will learn from faculty who are themselves policy-makers, inventors, and entrepreneurs involved in the most pressing issues facing society.

Through small, progressive steps begining with student gardens across campus, the Student Community Gardens hopes to create a fully developed Sustainable Food System at Stanford University that focuses on local sourcing and closed loop systems. In the future, the project will build a working farm on campus, establish product sourcing that prioritizes local and organic sources, and develop a biodiesel waste vegetable oil recycling system.

In 2004, the University received Santa Clara County 's Green Business Certification, recognizing that Stanford, with the major contribution of its residential dining halls and campus café operations, embraces cooperative solutions that protect the vast economic and environmental resources with which this community is blessed.

Making a Difference Studies

International Relations

Intelligence and US Foreign Policy
20th Century Eastern Europe
International Security in a Changing World
Globalization & Organization
Africa in the 20th Century

Theories & Concepts in International Relations
International Law and International Relations
Decision Making in International Crises
Palestine, Zionism, & the Arab-Israeli Conflict
Regime Change: Comparative Theories

Ethics in Society

Encourages students to reflect on fundamental issues of moral and political philosophy including: the nature and implications of treating people with equal dignity and respect; the scope of liberty; the legitimacy of government; and the meaning of responsibility. It extends moral concern and reflection across disciplines such as medicine, law, economics, international relations, and public policy.

Introduction to Moral Theory
Medical Ethics
Distribution of Income and Wealth
Character and the Good Life
Contemporary Theories of Justice

The Ethics of Social Decisions
Economics and Public Policy
Computers, Ethics, and Social Responsibility
Ethics and the Built Environment
Ethics of Development in the Global Environment

Urban Studies: Community Organization, Architecture & Urban Design, Urban Planning

Urban Economics
Environmental Justice in the U.S.
Education of Immigrants in Cities
Education for Liberation
The Politics of Development

Design & Construction of Affordable Housing
Ecological Anthropology
Spirituality & Non-Violent Social Transformation
Green Architecture
Utopia & Reality in Modern Urban Planning

Feminist Studies

Perils of Proclaimed Equality
Language and Gender
Gender, Power and Justice
Int'l. Women's Health & Human Rights
Goddesses and Gender in Indian Religion

Women, Sexuality, and Health
Women in the Health Care Debate
Women - Transition to Democracy: Latin America
Global Politics of Human Rights
Status, Expectations, and Rewards

Cultural & Social Anthropology

Ethics of Development in a Global Environment
Tibetan Ritual Life
Race and Medicine
Anthropological Approaches to Rights

Law, Rights and Subjectivity
Conservation & Community Development: Latin Amer.
Cultural Approaches to Education & Development
Environmental Justice: Nature, Identity, Politics

Environmental Engineering

Sustainable Water Resources Development
Big Dams, City Hall and The Sierra Club
Ethical Issues in Civil Engineering
Air Pollution Modeling
Energy Resources

Green Architecture
Watersheds and Wetlands
Environmental Policy Design & Implementation
Energy Efficient Building
Air Pollution: From Urban Smog to Global Change

Race and Ethnicity   Public Policy   Middle Eastern Studies

Apply by: 12/15

Student Body: 47% Minority   Average class size under 30 students
• Interdisciplinary   • Service-Learning

Office of Undergraduate Admission
Bakewell Building, 355 Galvez St.
Stanford University
Stanford, CA 94305-3020

650. 723. 2091
www.stanford.edu
admissions@stanford.edu

STERLING COLLEGE

100 Students   Craftsbury Common, VT

Sterlings Goal is "to build responsible problems solvers who become stewards of the environment as they pursue productive lives." Sterling College is a learning community that cultivates the wisdom, skills, and values needed for sustainable living. Sterling's motto, Working Hands~Working Minds, embraces integration of research and discussion, field studies, culture, history, and the dynamics of human relations in a learning environment that combines solid academics with experiential, hands-on learning. Through the study of the environment students are exposed to the traditional tenets of a liberal arts education in a way that is rich and meaningful. Sterling College students gain intellectual and physical competence, practical skills, and personal confidence in their ability to solve the problems we face in today's world.

Unique experiences engage students in adventurous and challenging situations. Each incoming class completes Winter Expedition—a three night camping trip celebrating the end of first semester. Winter Expedition and other similar experiences serve to develop group communication and leadership skills, encourage personal growth, and provide opportunity for students to explore the landscape surrounding the College through rock climbing, cross-country skiing, snowshoeing, and paddling.

Community is vital and students play an important role in creating and sustaining Sterling's evolving community. An integral part of the community and curriculum is a campus-wide Work Program. Students function as the work force of the College and are employed an average of six hours a week in one of over 100 different jobs. In exchange for work, students earn a $1,450 tuition and books credit. Sterling College believes that connecting people directly to their support system fosters greater care for the environment and its communities.

Sustainable Sterling is an effort directed toward greening the campus and infrastructure of the College. This initiative challenges the college community to model appropriately scaled and regionally suitable sustainable living practices. Projects include harvesting an average of 9,844 pounds of organic produce for the Sterling College kitchen from the campus gardens and local farmers, diverting an average of 15,410 pounds of food waste from the landfill by composting, encouraging sustainable transportation through a Green Bikes program, and use of Sterling's own harvested timber/lumber to build lean-tos, bike and garden sheds, and fencing.

For over twenty years the Internship Program has placed students in 45 states and 18 foreign countries. The 10-week environmental internship helps students gain real experiences with organizations such as federal land management agencies, sustainable farms, wildlife rehabilitation centers, or outdoor leadership programs.

Sterling College is not like most colleges. Strong academics and experiential learning opportunities create a dynamic and progressive learning environment. Grounded in an awareness of the world and its communities, Sterling College demands a forward-looking approach to learning, to growing, and to living. Throughout the curriculum, students focus on environmental studies, discuss sustainability, and learn how people can embrace the strength of community to create change in the world. In keeping with this philosophy, Sterling College offers the special programs listed below.

Global Field Studies immerse students in different cultures to learn about social ecology and environmental sustainability. Destinations include:

- Belize: Students travel to this small tropical country to study marine and rainforest ecosystems and explore their natural communities and related management issues.

- Iceland and the Scottish Isles: Students explore the ecology, ancient history, and culture of the North Atlantic through investigations into geography and geological processes. Stays in coastal villages allow for immersion in communities that embrace traditional folkways, with time for discussions with local peoples pressured by technology and a global economy.

- James Bay region of Quebec, Canada: Study is focused on hydroelectric development and its impact on the local ecosystems and native peoples.

- Japan: Students explore sustainable practices on the northern island of Hokkaido through visits to managed forests, organic farms, and Zen gardens; conversations with students and professors at Hokkaido and Obihiro Universities; and investigations into Japanese land use practices.

- Scandinavia: Students research environmental sustainability in Denmark, Iceland, Norway, and Sweden through visits to alternative energy sites, investigations of eco-villages, tours of industries featuring green technology, and discussions with members of non-governmental organizations dedicated to improving the environment.

- Lapland: Students travel above the Arctic Circle to Sápmi, as the indigenous Sámi call their homeland in Scandinavian Lapland, and explore the marine, forest, and tundra lifeways of traditional reindeer herders.

The Center for Northern Studies at Sterling College integrates field research with educational programs addressing the ecosystems and people of Artic and subarctic environments and the challenges of sustainable interaction in a global society. The Center offers study-away options to students from other colleges and supports the Northern Studies major.

The Sustainable Agriculture Semester immerses students in the daily rhythms and realities of farming. Focusing on sustainability, this summer semester is a program of work and study exploring holistic management of plants, animals, and land. The farm includes certified organic vegetable gardens, solar and wind powered barns, and a variety of livestock including sheep for food and fiber, goats, pigs, steers, poultry, and a draft horse team for light work.

The Mountain Cultures Semester combines trekking, mountaineering, service work, and homestays in local villages to explore cultural differences in attitudes toward natural and human resources. Prior destinations include the Solu Khumbu region of Nepal, Sikkim in India, and the Sierra Madre mountains of Mexico.

Each year Sterling College offers two full tuition scholarships to incoming students who have demonstrated an exemplary commitment to environmental service and volunteerism. Any student who has not previously attended Sterling College is welcome to apply.

> *Until the great mass of the people shall be filled with the sense of responsibility for easch other's welfare, social justice can never be attained.*
>
> Helen Keller

MAKING A DIFFERENCE STUDIES

CONSERVATION ECOLOGY

As humans continue to alter biodiversity in the environment, the need for well-rounded individuals who can present solutions to an increasing number of environmental problems grows. The major prepares students to study and understand the world from diverse points of view and use a variety of methods to create and communicate viable solutions to pressing problems. Maintaining or restoring habitats to support natural patterns in biodiversity is an important practical application in this field.

Wildland Stewardship
Fish and Wildlife Management
Geology
Vertebrate Natural History

Conservation Biology
Forestry
International Forestry and Wildlife Issues
Geographic Information Systems

NORTHERN STUDIES

More than ever, skilled professionals are needed to monitor, protect, and care for this fragile part of the planet. Northern Studies provides an ideal discipline for rigorous research in a pristine but also imperiled environment. The major combines research in all aspects of the circumpolar North while promoting a broad understanding of the diverse people, cultures, and history of the region.

Stories and Storytelling
Literature and Film of the North
Quaternary Studies
Winter Ecology

Indigenous Cultures of the Circumpolar North
Community Development in the Circumpolar North
Conservation Biology
Polar Biota: Flora and Fauna

OUTDOOR EDUCATION AND LEADERSHIP

This program combines the study of education and leadership theory and practice with technical outdoor travel and adventure skills. Students explore issues ranging from ethical controversies and risk management to program design. Students gain a solid background in ecology, environmental science, and recreational resource management.

Wilderness First Responder
Wilderness Canoe Tripping
Group Process for Outdoor Leaders
Education and Culture

Wildland Stewardship
Foundations of Outdoor Education & Leadership
Experiential Education Curriculum
Rockclimbing Techniques for Outdoor Leaders

SUSTAINABLE AGRICULTURE

Students learn the principles of science and economics that underlie agricultural systems and learn a variety of agricultural techniques and practices applicable to the small, diversified farm and homestead. Graduates typically work to develop innovative farming techniques and vibrant local economies and markets, while protecting natural resources such as soil and water quality and wildlife habitat.

Livestock Systems Management
Draft Horse Management
Global Agriculture
Plant and Soil Science

Organic Vegetable Production
Human Nutrition
Exploring Alternative Agriculture
Animal Science

Rolling Admissions   Early Action: 12/15

• Work College   • Team Teaching   • Self-Designed Majors   • Service-Learning • Field Studies
• Interdisciplinary Classes   • Green Campus   • Optional SAT's   • Vegetarian/Vegan Meals

Admissions Office
Sterling College
P.O. Box 72
Craftsbury Common, VT 05287

802. 586. 7711
800. 648. 3591
admissions@sterlingcollege.edu
www.sterlingcollege.edu

STETSON UNIVERSITY

2,250 Undergraduates   DeLand, Florida

"Commitment to values" is not just a phrase at Stetson University; it's a way of life. Stetson is committed to helping you grow and develop into a purposeful and values-driven member of society. You'll be challenged to reflect on why you hold the beliefs and values that you do. You'll explore diversity and gender equity, figure out how religion or spirituality fits into your life, and discover ways you can serve the world and other people. Liberal education at Stetson means liberating yourself from prejudice. It means studying with and living with people who have had life experiences different from your own.

Stetson starts by affirming the human dignity, worth, and equality of each member of the community. Through sharing life stories and the stories of our ancestors, we learn how people have been unfairly treated or privileged because of race, ethnicity, religion, economic class, or sexual orientation. Stetson is also committed to valuing women's voices, ensuring that University policies and practices are not discriminatory, and distributing resources equally between men and women.

When you go to college in a place as beautiful as coastal Florida, you can't help but be aware of your surroundings. As individuals and as a university, Stetson is committed to living in harmony with the environment. Students have many opportunities to participate in environmental programs, ranging from beach clean-up days to fish census research at local springs. Through its Florida Native Plant Initiative, the University is becoming a leader of a new approach to landscaping, allowing use of only native Florida flora on its 174-acre main campus.

In view of the unprecedented world environmental crisis, Stetson University has committed itself to incorporating principles of sustainable living on its campus; not to compromise the lives of future human generations nor diminish the health of planetary ecosystems. As a responsible institution of higher learning, Stetson intends to advance the ecological literacy of the university community by modeling environmental stewardship in its physical plant and by embodying sustainability in its institutional operations.

A core curriculum in liberal studies develops breadth of understanding and serious engagement with principles of ethical decision-making. The University is dedicated to promoting a lifelong commitment to social responsibility and integrating service learning into the curriculum. Students are encouraged to combine classroom learning with community service - so the things you learn in the classroom go hand-in-hand with the things you learn through community service. Because of this commitment to social responsibility, students, faculty, and staff have the ability to directly engage in activities that foster values and improve the campus, community, and world.

One of Stetson's central goals is to create an inclusive community where social responsibility is emphasized, and where groups work collaboratively rather than competitively. The Diversity Council works to foster change by recognizing that points of difference resulting from racial/ethnic background, gender, sexual orientation and religious heritage, encourage a celebration of the points of intersection. The Council promotes the belief that through the splendor of different experiences, we come to realize we are all members of one over-arching, values-driven community of learners. The Diversity Council (a group of faculty, staff and students) is committed to incorporating the essence and significance of the different backgrounds, perspectives and experiences of people from all walks of life into the culture of the institution.

MAKING A DIFFERENCE STUDIES

AQUATIC AND MARINE BIOLOGY

Stetson is situated in an area with springs, rivers, lakes, swamps, salt marsh and ocean ecosystems. Senior projects include studies of manatee, nesting ecology of turtles, and impact of artificial reef design.

Marine Biology
Invertebrate Zoology
Experimental Biology and Biostatistics
Conservation Biology
Ecology of our Changing Earth

Limnology (Freshwater Biology)
Aquatic/Marine Biology Internship
Ecology
Animal Behavior
Environmental Biology

ECONOMICS

Exploring Economies in Different Countries
Economies of Russia and China
Energy, Environment, and Economics
Economics, Freedom, and Human Values
Economic Problems of Latin America

Current Economic Policies and Issues
Political Economy of Southern Africa
Economics of Race and Gender
Economics, Ethics, and Religion
Public Finance

- **Humane Economics** Looks at the duality of humans by adding other-interest, cooperation, caring, and compassion to the standard course emphasis on self-interest, competition, individualism, and conflict. Emphasizes the melding of community service with study in the classroom.

LATIN AMERICAN STUDIES

Survey of Spanish American Literature
Economic Problems of Latin America
Environment and Development
Politics of the Developing World
Latin American Politics
Contemporary Mexico/Contemporary Spain

Mayan Culture
International Economics
Latin America in the Modern World
History of U.S. - Latin American Relations
Sociology of Developing Societies
Internship in the Mexican-American Community

APPLIED ETHICS/PHILOSOPHY (MINOR)

Ethical Decision Making
Environmental Ethics
Economics, Freedom, and Human Values
Management Ethics and Decision Making
The Ethics of Peace and War
Ethics in Religious Perspective

Feminist Ethics;
Ethics in Communication
Economics, Ethics and Religion
Environmental Politics;
Frontiers in Medical Ethics
Ethics and Technology

RELIGION

Spiritualities East and West
Race, Gender, Class, and Religion
Indo-Tibetan Buddhism
Islam: The Religion of the Prophet
History of American Christianity

Buddhism and Christianity: A Comparative Study
Frontiers in Medical Ethics
Varieties of American Religions
Charismatic Leadership in Religion and Society
Male and Female in Biblical Perspectives

Goddesses, Whores, Wives, and Preachers: The Feminine Voice in Religion

INTEGRATIVE HEALTH SCIENCE   INTERNATIONAL AFFAIRS   GEOGRAPHY   HISTORY

Apply by 3/15

- Self-Designed Majors   • Service-Learning   • Field Studies   • Green Campus

Stetson University.
Office of Admissions
Unit 8378, Griffith Hall
DeLand, FL 32723

800. 688. 0101
386. 822. 7100
admissions@stetson.edu
www.stetson.edu

Juniata College students engaging in a study of birds during which they band the birds for identification.

Grinnell's commitment to social responsibility has been a large part of its history. Students are encouraged to link community service to their academic interests. Here students raise money to help the needy.

Swarthmore College

1,500 Students   Swarthmore, PA

If you want to make a difference in the world, Swarthmore College will encourage and support you all the way. Swarthmore is widely known for academic excellence; what insiders also know is that the academics serve a larger mission to train students to ask hard questions, to explore how things are, and then to act to improve their world.

At Swarthmore, you'll get a philosophical and academic background that will prepare you for a life of service to your community. On a practical level, at Swarthmore you'll find scholarships for activists, funding for student-run social action projects, and a fully-staffed volunteer clearinghouse that matches students with organizations that need help. You can choose a concentration such as Peace and Conflict Studies or Environmental Studies which will prepare you to make a profession of changing the world. Courses in social action combine academic study with classes spent actually tutoring poor children or working with residents of a housing project to improve access to medical care. There's nothing as powerful as the combination of theory and personal knowledge: students come away knowing their own power and how to use it effectively.

Swarthmore's campus is populated by people who believe not only that they can make a difference, but that they must. Students often find in the College's Quaker traditions - a moral and social compass that inspires them to work for equality, peace, and justice. For many, Swarthmore's meaning lies in the clarification of their values and in the imperative to use those skills and values in the service of creating a better world. You'll meet professors who are involved in international struggles for peace and justice, and students who spend their breaks not in Aspen, but in Guatemala or Northern Ireland.

Swarthmore's academic atmosphere is as exhilarating as it is demanding, because every course is informed by the belief that things can change if one is willing to take risks and do the work. Cynicism is blessedly rare, and there are many opportunities and support systems for idealism. Students may apply for Lang Scholarships of up to $10,000 to support a social action project which they design and carry out. For instance: a housing rehabilitation project started by a Lang Scholar over ten years ago is now carried forward by the people who bought the houses at low cost through the project. Any student may apply for a grant up to $1,000 for a social service project of their own design.

CIVIC (Cooperative Involvement as Volunteers in Communities) runs seven volunteer programs and puts students in touch with 200 other organizations that need volunteers - from soup kitchens to AIDS care. CIVIC teaches the skills and sensitivities volunteers need to be effective.

There are many other opportunities at Swarthmore, and students can make of them what they will. Follow the lead of the student who built her entire senior year around a project to make health care accessible in hard-hit housing projects. She researched residents' needs and preferences, organized care with a local hospital, identified and trained people who are willing to help their neighbors tap into the system, and wrote papers on her experience-all for credit.

To have meaning beyond the lives of its graduates, a great college must serve the interests of the larger world. Swarthmore's educational and intellectual excellence - coupled with its ethical, moral, and social values - have provided generations of leaders in every imaginable field. These values are not just those of today's Swarthmore; they have roots in its history and traditions. The College has thrived through its uncompromising commitment to offering a liberal arts education of the highest quality - an education that has consistently helped students learn to question and explore, to think critically, to develop their imaginations, and to act responsibly and with conviction. They are both its legacy and its future.

MAKING A DIFFERENCE STUDIES

ENVIRONMENTAL STUDIES

Students take related courses as diverse as religion and engineering, and conclude with a practical senior project. One recent project: building a prototype house of straw bales - strong, well-insulated, cheap, biodegradable, and not prone to fire, rats, or mildew.

Sustainable Systems Analysis

Water Quality and Pollution Control

Religion and Ecology

Swarthmore and the Biosphere

Psychology of Environmental Problems

The Environment and Contemplative Practices

Marine Biology

Solar Energy Systems

Economics of Environment & Nat. Resources

Problems in Energy Technology

PEACE AND CONFLICT STUDIES

As a college founded by Quaker pacifists, Swarthmore has a strong tradition of pacifism buttressed by a large and comprehensive peace library.

Prejudice and Social Relations

Power, Authority and Conflict

Race and Foreign Affairs

War and Peace

Nonviolence and Social Change

Economic Development

Indigenous Resistance & Revolt in Latin America

Buddhist Social Ethics

Peace Movement in the US: Women & Peace

Human Rights, Refugees & International Law

PUBLIC POLICY

Ethics and Public Policy

Polling, Public Opinion, and Public Policy

Environmental Politics and Policy

Defense Policy

Politics of Population

Urban Education

Race, Ethnicity, Representation, & Redistricting

Labor and Social Economics

China and the World

Economic Development

Global Policy and International Institutions: Hunger and Environmental Threats

SOCIOLOGY AND ANTHROPOLOGY

Bioethics: A Sociological Perspective

Explorations of Diaspora Populations

Islam in Global Context

Explorations of Diaspora Populations

Latin American Urbanization

Social Inequality

Psychological Anthropology

Language and Culture

Ethnoecology: The Resurrection of Traditional Environmental Knowledge

EDUCATION

Educational Psychology

Environmental Education

Political Socialization and Schools

Gender and Education

Literacies and Social Identities

Child Development and Social Policy

Social and Cultural Perspectives in Education

Counseling: Principles and Practices

Political Economy of Education Urban Education

Race, Ethnicity and Inequality in Education

WOMEN'S STUDIES   PUBLIC POLICY   ECONOMICS

Apply by 1/1   Early Decision 11/15

Student Body: 32% Minority

• Service Learning   • Self-Designed Majors   • Team Teaching   • Interdisciplinary Majors

• Field Studies   • Vegetarian Meals

Office of Admissions

Swarthmore College

500 College Avenue

Swarthmore, PA 19081-1390

610. 328. 8300

800. 667. 3110

www.swarthmore.edu

admissions@.swarthmore.edu

TUFTS UNIVERSITY

5,000 Undergraduate Students   Medford, Mass.

Since its founding in 1852, Tufts University's commitment to using knowledge, skills, and scholarship for active public leadership has broadened traditional definitions of service, citizenship and education. At Tufts, the responsibility of each individual to their local, national, and international communities is a basic tenet of the University's mission and philosophy. Public service is promoted across the curriculum from the College of Engineering and the Sackler School of Biomedical Sciences, to the College of Liberal Arts, the Fletcher School of Law and Diplomacy, and the Urban and Environmental Policy Program.

Tufts is a community of scholars dedicated to change through service. Many courses and departments employ community service as a method of enhancing classroom learning and performance of service. Service-learning courses can be found in Education and Child Study, as well as in Mechanical Engineering and Chemistry.

John DiBiaggio, former President of Tufts and ardent supporter of service learning was committed to making public service a hallmark of a Tufts education: "We are using all the best educational innovations of this century to produce a corps of thinking, caring men and women dedicated to bettering their society." Tufts works to enhance the public service education, research, and community outreach activities of students and faculty through the Lincoln Filene Center, the Public Service Task Force, the Center for Environmental Management among others. Sophomore, junior, and senior year students accepted into Citizenship and Public Service Scholars Program, an innovative leadership program, commit to rigorous community project work, training, and knowledge development.

Building on a tradition of service, Tufts' students engage in developing new initiatives for public service. Many organizations not only participate in, but create venues for, community service. Tufts' largest and oldest community service organization is the Leonard Carmichael Society with a core membership of 700 students participating in ongoing programs. Many cultural groups, such as the Pan-African Alliance and the Asian Community at Tufts, have long-standing service commitments to nearby ethnic communities. Groups such as Environmental Consciousness Outreach and Oxfam Cafe also inform the student body on local, national, and international challenges to community and the environment.

Tufts' commitment to citizen education does not simply start with matriculation and end with graduation; through the Community Service Option, students may dedicate their time, and energy to serving social needs before, during, and after their years at Tufts. Newly accepted students may defer admission for one year if they commit to a minimum of twenty-five hours of community service during that time.

Tufts Dining Services is improving the sustainability of the products served in dining halls and sold at campus stores and cafes. Current initiatives include revised menus with a greater range of locally-grown products, more organic offerings in dining halls, and the designation of one on-campus cafe as an all Fair Trade venue, in addition to the availability of Fair Trade coffee in all dining locations. Tufts is also implementing expanded composting and recycling services.

Tufts was the first university to adopt a new set of strenuous climate change goals drafted by international leaders from the U.S. and Canada. Tufts was also the first university to join the Chicago Climate Exchange. And for the last several years, Tufts has ranked as one of the top Peace Corps suppliers among universities its size.

MAKING A DIFFERENCE STUDIES

ENVIRONMENTAL STUDIES: ENVIRONMENTAL SCIENCE, ENVIRONMENT & TECHNOLOGY, ENVIRONMENT AND SOCIETY

Environmental Biology
Time, Nature, and Humanity
Pollution Prevention Management
Sustainable Development
Marine Biology

Population and Community Ecology
Bioethics
Politics of Environmental Policy in the U. S.
Environmental Health and Safety
Politics of Sustainable Communities

COMMUNITY HEALTH

How anthropology, medicine, history, sociology, psychology, economics, ethics, political science, public health, and biology, affect communities' strategies to promote health and cope with disease.

Domestic Violence
Community Health: Theory & Practice
Policy for Aging Populations
Challenge of World Hunger
Humanitarian Policy & Public Health

Intro to Hazardous Materials Management
Religion, Health and Healing
Health, Ethics and Policy
Health of New Immigrants
Emerging Global Health Crisis

CIVIL AND ENVIRONMENTAL ENGINEERING

Intro to Environmental Engineering
Hydrology & Water Resource Engineering
Bioremediation: Natural and Enhanced
Pollution Prevention Management
Occupational and Environmental Health

Intro to Hazardous Materials Management
Groundwater Hydrology
Earth Support Systems
Air Pollution
Public Health

CHILD STUDY

The Child and the Education Process
Personal-Social Development
Language and the New Immigrant
American Sign Language and the Deaf
Social Policy for Children and Families

Developmental Crises
Community Field Placement
Fostering Literacy Development
Child Advocacy Educational Rights
Rights of Children to Social Services

INTERNATIONAL RELATIONS

Topics in International Development
Economics of Food & Nutrition Policy
International Global Human Rights
Cross Cultural Political Analysis
Cold War America

Natural Resources & Enviro Economics
Sociology of War and Peace
Political Economy of World Hunger
Non-Governmental Actors in Int'l. Relations
Re-Building the European Union

PEACE AND JUSTICE

Dissent and American Foreign Policy
Peace, Justice & Social Change
Inner Peace, Outer Action
Enviro Justice, Security & Sustainability

Global Justice
Cultural Legacies of the Atomic Bomb
International Conflict Management
Active Citizenship in an Urban Community

WOMEN'S STUDIES   AMERICAN STUDIES   ARABIC   ECONOMICS

Apply by 1/1
• Self-Designed Majors • Interdisciplinary Classes • Service Learning
• Theme Housing • Green Campus

Office of Undergraduate Admissions   617. 627. 3170
Tufts University   admissions.inquiry@ase.tufts.edu
Medford, MA 02155-7057   www.tufts.edu

UNITY COLLEGE

500 Students   Unity, Maine

Unity College recognizes that we are custodians of a fragile planet. The College intends to graduate individuals with firm values, a sense of purpose, and an appreciation of the web of life. Unity graduates are professionally effective and environmentally responsive, recognizing their responsibilities as passengers on this fragile planet. They understand that, as global citizens, they must assume a leadership role in the stewardship of the earth.

Unity College exists for the student whose love of the outdoors is reflected in career choices. Unity students typically place a premium on jobs that do not require sitting behind a desk, thus Unity combines academic rigor with equally demanding field experience. Education at Unity can be the first step to a position with a state park, wildlife refuge, nature education center, or wilderness recreation organization.

In addition to the required course work in their field of concentration, all students are required to complete the Unity Environmental Stewardship Curriculum. A common core integrates the development of broad-based lifelong learning skills with the exploration of the themes of environmental stewardship.

Unity students come from diverse backgrounds, but they share a spirit of independence and a love of nature. They are individuals who welcome the opportunity to participate actively in their education and in the life of a small college community. To succeed at Unity College, students must bring a willingness to have their ideas questioned – and possibly changed. Students must be prepared to accept new challenges that expand their limits. Climbing an ice-covered mountain demands courage and commitment; waking up at 4 a.m. to go out in the field and conduct a small mammal survey requires determination.

Unity College has a special location: the mountains, lakes, and rocky coast of Maine offer innumerable opportunities to camp, hunt, hike, canoe, and fish. At Unity, students experience the personal growth that comes from awareness of the connections linking human beings with the natural environment. Nearby habitats as diverse as ocean, mountains, freshwater wetlands, and lakes provide the opportunity for hands-on study of a variety of ecological systems.

Most Unity students gain work experience in their major field as part of their education. Students may choose credit-bearing internships, cooperative education work experiences, or summer employment to supplement classroom learning. Positions with state and federal agencies, businesses, or nonprofit organizations enable students to apply academic knowledge to real working situations. Typical internships have included work with the Environmental Defense Fund, the American Rivers Conservation Council, and the U.S. Environmental Protection Agency. Other internships have included Hurricane Island Outward Bound, Connecticut Audubon Society and Volunteers for Peace

Unity's campus has a sense of open space that reflects the value the College places on the outdoors. The 200-acre campus has an agrarian feel; in the warm months cows graze adjacent to the residence halls. Over 100 acres of campus land have been designated a tree farm used for educational and recreational purposes. In addition to its campus property Unity owns more than 320 acres of land including frontage on Lake Winnecook, a Wetlands Research Area, and a 230-acre tree farm off-site.

Making a Difference Studies

Environmental Policy

Environmental Analysis
Environmental Resource Law
Natural Resource Policy
Technical Writing
Social Problems

Land and Water Law
Geology of Environmental Problems
Freshwater Ecology/Limnology
Advocacy, Ethics and the Law
State & Local Government

Landscape/Horticulture

Environmental Plant Physiology
Landscape Fundamentals
Forest Tree Diseases & Insects
Sustainable Landscape Horticulture
Soil Fertility

Designing with Nature
Plant Health Care
Arboriculture
Designing with Nature
Plant Diseases and Insects

Adventure Education Leadership

Wilderness First Responder
Leadership
Group Process
Cross Country Skiing
Rock Climbing

Wilderness Expedition Skills
Outdoor Adventure Education
Enviro Education: Methods & Materials
Map and Compass
Mountaineering

Conservation Law Enforcement

Introduction to Criminal Justice
Courtroom Procedures and Evidence
Marine Law Enforcement
Geology of Environmental Problems
Environmental Law
Wildlife Law Enforcement

Conservation Law Enforcement
Firearms Training
North American Wildlife
Interpersonal Relations
Wildlife Techniques
Conservation Biology

Environmental Education

Environmental Education students pursuing teacher certification meet additional requirements

Teaching Science in Secondary Schools
Environmental Ed: Methods & Materials
American Outdoor Experience
Educational Psychology
Community Leadership

Foundations of Education
Instruction Practices & Curriculum Development
Researching Local Places
Current Environmental Education Problems
Interpretation Methods

Parks, Recreation & Ecotourism

Park Planning, Design & Maintenance
Conservation Biology: Aquatic
Wildland Recreation Policy
North American Wildlife
Visitor and Resource Protection

Professional Development in Park Management
Park Administration and Operations
Environmental Resource Law
Ecotourism
Geology for the Naturalist

Wildlife Conservation   Ecology   Forestry   Aquaculture & Fisheries   Teaching

Rolling Admissions
• Team Teaching   • Service Learning   • Field Studies   • Interdisciplinary Classes
• Individualized Majors   • Vegetarian Meals   •   Environmental Scholarships   • Greening Campus

Director of Admissions
Unity College
Unity, ME 04988-0532

800. 624. 1024
www.unity.edu
admissions@unity.edu

UNIVERSITY OF VERMONT

10,000 Undergraduates   Burlington, Vermont

"The University is steeped in the traditions and values of Vermont: practicality, environmental stewardship, civic duty, fairness, social justice, and respect for individuality. It is deep within our ethos to make a difference on the things that matter, from acid rain to drug addiction to the memory of the Holocaust," says Daniel Fogel, President of UVM. The University instills a combination of pragmatism and idealism necessary to have a positive impact on the world.

UVM has long been a national leader in study of the environment. Environmental Studies is a University-wide curricula offering several academic programs. It is one of UVM's most distinctive and popular academic programs – unique in its breadth and interdisciplinary nature. The program includes undergraduate education, research, and community service programs dedicated to the study and improvement of cultural and natural environments.

The School of Natural Resources is actively committed to diversity; biodiversity in natural communities and cultural diversity in human communities. SNR's innovative curriculum is a four-year sequence integrating ecology, human perspectives, ecosystem management, natural resource policy and environmental assessment. Students are challenged to use their knowledge of natural and social science concepts to solve real-world problems. The School includes programs in: Environmental Studies, Forestry, Natural Resources, Recreation Management, Resource Economics, Water Resources, and Wildlife and Fisheries Biology, and provides a holistic framework and field studies that complements traditional natural resources curricula.

UVM reaffirmed its commitment to environmental values by hiring a full time coordinator for its Environmental Council which recommends ways the University can reduce environmental impacts and expand environmental research, education, and service. Student projects include reducing junk mail, designing ecologically sound buildings, and socially responsible investing. The council is working on indicators of sustainability for UVM, a campus arboretum, use of hazardous materials in laboratories, as well as sustainable forestry initiatives with local sustainable forestry businesses.

A strong environmental ethic pervades the institution, informing not only curriculum and research, but also how the university does business. This commitment is reflected in the implementation of a "green" building policy that sets high standards for design, construction, and operating efficiency of new buildings to meet U.S. Green Building Council standards.

UVM's Center for Service-Learning provides structured experiential programs and volunteer placements within the context of public service. Students get involved in the community by filling real needs and link their experience with a structured academic program. Typical placements involve health and human services, law and justice, or governmental, environmental and educational organizations.

The Community Service Program provides ways for students to get involved as volunteers. They participate in one-time events such as Hunger Clean Up or Into the Streets, work several hours per week at a local agency, or make a year-long commitment. The Alternative Spring Break allows students to increase their social awareness through service in an economically disadvantaged environment away from Vermont. Reflection on and examination of the cultures and circumstances are built into the program. The Center also offers a Community Service Trek, a week-long experience for incoming first-year students prior to the first week of classes.

MAKING A DIFFERENCE STUDIES

AGRICULTURAL & RESOURCE ECONOMICS: COMMUNITY & INTERNATIONAL DEVELOPMENT

Sustainable Community Development
Communities in Modern Society
World Natural Environments
Solar Strategies for Building Construction
Project Planning & Development

World Food, Population & Development
Law, Ethics and Responsbility
Anthropology of Third World Development
Community Leadership Organization & Devp't.
Economics of Sustainability

NATURAL RESOURCES

Eco Design & Living Technology
Water as a Natural Resource
Int'l Problems in Natural Resource Mgm't.
Wilderness & Wilderness Management
Race & Culture in Natural Resources

Effect of Human Activities on a Lake
The American Wilderness
Global Environmental Assessment
Ecological Aspects of Nat. Resource Conservation
Legal Aspects of Environmental Planning

WILDLIFE AND FISHERIES BIOLOGY

Wildlife Conservation
Fisheries Biology and Management
Florida Ecology Field Trip
Uplands Wildlife Ecology

Conservation Biology
Wildlife Habitat & Population Measurements
Wetlands Ecology & Marsh Management
Principles of Wildlife Management

HUMAN DEVELOPMENT & FAMILY STUDIES

Contemporary Issues in Parenting
Public Policy and Programs for Elders
Social Context of Development
Aging: Change & Adaptation

Intro to Early Childhood & Human Development
Family Ecosystems
Personal & Family Development in Later Life
Human Relationships and Sexuality

SUSTAINABLE LANDSCAPE HORTICULTURE

Introduction to Ecological Agriculture
Biological Control
Landscape Design
Permaculture
Ecological Farm Management

Entomology and Pest Managemen
Soil and Water Pollution and Bioremediation
Greenhouse Operations and Management
Agroecology
Ecological Agriculture Internship

ECONOMICS

Emphasis placed on evaluating alternative policy solutions to problems, such as globalization and poverty, gender and racial discrimination in labor and capital markets, and environmental pollution.

Capitalism and Human Welfare
Law and Economics
The Vermont Economy
Globalization and Poverty

Economics of Gender
Election and the Economy
Health Economics
Political Economy of the Environment

SOCIAL WORK   ENVIRONMENTAL STUDIES   TEACHING CREDENTIAL: ENVIRO STUDIES (7-12)

Apply by 1/15   Early Decision: 11/1
• Service Learning   • Field Studies   • Self-Designed Majors
• Organic Gardens   • Theme Housing   • Green Campus

Admissions Office   802. 656. 3370
University of Vermont   www.uvm.edu
Burlington, VT 05401-3596   admissions@uvm.edu

WARREN WILSON COLLEGE

800 Students   Asheville, North Carolina

Warren Wilson College is located on a beautiful 1,100-acre campus in a mountain valley that American Indians called "Swannanoa," meaning "land of beauty." Over the years the setting has inspired community, creativity, learning, and a sense of harmony with the environment. The mission of Warren Wilson College is to provide a liberal arts education combining academic study, participation in a campus-wide work program, and required service-learning. Each component of this triad plays an important role in the education of the whole person — within a learning environment that promotes wisdom, understanding, spiritual growth and contribution to the common good.

Warren Wilson College affirms a commitment to spiritual growth and social responsibility; and invites to its educational community individuals who are dedicated to personal and social transformation, and to stewardship of our natural environment.

Students have constituted the core work-force for the College since its founding more than a century ago. Today each residential student works 15 hours each week on one of more than 100 work-crews that help run the college, and the work helps offset the cost of room and board. The work-crews give students experiential learning opportunities in their fields of study. For example, pre-veterinary students care for the pigs and cattle on the 300-acre College farm.

The work crew is not the only commitment Warren Wilson students make outside the classroom. Each student is responsible for giving 100 hours of community service in the Asheville community, their own home town, or in another country before graduation. The College believes that service to society enables students to make a difference in the world and to better understand the needs of the others. Service projects include working at homeless shelters, building homes with Habitat for Humanity, serving as Big Brothers and Big Sisters, establishing tree plantations in Nicaragua, and developing water collection systems in Kenya.

Warren Wilson's student body of 800 comes from 40 states and 14 countries. The College also provides many opportunities for students, faculty, and staff to learn about different cultures well beyond the campus, whether they be in a different part of the United States or a different part of the world.

The Warren Wilson WorldWide Program gives each student a chance to work, learn, and serve abroad. From summer- to semester-long trips in countries ranging from Ireland to India, the WorldWide program offers cross-cultural experiences that help students discover how their academic studies and the College mission triad come alive in the field, in our global community, and in connection with our fragile planet.

Ninety percent of students and 40 percent of faculty and staff live on campus. Because students, faculty and staff live, work and serve together, there is a strong sense of community. The size of the college enables students and staff to be involved and challenged with community leadership roles. The staff meets biweekly for a staff forum at which issues, goals, and ideas are communicated and acted upon. The student caucus also plays an important role in the college's short- and long-term plans. It meets each week to discuss student issues, to communicate ideas and concerns to the administration, and to make policy recommendations.

There is plenty of student teacher attention with a low ratio of 13:1. Not only are classes small, but there are ample opportunities for independent tutorials.

Open to Warren Wilson sophomores and juniors on a competitive basis, the Environmental Leadership Center Internship Program is designed to instill in students a keen understanding that they are part of something greater than themselves. Internships give students the opportunity to work hard and serve well in superb institutions led by dedicated environmental scientists, scholars, researchers, educators, and activists. Upon their return, interns share their experiences with civic clubs, churches and schools, creating a ripple effect of environmental awareness.

Community members meet often to address issues concerning sexism, diversity, peace issues and other global and local topics. Students and staff are particularly sensitive to environmental issues. Warren Wilson has been recycling on campus for more than a decade. Student work-crews are completely responsible for the program, which includes curbside pickup for campus buildings and residences. The Eco-Dorm, a dormitory planned by both students and the administration was be constructed with sustainable principles in mind.

Students and staff have participated for more than 20 years in the archaeological excavation of an American Indian village on the campus. Further reflecting the special heritage of its Southern Appalachian location, Warren Wilson offers a program in Appalachian music including instruction in the more common instruments used in the genre. Students and staff join together to create an Appalachian String Band which performs for campus activities.

Capitalizing on its mountain location Warren Wilson is in partnership with North Carolina Outward Bound, and the outdoor leadership major has become one of the College's most popular fields of study.

The College's location just outside Asheville, in the Blue Ridge Mountains, provides many fascinating opportunities for students including kayaking, mountain biking, caving, and rock climbing. On weekends students may stay on campus to enjoy a play, a performance or music, see an art exhibit, go to dances, or create their own entertainment. Or they may go to downtown Asheville for a poetry reading, a movie at the Fine Arts Theatre, or a meal at one of the many restaurants in and around Asheville. A shuttle bus is available for students all weekend long to and from Asheville.

One applicant to the college wrote: "I'm lured to Warren Wilson College because of many things: the triad, the location, the classes, the cows, the kindness of the staff and students. I have found in my visit to the College a respect for life that coincides with my own. Very simply, I felt at home there, I felt that I had found an environment that would allow me to grow, that would unbiasedly witness a portion of the continuous evolving of my life." All of these things combine to make Warren Wilson College the community and learning environment that it is, a place where students come to grow.

Making a Difference Studies

ENVIRONMENTAL STUDIES: ENVIRONMENTAL ANALYSIS; ENVIRO. EDUCATION; PLANT BIOLOGY & HORTICULTURE; FOREST RESOURCE CONSERVATION; ENVIRO. POLICY; WILDLIFE BIOLOGY

Horticulture

Forest Biology

Community and Regional Studies

Wilderness: Past and Prospects

Environmental Impact Assessment

Thinking Globally, Acting Locally

Sustainable Farm Management

Conservation of Natural Resources

Aquatic Ecology and Water Pollution

Sustainable Development & the Politics of Growth

Introduction to Environmental Education

Environmental Policy

Wildlife Management

Methods & Materials in Environmental Education

- **Environmental and Ecological Economics** Explore the relationship between human social and economic systems and the environment. Analyze how markets fail, causing many environmental problems, how markets can be harnessed, and how various government strategies can lead to better management of environmental resources and ecosystem services. Topics such as resource valuation, cost-benefit analysis, and multi-criteria analysis are discussed as well as alternative government policy approaches.

- **Faculty Bio**: Dr. Mark V. Brenner (B.S., U of Wisconsin - Stevens Point, M.S. and Ph.D., U of Washington) is the chair of the Environmental Studies Department. Mark's specialty is aquatic ecology and the ecological effects of pollution. He has assisted a number of students with research projects related to aquatic ecology and pollution. Currently Mark is working with waste recycling research, composting techniques, and waste from aqua-culture. For fun Mark plays on Warren Wilson's volleyball team and leads the Discovery Through Wilderness - Pacific NW trip.

BIOLOGY

Field Natural History

Field Ornithology

Evolution

Plant Morphology

Ecology

Animal Behavior

Immunology and Infectious Disease

Special Topics in Biology

PEACE STUDIES

Introduction to Peace & Conflict Studies

Lifestyles of Nonviolence

Resolving Conflict: Global and Local

Special Topics in Peace Studies

Politics of Peace

Current Issues of Peace and Justice: America

SOCIAL WORK

The Aged: Issues and Interventions

Social Welfare as a Social Institution

Micro-Practice: Individuals

Field Instruction

Substance Abuse: Issues and Interventions

Human Behavior in the Social Environment

Micro-Practice: Groups and Families

Social Work in the International Community

Macro-Practice: Communities, Organizations, and Policy Development

RELIGION

Social Ethics in Story Theology

Religious America: Four Distinct Paths

Eastern Religions

Christ and Contemporary Culture

Heaven on Earth: Religious Lifestyles in 19th Century America

- **The Sacred/Secular Search** Explores fundamental questions concerning the nature of religion. Eastern and Western religions, innovative and traditional examples of religious practice are examined. Particular attention is paid to the relationship between "religious" and "secular" claims upon one's time and energy; diverse rivals for our "ultimate concern" are studied, whether or not they bear overt religious labels.

GLOBAL STUDIES

This interdisciplinary field provides a foundation for further study and work in private or government international agencies, conflict resolution, and global development.

Economic Development
Mahatma Gandhi
Human Behavior in Social Environment
Eastsern Thought
Intercultural Communication
Native Peoples of Mexico and Guatemala

Gender, Development and the Environment
Worlds of Change
Comparative Governments: Third World
Environmental Politics in Global Perspective
Development Agencies at Home & Abroad
Environmental Sociology

- **International Development Practicum** This course involves participation in a work-study overseas service field project of the international development program. Emphasizes providing a useful service to a local community program through use of appropriate skills.

APPALACHIAN STUDIES

Introduction to Appalachian Studies
Appalachian Folk Arts
Archaeological Field School
Southern Appalachian Term

Folk Tales and Storytelling
Appalachian Folk Medicine
Native Americans of the Southeast
Introductory Anthropology

OUTDOOR LEADERSHIP

Prepares you for a leadership role in the professional field of outdoor adventure education. Focus on education, facilitation, and experiential learning methodologies. Interpersonal skills and leadership skills such as group process, conflict resolution, program planning, and administrative issues.

Leadership for Adventure Education
Wilderness Skills and Techniques
Rock Climbing
Group Process
Program Planning and Design
Winter Camping

Outdoor Recreation Activities
Wilderness First Responder
Initiatives for Adventure Education
Outdoor Leadership Internship
Survey of Exceptional Child Education
Org. & Admin. of Adventure Education Program

- **Faculty Bio** Ed Raiola (B.A., CA State U; M.A., U of N. Colorado; Ph.D., Union Graduate School) I consider myself a catalyst: an educator who facilitates opportunities for people to challenge their expectations and preconceived limitations about what they can and cannot do. All of us need to keep growing and learning in order to make a positive difference in society. I see education in general and outdoor education in particular as encouraging people to become responsible choice-makers. Without knowledge or emotion relating to the earth, we lose a sense of commitment and loyalty to it. Hobbies: biking, cooking, travel, hiking and mountaineering.

HISTORY AND POLITICAL SCIENCE

The Holocaust
Civil War and Reconstruction
Poverty and the American City
Politics of Developing States

Latin American Civilization
History of Black Experience in America.
Mahatma Gandhi: Experiments With the Truth
Amer. Immigrant Experience Thru Ethnic Lit.

HUMAN STUDIES   PHILOSOPHY   PSYCHOLOGY   3/2 PRE-FORESTRY WITH DUKE

Apply by 3/15   Early Decision 11/15   Avg.# of students in a first year classroom: 15
- Work College   • Service-Learning   • Field Studies   • Required Community Service
- Third World Service-Learning   • Vegetarian /Vegan Meals   • Green Campus
- Eco Dorm   • Organic Gardens

Office of Admission
Warren Wilson College
P.O. Box 9000
Asheville, NC 28815-9000

828. 298. 3325
800. 934. 3536
admit@warren-wilson.edu
www.warren-wilson.edu

WASHINGTON STATE UNIVERSITY

16,000 Undergraduates   Pullman, Washington

Founded by the Legislature in 1890 as the State's land-grant university, Washington Sate University is today a four-campus university with a growing national reputation. WSU offers a liberal arts education balanced with practical instruction in professional and technical fields. Quality teaching and a special student experience in and out of the classroom are hallmarks of a WSU education.

WSU has a number of unique programs that prepare students to make a difference in society. For example, the University offers:
- The nation's most comprehensive educational program in pollution prevention;
- A speech and hearing program training Native American students to work with their own people who have 5 to 15 times more communication disorders than the general population;
- Sustainable agriculture and integrated pest management programs.

WSU is known for teaching and research that makes a difference in people's lives, and in the state's industries and professions. Current studies range from cancer prevention to disease-resistant crops and qualities of successful marriages, education reform to animal health. Faculty work in an array of developing countries on agricultural, animal health, and educational projects to improve the quality of life.

The Department of Natural Resource Sciences at WSU seeks to advance and impart knowledge of ecosystems and natural resources, their attributes and functions, ecological and societal values; and their management in an ecologically, socially and economically sound, sustainable manner. This mission is pursued through interdisciplinary programs in the fields of forestry, wildlife ecology, range management, wildland recreation management, and related biophysical and social sciences. The Department emphasizes individualized student advising, field studies and other forms of experiential learning.

The WSU Center for Sustaining Agriculture & Natural Resources develops and fosters agriculture and natural resource management that is economically viable, environmentally sound, and socially acceptable through interdisciplinary relationships between WSU, growers, industry, and environmental groups. The WSU Native Plant & Landscape Restoration Nursery helps conserve the biological diversity of endangered Palouse Prairie and western native plants, and supports the ecological restoration of sustainable landscapes in the Pacific Northwest.

International elements can be seen in many of WSU's academic programs. They are part of a comprehensive effort to increase student understanding of diverse cultures, economies, political systems, and environments. A pair of world civilization courses, required for undergraduates, is at the heart of WSU's nationally recognized core curriculum. Six students in engineering students worked with WSU's Engineers Without Borders to design schools that will be rebuilt in the Indonesian region destroyed by the December 2004 tsunami. EWB@WSU is currently studying the feasibility of developing sustainable projects in Colombia such as providing rural school buses run on bio-fuel.

Dining Services supports the University's sustainability initiative by using locally grown, minimally processed ingredients, selling Fair Trade coffee and recycling.

Opportunities for camping, backpacking, biking, and winter sports abound. A half-dozen mountain ranges surround you, and extensive national forest land lies just to the east, as do Glacier and Yellowstone National Parks. If you like to get wet, you are in the middle of world-class floating and kayaking waterways, numerous lakes, rivers and mountain streams.

MAKING A DIFFERENCE STUDIES

ENVIRONMENTAL SCIENCE & REGIONAL PLANNING

Environmental Health Assessment
Environmental Impact Statement Analysis
Environmental Ethics
Environmental Policy
Environmental Psychology

Natural Resource Policy & Administration
Energy Production and the Environment
Human Issues in International Development
Economic Development & Underdevelopment
Natural Resource Economics

COMMUNICATION AND JOURNALISM

History of Mass Communications
Gender and the Media
Ethics in Mass Media
Language and Human Behavior
The Costs of Free Speech

Mass Communications and Society
Intercultural Communication
Stereotypes and The Media
Mass Media and the First Amendment
Reporting of Public Affairs

ENVIRONMENTAL AND RESOURCE ECONOMICS AND MANAGEMENT

Issues in forest management, water use, pollution, land use, fisheries, recycling, and hazardous wastes.

Public Finance
Environmental Economics
Natural Resource Economics
Financial Management

Sustainable Development
Economic Analysis of Environmental Policies
Natural Resource & Environmental Policy & Law
Technical/Professional Writing

ENTOMOLOGY: INTEGRATED PEST MANAGEMENT

Pest Management Internship
Insects and People
Toxicology of Pesticides
Urban Entomology
Pesticides and the Environment

Urban Entomology
Beekeeping
Systems of Integrated Pest Management
Insect Ecology
Introduction to Biological Control

ORGANIC AGRICULTURE SYSTEMS

Prepares not only aspiring growers of organic food, but also students who are interested in related industries, such as direct marketing, global marketing, or food or environmental quality.

Organic Farming & Gardening
Small Acreage Farming
Practicum in Organic Agriculture
Ecology & Management of Weeds
Living System

Sustainable Agriculture
Field Analysis of Sustainable Food Systems
Nutrition for Living
Agricultural Entomology
Natural Resource Ecology

CHILD/CONSUMER/FAMILY STUDIES

Patterns of Chicano Families
Family Housing Decisions
Families in Crises
Perspectives on Aging
Management Experiences With Families

Guidance of Young Children
The Child and Family in Poverty
Women in Management
Curriculum for Young Children's Programs
Adolescent and Early Adult Development

CONSERVATION BIOLOGY   ENVIRO. ENGINEERING   PEACE STUDIES   WOMEN'S STUDIES

GEOLOGY   WILDLIFE   SUSTAINABLE AGRICULTURE   FORESTRY   WILDLAND RECREATION

Apply by 3/1

• Co-op Education   • Service-Learning   • Team Teaching   • Self-Designed Majors   • Vegetarian Meals

Director of Admissions
Washington State University
Pullman, WA 99164

888-468. 6978
www.wsu.edu
admiss2@wsu.edu

WESLEYAN UNIVERSITY

2,750 Students   Middletown, Connecticut

Wesleyan prepares students to face a rapidly changing world with confidence and the sense of responsibility to want to make the world a better place. Students gain that confidence from a strong education in the liberal arts and sciences - an education that engenders the ability to engage in critical thinking, to communicate effectively, to find creative solutions to problems, to develop the imagination to see the world as others see it, and to make ethical judgments that come from deep within one's character. Liberal education offers the underpinning for democracy in a time when technical specialization may make the common interest increasingly hard to discern.

Nationally known for its long-standing commitment to a multicultural student body, Wesleyan's students boast a diversity of ideas, interests, and viewpoints, together with their diverse socio-economic, geographic, and international backgrounds. The interaction of these factors on a small campus, coupled with top-notch academic departments, enables Wesleyan students to understand "the big picture." Wesleyan graduates are involved at all levels of public and private service, education, community organization, and academia.

Wesleyan's Science in Society curriculum has been designed to help students explore systematically the interrelations between scientific knowledge, society, and the quality of human life. The Earth and Environmental Science department emphasizes field work on the coast and inlands of Connecticut, and is known for the cohesiveness that its field experiments help create. Faculty have taken students to Central America, Newfoundland, Montana, Greece, Italy and elsewhere.

Students have been involved in a broad range of internships in hospitals, museums, television stations, architectural firms, publishing companies, and educational institutions. The College Venture Program places students for 3-6 months in positions such as advocate for the homeless, research assistant, and teaching. Students are encouraged to become involved with the local community and to use the Office of Community Service as a resource for volunteer opportunities. The OCS supports for student-run tutoring programs, and offers mini-grants to students who create programs for local children, and sponsors service projects.

The Center for Afro-American Studies sponsors a wide range of academic, social, and cultural events open to the entire university community. The Center's events includes a lecture series, jazz concerts, dance performances, art exhibits, a spring film series, and a Fellows Program designed to encourage students and faculty members to meet informally.

The Mansfield Freeman Center for East Asian Studies presents a continuing program of exhibitions, concerts, courses, lectures, and special events. The Center is a place to meet distinguished visitors and faculty, and to learn from first-hand observers about current political and cultural events — from the repercussions of Tiananmen Square to contemporary theater and philosophical trends.

The First Harvest Cafe features freshly prepared vegetarian, vegan, and organic food for lunch and dinner. Several locally sourced foods are used by dining services including cheese, milk, garlic and spring water. A small organic garden plot started by students is expanding to a full acre, and grows 80 different vegetables and herbs.

MAKING A DIFFERENCE STUDIES

EARTH AND ENVIRONMENTAL SCIENCE

Physical Geology: Our Dynamic Earth

Geology of Connecticut

Coastal and Estuarine Environments

Climate Change and Human History

Water Resources

Introductory Oceanography

Conservation of Aquatic Ecosystsems

Principles of Geobiology

Remote Sensing

Earth's Changing Climate

LATIN AMERICAN STUDIES

Contemporary Urban Social Movements

Colonialism & Its Consequences in the Americas

Latin American Economic Development

Cuba's Afro-Creole Religions

Justice, Forgiveness and Reconciliation

Exile, Immigration & Latino & Hispanic Literatures

Power and Resistance in Latin America

Globalization, Democracy & Social Change

Liberation, Theology, Pentecostalism, and other Christianities in the Americas and Africa

Vulnerability, Development and Social Protection in Latin America

SOCIOLOGY

Women, Health and Technology

Theories of Capitalism and Globalization

Community Research Seminar

Environmental Sociology

The Health of Communities

Race and the American Legal System

Postcolonialism and Globalization

Music in Social Movements

Education and Inequality

The War in Iraq

Migration & Cultural Politics: Caribbean Immigrant Experiences in the U. S.

ANTHROPOLOGY

Being and Becoming Human

Color in the Caribbean

Feminist Ethnographic Writing

Black Feminist Thoughts and Practices

Anthropology of Development

Imperial Encounters

Anthropology and Contemporary World Problem

Gender in a Transnational Perspective

The Anthropology of Globalization

Indigenous Sovereignty Politics

Ethnicity, Nationality, Identity

Cultural Analysis

INTERNATIONAL RELATIONS

Economics of the Environment

Nationalism

UN Peacekeeping

International Political Economy

Post-Colonialism and Globalization

Globalization

War, Technology and Society

Politics of Terrorism

Ethnonational Conflict

World Economy: Migration, Race & Ethnicity

EAST ASIAN STUDIES

Introduction to East Asian Music

Traditional China

Taoism: Visionaries and Interpreters

Salvation and Doubt

Japanese Film & Japanese Society

Japanese Literature 1700-1945

Tibetan Buddhism

Twentieth Century Japan

Women in Buddhist Literature

Politics & Political Development in China

AFRICAN AMERICAN STUDIES   RUSSIA & EAST EUROPEAN STUDIES

Apply by 1/1

• Self-Designed Majors   • Interdisciplinary Majors & Classes   • Co-op Studies

• Theme Housing   • Vegetarian Meals   • Organic Garden

Admissions Office

Wesleyan University

Middletown, CT 06457

860. 685. 3000

admissions@wesleyan.edu

www.wesleyan.edu

WESTERN WASHINGTON UNIVERSITY

FAIRHAVEN COLLEGE   400 Students Bellingham, WA

Fairhaven College is an undergraduate learning community within Western Washington University, defined by five attributes: 1) interdisciplinary study; 2) student-designed studies and evaluation of learning; 3) examination of issues arising from a diverse society; 4) development of leadership and a sense of social responsibility; and 5) curricular, instructional, and evaluative innovation. Students will be encouraged to find their connection with the world, to understand relationships of thought and action, theory and experience, to cultivate opportunities to apply what they learn, and to develop a strong sense of themselves as individuals in a community, including the benefits and responsibilities that come from membership in it

Fairhaven's interdisciplinary curriculum is centered on the process of inquiry as well as on the development of knowledge. Classes are small and most are held in a seminar format where the use of primary sources and student participation is essential. Classes are interdisciplinary and often problem-focused. Students learn to engage respectfully in discussion, to value and respect different world views, and to appreciate multiple voices reflecting the diversity of experience in our society. Narrative self-assessments and written faculty evaluations of student learning replace letter grades.

Fairhaven students can choose to develop a self-designed interdisciplinary concentration integrating several areas of study, or an established major in another college within WWU. Fairhaven places responsibility for program design and development in student hands and allows you to incorporate independent study projects, internships or study abroad. Recent Concentrations have included: Latin American Studies; Inequality and Social Change; and Contemporary Political and Economic Issues in Native America. Recent seminars include: Pacific Rim Studies; Regional Ecologies; Art & the Environment; and Organic Gardening.

Independent Study projects enable students to take responsibility for the direction and content of their education. These projects have included: Wilderness First Aid; Alternative Healing; Wetlands Restoration; History of Native American Education; and Grant Writing.

HUXLEY COLLEGE OF ENVIRONMENTAL STUDIES   500 Students

Are you concerned about the environment and like the challenge of problem solving with others, do you want a career where you can make a difference? The faculty, staff, and students at Huxley College of Environmental Studies share your genuine concern for the environmental well-being of the earth. Students from around the world come to Huxley College with a commitment to hands-on environmental problem solving. Established in 1968, Huxley is one of the oldest environmental colleges in the nation. The College's academic programs reflect a broad view of our physical, biological, social, and cultural world. Courses at Huxley are primarily upper-division (junior and senior level) and admission is competitive.

The College teaches and researches, in an interdisciplinary and systematic way, the complex issues and problems of the natural environment and its social overlay. Huxley is a gathering place and focus for those genuinely concerned about the environmental well-being of the earth. Majors include Environmental Economics, Environmental Journalism, Emergency Management, along with a new minor in Sustainable Planning and Design.

Making a Difference Studies

Fairhaven: Society and the Individual

Rights, Liberty & Justice in America
Global Migration
Psychology of Mindfulness & Well-being
Disposable People
Cross-cultural Shamanism
Shifting Direction: Ecocultural Principles for Global Democracy

Contemporary Native American Issues
Children of a Changing World
Vietnam War Redux
Human Rights, World Visions
African-American & Caribbean Women Feminism

Science and our Place on the Planet

Marine Bird Pop Ecology
Studying Nature Through Photography
Biological Perspectives on Parenting & Childbirth

Applied Conservation Biology
Visioning Sustainable Futures

Humanities and the Expressive Arts

Memoir: Childhood in America
Public Art

Art and Social Activism
Art and the Environment

Huxley: Environmental Studies - Mass Communication & Environmental Education

Environmental Disturbances
Environmental History and Ethics
Environmental Education & Curricula
Social Impact Assessment
Environmental Interpretation Methods

Human Ecology
Community Based Environmental Education
Environmental Journalism
Environmental Impact Assessment

Environmental Science: Aquatic/Terrestrial Ecology; Environmental Chemistry/ Toxicology

Ecology
Environmental Physiology & Biochemistry
Air Pollution
Water Quality Lab
Intro. to Marine Pollution & Toxicology

Ecosystem Restoration
Energy & Energy Resources
Environmental Impact Assessment
Conservation of Biological Diversity
Effects of Global Climate Change

Planning & Environmental Policy: Planning; Geography; Enviro & Resource Mgm't.

Public Opinion & Enviromental Issues
Environmental Systems
United States Environmental Policy
Parks and Protected Areas
Land Use Law

Natural Resources Management
Urban Economics
Environmental Dispute Resolution
International Environmental Policies

Environmental Studies: Economics concentration

Economics, Environment & Natural Resources
Population and Resources
Energy Economics
Environment and Resource Policy

Developing World
Environmental Economics
Wetlands for Wastewater Treatment

Sustainable Community Development   Island of Kefalonia, Greece - Study Abroad program
Multidisciplinary applied studies targeting students in sustainable design, urban planning, enviro. studies, landscape design/architecture, natural resources mgm't, green building, community/int'l development...

Apply by 3/1

Admissions Coordinator
Fairhaven College
Huxley College
Western Washington University
Bellingham, WA 98225-9118

360. 650.3680
www.wwu.edu/depts/fairhaven/
360. 650.3520
www.wwu.edu/depts/huxley/
www.wwu.edu

WILDLANDS STUDIES

UC, Santa Barbara

Wildlands Studies is a unit of the University of California, Santa Barbara's Extended Learning Services. The program offers you the opportunity to join field teams in a search for answers to important environmental problems affecting endangered wildlife and threatened wildland ecosystems. Wildlands Studies offers onsite field research projects throughout the US and around the world. You can choose among 25 wildlife, wildland, and wildwater projects in the US Mountain West, Alaska, Hawaii, New Zealand, Fiji, Canada, Belize, Thailand, or Nepal.

Wildlands Studies projects are exciting and challenging opportunities for which previous fieldwork experience is not required. In backcountry settings, you will acquire and directly apply field study skills while examining firsthand the issues of wildlife preservation, resource management, conservation ecology, and cultural sustainability.

Your fellow team members will come from diverse US and Canadian locations, a mix that provides ample substance for trailside conversations and new friendships. In most cases there will be no more than 9-14 team members working with project faculty. Small teams are best suited for sharing energies, responsibilities, and discoveries.

Wildlands Studies projects occur entirely in the field, and while there is time for solitude and relaxation, they are not vacations. Fieldwork sometimes means long days and uphill trails in weather that is not always ideal, but that is a rare and fascinating opportunity to explore wildland firsthand while striving toward shared goals with experienced researchers and new friends. Students earn 5-12 transferable upper division semester units per project. Units earned may be eligible for transfer credit to both semester and quarter system colleges. (5 quarter units equals 3 1/3 semester system units.)

As concerned students you can join a Wildlands team and help in the effort to solve critical problems facing wildlands and wildlife populations. Wildlands Studies programs afford a rare chance to gain an intimate introduction to the ecology of fascinating and remote ecosystems, while taking part in field studies of significance to the region's future.

Wildlands programs will expose you to a stunning flux of new information. In the field you will discover how boundaries separating subjects – like wildlife behavior, conservation biology, and cultural ecology – tend to dissolve, and information appears as a richly integrated text. Using an interdisciplinary approach of rigorous ecosystem/wildlife observation and experimental field investigation, students consider the complex network of interrelated biological, ecological, and social processes which shape wildernesses and the wildlife populations they support.

A cooperative, experiential approach is at the heart of WS's educational philosophy. Education is most effective when students are involved in the learning with all their faculties. The way in which learning occurs is as important as the content of any particular discipline. Wildlands approaches field studies the same way you might approach a glacier, a fern, or a friend: first with direct experience and observation, then with questions about how the conclusions drawn tie into personal and global conditions.

MAKING A DIFFERENCE STUDIES

Wildlands Studies field programs take place year round, and run from approximately 3 weeks during the summer to a full academic or summer term.

MOUNTAIN ECOSYSTEMS OF CHINA AND THAILAND

Take part in a rare, on-site examination of China and Thailand's spectacular ecosystems and the environmental challenges they face across a broad spectrum of wildland environments. Field study takes place at sites on an ecological transect from the tropical monsoon forests of Thailand, across the Yunnan Plateau to the southeastern margin of Tibet. This transition from tropical Asia into the Eastern Himalayan region is one of the most enthralling on earth. High biological diversity, tremendous biotic/cultural variability over short distances, and acute environmental challenges make this an ideal site for a field project in natural history, human ecology, and conservation biology.

Participants receive firsthand exposure to ongoing case studies in conservation, development, and cultural sustainability. Examples include community forestry and habitat restoration in northern Thailand, community-based conservation in China and the uneasy relationship between spirituality, tourism, and conservation in Yunnan China/eastern Tibet.

YELLOWSTONE ENDANGERED SPECIES

Combine firsthand field observation and evaluation — of the ecological relationships and habitat needs for recovery in the wildlands of the Greater Yellowstone Ecosystem — of the Gray Wolf, the Grizzly Bear, the Bald Eagle and the Peregrine Falcon. Working in the largest essentially intact ecosystem in the temperate zones of the earth, team members will gain a firsthand understanding of the ecological parameters and wildlife management-complexities surrounding efforts to recover Yellowstone's endangered wildlife.

THAILAND ECOSYSTEMS AND CULTURES

Students take part in a rare onsite examination of Thailand's wild ecosystems and the environmental challenges they face. Working onsite, the team will use several of Thailand's National Parks as models to investigate the biological ecology of Southeast Asia, and how the Thai people's interaction with wild nature shapes emerging conservation strategies. The goal during the ten weeks in Thailand is to explore how the people of Southeast Asia might hope to balance economic development, biological conservation, and cultural survival.

HAWAII ISLAND FIELD PROGRAM

Fieldwork will center on the "Big Island" of Hawai'i, geologically one of the youngest spots on earth with active volcanoes, lava landscapes and black sand beaches as intriguing today as they were in the earliest days of Hawai'ian society. Investigate key ecosystems on Kaua'i, Mau'i, and Moloka'i: Kaua'i's renowned Na Pali Coast and Kalalau Valley; Mau'i's Haleakala Volcano; Moloka'i's spectacularly rugged environments still largely untransformed by visitor use impacts. Focus on the unique interactions among life, land and ocean in the living laboratory of Hawai'i. Examine numerous and complex threats to diverse native species and effects of outside contact on Hawaiian environment and culture.

Himalayan Ecosystems   Big Sur Wildlands   Costa Rica   New Zealand   Baja California
Birds of Prey & Bighorn Sheep   Chile   American Wildwaters   Belize   Alaska

Wildlands Studies
3 Mosswood Circle
Cazadero, CA 95421

707. 632. 5665
info@wildlandsstudies.com
www.wildlandsstudies.com

U OF WISCONSIN, STEVENS POINT
COLLEGE OF NATURAL RESOURCES

1,350 CNR Students   Stevens Point, Wisconsin

The College of Natural Resources (CNR) is the largest undergraduate program in natural resources in the United States. It began in 1946 with the nation's first conservation education major. The conservation education program provided a broad background in natural resources management, ethics, and philosophy for high school teachers. The strength of the program is the interdisciplinary education of its students. All students take coursework in forestry, wildlife, water resources, and soils before focusing on their major. All of CNR's faculty are committed to undergraduate education; over one fourth have received the coveted excellence in teaching recognition at UW Stevens Point.

UWSP is located on the north edge of Sevens Point in Portage County, the geographic center of Wisconsin. Portage County is located within an ecological "tension zone" that separates northern plant and animal communities from those in the south. As a result, the county has a rich diversity of flora and fauna.

The College emphasizes field experience in all curricula and operates three field stations. Treehaven, a 1,200 acre field station near Tomahawk, Wisconsin, serves as a year round conference center as well as a base for our summer camp and short courses. All CNR students participate in a six week summer camp field experience at Treehaven or attend a similar program in Europe. The Central Wisconsin Environmental Station is a 500 acre facility on Sunset Lake is a year-round conference and education center. A 200 acre nature preserve, adjacent to the campus provides a field laboratory for many classes.

College of Natural Resources international programs allow students to gain a global perspective on resource management. The three international programs coordinated by the CNR are: the European Environmental Studies program in Poland and Germany; a semester abroad in Australia, New Zealand, and the Fiji Islands; and an interim trip to study rain forest ecology in Costa Rica. CNR is actively involved in sustainable development initiatives overseas, working with both the forestry industry and indigenous peoples in Chile, and attended the World Summit on Sustainable Development at Johannesburg as a Non-Governmental Agency.

The Global Environmental Management Education Center (GEM) is a center for world class curricula and outreach education services in natural resources and environmental management. GEM's purpose is pioneering and applying practical learning methods and technology to solve natural resource problems by linking faculty, students, and citizens worldwide. GEM serves students and stakeholders with curricula and outreach programs that are integrated and international using the tools of technology and communication to solve real world problems. GEM is building hope for the future through its work on sustainability, international programming and leadership development. The Student Ambassador Program is an exciting and innovative, student-centered initiative. To date, nearly two dozen students — many of them undergraduates — have been awarded GEM Student Ambassadorships for projects or research in Costa Rica, Kenya, Peru, Puerto Rico, South Africa, Guyana, South Pacific, and the U.S.

Graduates of the CNR are in great demand. Students have many job offers and overall, 90% either go to graduate school or find jobs in their fields.

MAKING A DIFFERENCE STUDIES

WILDLIFE

Wildlife Ecology and Conservation Biology
Wildlife and Society: Contemporary Issues
Wildlife Diseases
Wildlife & Fish Population Dynamics
Ecosystem Management & Restoration Ecology

Wildlife of North America
Principles of Captive Wildlife Management
Management of Wildlife Habitat
Captive Wildlife Management
Wetlands Ecology and Management

RESOURCE MANAGEMENT

International Resources Management
Youth Agency Administration
Peoples of Central & South America
Resource Economics
Energy Education

Environmental Mgm't. for Homeowners
Urban and Regional Planning
Latin American Development
Integrated Pest Management

WATER RESOURCES: WATERSHED MANAGEMENT/FISHERIES

Topics in Groundwater
Contaminant Hydrogeology
Watershed Management
Environmental Analysis
Biological Assessment of Water Quality
Aquatic Ecosystem Evaluation

Design of Constructed Wetlands
Groundwater Management
Environmental Toxicology and Risk Assessment
Fisheries Management
Wildlife and Fish Population Dynamics

SOIL AND LAND MANAGEMENT

Soil conservation, soil mapping and classification, nutrient management in agriculture, wastewater treatment, solid waste and hazardous waste management and recycling, septic systems, and wetlands.

Forest Soils
Erosion Control in Construction
Soil Management for Resource Sustainability
Soil and Plant Analysis

Soil Conservation and Watershed Inventory
Soil Survey Interpretations for Land Use Planning
Site Restoration at Water Crossing Facilities
Bioengineering in Streambank & Channel Restoration

FORESTRY

Forest Pathology
Fire Management and Ecology
Forest Tree Improvement
Land Ecology
Native American Forestry

Forest Protection
Forest Ecosystem Ecology
Urban Forestry
Forest Recreation and Tourism
Urban Trees and Shrubs

NATURAL RESOURCES: ENVIRONMENTAL EDUCATION & INTERPRETATION

Foundations of Environmental Education
Park Interpretation
Intro to Environmental Study & Enviro. Ed.
Leadership Development in Natural Resources
Interprative Media
Environmental Education Teaching Methods.

Natural Resources and Public Relations
Oral Interpretation Methods
Youth Agency Administration
Natural Resource and Public Relations
Environmental Education Practicum
Environmental Education Teaching Methods.

Rolling Admissions
• Field Studies   • Life Experience Credit   • Study Abroad

Admissions Office
Rm. 102 Student Services Center
UW - Stevens Point
Stevens Point, WI 54481

715. 346. 2441
admiss@uwsp.edu
www.uwsp.edu/cnr/index.htm

WOODBURY COLLEGE

150 Students   Montpelier, Vermont

Woodbury College specializes in practice-based programs in fields where graduates can make real change in the world. Woodbury offers hands-on, skills-based programs in conflict resolution, advocacy, community development, human services, prevention, and legal and paralegal studies. At Woodbury, students will find a warm, enthusiastic community of non-traditional and adult students who are learning new skills to make a difference for themselves, and for the world.

Woodbury College seeks to give adults a supportive educational environment in which dynamic learning experiences can occur. By combining theory with practice, and providing individual attention and mentoring, the programs foster the knowledge and technical competency adult learners need to prepare successfully for work, further education, and active community participation.

Small classes, personal and respectful attention, and practice-oriented learning are keys to the Woodbury experience. Woodbury's outstanding faculty are leaders in their fields, and as practicing professionals, they bring insight, enthusiasm, and rich current knowledge to their teaching.

Woodbury's programs are designed for non-traditional students who prefer compressed programs of study. The college offers weekend and weekday programs leading to associates degrees, bachelors and masters degrees, or post-bachelors-degree professional certificates. A full program of study at Woodbury requires approximately two days per week of class time. Students are then free for work, volunteer activities, family time, or school-related projects.

If you're both creative and analytical and are interested in tools to help create a more peaceful society, you may wish to consider a career as a conflict management professional. In today's litigious society, mediation and conflict management are increasingly seen as effective ways to resolve family disputes, settle divorces, reduce neighborhood violence, improve community conditions, address business and environmental disputes, and reconcile crime victims and perpetrators.

The college's hands-on approach to learning gives students a chance to learn by doing. All students participate in an internship in a community organization, court, state agency, law office, corporations, or other location. The internship gives them an opportunity to refine their skills in a field-based learning experience, explore potential careers, and make connections for new career paths.

Graduates are working in varied fields, including community dispute resolution, advocacy, victim-offender mediation, child sexual abuse prevention, school volunteer coordinator, human rights mediator, family court manager, probation officer, AIDS education coordinator, disability advocate etc.

Woodbury College is located in the heart of Vermont, the Green Mountain state, in Montpelier, the country's smallest state capital. Students enjoy easy access to hiking, biking, canoeing, snow-shoeing, snow-boarding, ice skating, skiing, and other outdoor sports, and at the same time benefit from a vibrant small-city atmosphere. The city hosts several independent booksellers, independent and commercial movie houses, a large and thriving food cooperative, art galleries, a resident professional theater company, coffee shops, and other amenities.

Making a Difference Studies

Prevention & Community Development

Learn to build community strengths to support health and well-being. Prepares students to work with individuals, families, and communities to create the conditions that lead to health and well-being. Associate's Degree, Bachelor's Degree, Certificate.

Prevention Theory & Practice
Child Development
Meeting Facilitation
Assessment & Evaluation
Public & Nonprofit Organizations

Developing Community
Adolescent Development
Economics as if Community Mattered
Addictions & The Family
The Psychology of Adult Development

Legal and Paralegal Studies

Work in law firms, government or investigative agencies, courts, victim advocacy agencies, nonprofit organizations, and everywhere else legal work is done. Associate's and Bachelor's Degree, Certificate.

Elder Law
Legal Research & Writing
Professional Ethics
Mediation, Negotiation & Dispute Resolution
Environmental Law
Juvenile Law
Medical & Health Law

Legal Analysis
Litigation
Legislative & Public Interest Advocacy
Employment Law
Family & Divorce Law
Real Estate Law
Mental Health & Disabilities Law

Advocacy

Graduates are prepared to work effectively to resolve problems facing children, elders, women, the homeless, people with low incomes, and other under-represented populations. Topics in law, community studies, communication, and conflict resolution. How to protect and advance legal and human rights through persuasion, legal & administrative process, networking, and consensus building.

Interpersonal Communication
Social Security Disability Law
Meeting Facilitation
Fostering Family Involvement in Education and Social Support

Child Support Law
Culture & Society
Coalition Building

Mediation and Applied Conflict Studies (Masters Degree Program)

Blends low-residency classes in Vermont, online learning, and practical applications in the student's home community to offer one of the strongest mediation programs in the country today.

Interpersonal Conflict
Negotiation
Mediation Skills with Supervision
Trends and Issues
Legal Issues and Mediation
Advanced Practice

Conflict Intervention Skills
Principles of Conflict Analysis
Research Methods
Ethics and Impartiality
Special Topics
Capstone Project

Rolling Admissions
Average age: 35   Age range: 18-70
• Optional SAT's • Interdisciplinary Classes   • Self-Designed Majors   • Service Learning • Green Campus
Short-term programs in summer and during year

Admissions Director
Woodbury College
660 Elm Street
Montpelier, VT 05602

800. 639. 6039
www.woodbury-college.edu
admiss@woodbury-college.edu

YALE UNIVERSITY

5,400 Undergraduates   New Haven, Connecticut

At Yale, education is achieved by dialogue – between roommates and class-mates; between students, teachers and texts, and between the university and the city in which it is located. The richness of this dialogue reflects the richness of the Yale community, which attracts talented students from all over North America and the world. Everyone at Yale encounters difference and is challenged in his or her assumptions and beliefs.

Equally important, professors at Yale are dedicated to undergraduate teaching. Quality student-faculty relationships are often cited as one of Yale's strengths, as are it's small classes. Every student's course of study is self-selected and unique. Without requiring specific courses, each student takes a broad sampling in humanities, arts, sciences, and social sciences.

Students also learn about being part of a larger community that extends beyond the campus to include New Haven. More than 55 percent of the student body is involved in volunteer work in this community, whether addressing critical social issues, tutoring at a local school, or volunteering at a soup kitchen. Dwight Hall, the umbrella organization for community-service groups, is the largest such organization on any college campus in the US.

Yale stays abreast of new philosophies of education and recognizes that, in a complex world, people need to develop a broad cultural and ethical awareness. Interdisciplinary majors respond to these and other issues: International Studies focus on global socioeconomic, environmental, and political change; Ethics, Politics, and Economics examines the institutions, practices, and politics that shape our world.

In more than 200 undergraduate social, political, and cultural groups students are able to voice opinions about campus, national, and international issues. Among these organizations are cultural houses for Yale's minority communities, and groups like the Student Environmental Coalition, the Yale Hunger and Homelessness Action Project, and the Journal for Human Rights.

The Reach Out Summer Fellowship program seeks to enrich academic study and foster a sense of global responsibility at Yale by encouraging students to explore the social justice and community service dimension of globalization. Through self-designed fellowships at non-profit organizations in the developing world, students explore these issues first-hand while furthering the work of the host NGOs and developing the skills they need to work against poverty, environmental degradation, human rights abuses, and injustice internationally.

The academic study of the international world and firsthand experience of foreign cultures are crucial for citizens of the global future. No Yale student can afford to remain ignorant of the forces that shape our increasingly transnational world. Yale's efforts to create a global university start from the premise that the world has become increasingly interconnected—not simply economically and geopolitically but also in the experience of daily life, through the immediacy of events that are broadcast worldwide and through the confrontation of cultures, ideas and values.

Starting in 2006 sustainable and organic foods are served at every meal in every dining hall. Yale is committed to sourcing seasonal and/or regional ingredients which support the local economy and protect the long-term health of the environment. Yale has also launched a Green Cleaning pilot program to minimize the environmental and health effects of cleaning products.

Yale's bus fleet is currently running on a mixture of 20% biodiesel and ultra low sulfur diesel. Yale is one of the first universities in the country to run on this fuel blend. Yale is committed to a level of investment in energy conservation and alternate energy sources that will lead to a reduction in its greenhouse gas emissions by 10% below 1990 levels by the year 2020.

Making a Difference Studies

Ethics, Politics and Economics

Constructive responses to natural and social hazards, allocation of limited social resources (medical care) or morally sensitive political issues (affirmative action) require close knowledge of political, economic and social dimensions, and a capacity to think rigorously about the basic questions they raise.

Global Firms and National Governments

The Idea of Progress Reconsidered

Money and American Elections

Left Radicalism in the Twentieth Century

Reflections on Zionist Political Philosophy

Professional Ethics

Globalization & Democratic Governance of the Economy

Gender Issues in the Modern Middle East

Welfare Econ. Social Choice, & Political Philosophy

Witnessing Human Rights Violations & War Crimes

War and Public Health

Moral Choices in Politics

Political Economy of Inequality and Growth

Economics

Labor Economics and Welfare Policies

Economic Development of India

Urban Economics

Issues in Health Economics

Economic History of Latin America

Health & Social Consequences of Economic Devlp't

Economics of Natural Resources

Economics of Aging

The Economics of Corporate Control

Poverty Under Post-Industrial Capitalism

International Studies

Critique of Political Violence

Violence and Civil Strife

Science, Arms and the State

Genocide: An Interdisciplinary Perspective

Nationalism and Identity

Moral Values in Civil Society

Economics of Developing Countries

Amer. Missionaries & W. African Christianity

Terrorism in America, 1865-2001

Citizenship and the Military in Latin America.

Ethnicity, Race, and Migration

Modernisms and Decolonialization

Structures of international Migration

Ethnic Cleansing in East European History

Vietnamese Culture, Values, and Literature

Urban Poverty and Policy

New Immigrants in the United States

Diaspora and Center in Cross-Cultural Perspective

Asia & the Environment in an Era of Globalization

Racializing Britain from WW II to the Present

Revolutionary Change in 20th Century Latin Amer.

History of Mexican Americans Since 1848

Southern Africa: Ethnography of Social Change

Public Health (a 3/2 accelerated masters degree option is available)

Medical Anthropology

Stem Cells: Science & Politics

The Engineering and Ownership of Life

Epidemics in Global Perspective

The Political Economy of Health Care

World Food Issues

Anthropological Perspectives on Gender & Health

Medicine and Society in American History

Epidemics & Society in the West Since 1600

Global Problems of Population Growth

War and Public Health

Moral, Religious and Social Issues in Bioethics

Enviro. Engineering   Environmental Studies   Geology & Geophysics   History

Political Science   Women's Studies   Anthropology

Apply by 12/31   Early Action 12/15

• Self-Designed Majors   • Interdisciplinary Classes   • Team Teaching   •Vegetarian/Vegan Meals

Office of Undergraduate Admissions

Yale University

P.O. Box 208234

New Haven, CT 06520-8234

203. 432. 9316

www.yale.edu

student.questions@yale.edu

ALPHABETICAL COLLEGE INDEX

Geographic College Index

ALASKA
Jackson College

ARIZONA
Prescott College

ARKANSAS
Hendrix College

CALIFORNIA
Humboldt State University
Monterey Bay - California State
New College of California -
Pitzer College
Rudolf Steiner Institute
University of CA, Santa Cruz
Stanford University

COLORADO
Naropa University
University of Colorado at Boulder

CONNECTICUT
Connecticut College
Wesleyan University
Yale University

FLORIDA
Stetson University

INDIANA
Earlham College
Goshen College
Manchester College

IOWA
Grinnell College

KENTUCKY
Berea College

MAINE
College of the Atlantic
Unity College
University of New England

MARYLAND
National Labor College

MASSACHUSETTS
Clark University
Hampshire College
Tufts University

MINNESOTA
Bemidji State University
Carleton College
St. Olaf College
U. of Minnesota at Minneapolis

NEW JERSEY
Rutgers State - Cook College/SEBS

NEW MEXICO
EcoVersity

NEW YORK
College of Environmental Science & Forestry
Cornell University: School of Labor Relations
Eugene Lang College
Long Island U --Friends World
Paul Smiths College
Sarah Lawrence

NORTH CAROLINA
Guilford College
Warren Wilson College

OHIO
Antioch College
Oberlin College

OREGON
Lewis and Clark
University of Oregon at Eugene
Portland State University

PENNSYLVANIA
Bryn Mawr
California Univ. of Pennsylvania
Juniata College
Swarthmore College

RHODE ISLAND
Brown University

VERMONT
Green Mountain
Middlebury College
Sterling College
University of Vermont
Woodbury College

VIRGINIA
Eastern Mennonite College

WASHINGTON
The Evergreen State College
Seattle University
Washington State University
Western Washington U - Fairhaven / Huxley

WISCONSIN
Beloit
Northland College
University of Wisconsin --Stevens Point

CANADA
Menno Simons College

TRAVEL & SUMMER PROGRAMS
Audubon Expedition Institute
Center for Global Education
Living Routes
Sierra Institute
Wildlands Studies

About Miriam Weinstein

Miriam Weinstein, mother of four, lives with a very fluffy cat in San Anselmo, California. She has an avid interest in the intersection of education, spirituality and activism. Involved in social causes since her early teens, she went on many peace marches for disarmament, and on picket lines and demonstrations for civil rights, and later on, became an ardent environmentalist.

Ms. Weinstein was founder and director of the Eco Design & Builders Guild of the San Francisco Bay Area, one of the first "green building' networks. She organized green building workshops, sold green building materials and produced one of the first green building product showcases in the U.S.

Miriam describes herself as an educated tree-hugging organic foodie who recycles conscientiously. A graduate of New College of California, she has been publishing *Making A Difference College Guides* since 1992.

Her eldest daughter completed a Fulbright Fellowship studying Civic Values in Education in Bulgaria, followed by a fellowship with UNESCO in Paris. She earned a Masters Degree in International Education from Teachers College at Columbia University.

Her eldest son graduated from Warren Wilson College, and in between his journeys has worked as an environmental educator and in after-school settings.

Miriam's youngest son, while on his wanderings in Asia taught English to school children in Thailand. Recently married, he now attends college studying to be a fireman.

Miriam's youngest daughter attended Warren Wilson College for two years, sojourned in India for a year, and is now finishing her undergraduate education in the Consciousness, Healing, Ecology program at New College of California.

Ms. Weinstein's cat studies how to jump on the printer, sit on laps, and sleep on top of computer monitors. She doesn't wander.

Miriam Weinstein, author of Making A Difference College Guide since 1992, now offers private college counseling. If you are in the San Francisco Bay Area, counseling is available in Marin County. Counseling can also be done by telephone and email if you are located elsewhere. Please contact Ms. Weinstein at mw@sageworks.net to inquire.